Praise for
THE CRISIS CASEBOOK

"A is for Alaska Airlines, Amazon, Apple and more in this rundown of crisis management for dozens of brand names. The author draws on decades of experience as a leadership strategist assessing what works. Alphabetized for easy access, T is for Taylor Swift, her music and her business sense, and Z is for Zelensky, president of Ukraine, adept at telling his country's story. Who did it right and who fell short is spelled out in *The Crisis Casebook*, an easy read that offers a roadmap for success."

Eleanor Clift, *Daily Beast* columnist and co-author of *Selecting a President*

"Having managed a crisis and maybe created a few at the White House, I can say that studying this crisis casebook will help anyone who is in a position vulnerable to unanticipated risk and inadequate preparation."

Mike McCurry, Former White House Press Secretary (1995–98)

"In today's always-on world of real-time media, a public relations crisis can occur instantly. Unless you are prepared for a quick response, you will be seen as uncaring (or worse). In *The Crisis Casebook*, Edward expertly analyzes the PR successes and failures of some of the biggest brands so we can learn from what they did right and wrong. It should be required reading of any brand manager and public relations executive."

David Meerman Scott, bestselling author of *The New Rules of Marketing and PR*, available in 29 languages from Albanian to Vietnamese.

"In *The Crisis Handbook*, Edward Segal draws upon extensive experiences, exhaustive research and excellent insights to help people, campaigns and companies navigate the dangerous terrain of crises.

Segal's succinct case studies illuminate the multitude of ways controversies and catastrophes can afflict businesses and organizations large and small, and he couples each saga with sage advice.

You can't help but come away from this book ready, willing, and able to tackle crises head-on. With *The Crisis Handbook* at your side, helplessness is replaced by hope, and despair is overcome by determination. The book is not only a must-read—it's a must-have at the ready when crises happen."

Jim Kennedy, a former spokesman for Bill and Hillary Clinton, Sony, and News Corp

"Edward Segal has done it again! What an amazing resource for communication practitioners and organizational leaders alike. The cases reflect the kinds of crises today's organizations face today and you will undoubtedly see your organization in many of them.

Edward not only captures and analyzes the experiences of other industry leaders so you can learn from them, he also provides rules to follow and pathways to build your own library of proven tools that will help you recognize, plan for, implement, and track crises affecting—or will likely affect—you and your organization. I can't wait to get this resource in the hands of my students as it provides the examples and lessons learned that will make them crisis ready communication leaders of the future."

Mitchell Marovitz, director and professor, Communications, Journalism, and Speech Program at the University of Maryland Global Campus

"Edward Segal's *The Crisis Casebook* is a practical, insightful guide to not only tackling the challenges but also seizing the opportunities associated with crisis management. Through real-world examples and expert observations, Segal explores how effective communication shapes business outcomes, builds trust among stakeholders, and leads organizations through uncertainty.

As a business communication scholar, I value how this book equips leaders with the necessary tools to make bold, informed decisions when the stakes are high. It's a must-read for anyone who wants to navigate crises with confidence and clarity."

Carla Bevins, Associate Teaching Professor of Business Management Communication at Carnegie Mellon University's Tepper School of Business

"*The Crisis Casebook* offers dozens of real-world examples and lessons on how others created or managed a wide range of crisis situations. Written by crisis management expert Edward Segal, this is my go-to resource to profit from the experiences of others and find ways to address crisis-related challenges and concerns. History shows that another crisis is always around the corner. That's why the sooner you read this book, the sooner you will be prepared for what comes next. Always keep *The Crisis Casebook* close by!"

Arnold Sanow, Author, *Get Along with Anyone, Anytime, Anywhere*

"Buckle up for the ultimate crisis playbook that's part corporate thriller, part leadership manual! Edward Segal does not just tell stories—he decodes the DNA of organizational survival in a world where one tweet can topple an organization.

The Crisis Casebook is your backstage pass to the most memorable corporate moments, unpacking how brilliant (and not-so-brilliant) leaders navigate make-or-break situations. It's like having a front-row seat to the most intense chess match, with insights that will make you rethink everything you know about leadership, resilience, and the razor-thin line between disaster and triumph. This is not just a book—it's a masterclass in turning potential catastrophes into comeback stories."

Lakesha Cole, Principal publicist at she PR

"If you wonder if there is a compilation of crises that have been managed well – and not so well – wonder no more!

The Crisis Casebook is, without question, what you are looking for: the classic, comprehensive compendium of crises and responses (successful and not successful at all!). It's by Edward Segal, one of America's premier, crisis management experts and the authoritative, crisis management commentator who has been read by millions on *Forbes.com*.

Segal's new book is a crisis management primer, filled with signature insights and learning moments. Knowing about and learning from others' crisis response failures is a safety net against making similar errors yourself. *The Crisis Casebook* reads like a thrilling novel and imparts meaty lessons on every page about what to do, what not to do, and how best to be prepared to address your crisis when it comes. Because, in one form or another, it often comes for us all."

David Nellis, CEO, ROI Advertising

"*The Crisis Casebook* underscores Edward Segal's standing as one of the world's leading authorities on crisis management.

Segal argues that relying on the strategies of hope, luck, avoidance, or denial during a crisis worsens problems instead of solving them. Alarmingly, many executives fall back on these inadequate measures as their primary crisis management plans.

The Crisis Casebook includes dozens of examples of how well-known companies and brands responded to a variety of risks and threats. At the heart of the examples are two critical questions: "What was the right thing to do?" and "What can you learn from the crisis?"

Coni K. Meyers, founder and president of BePreparedBeReady.org

"Businesses face countless types of crises, some predictable, others not. In *The Crisis Casebook*, Edward Segal offers his insights and advice into crisis management for scores of catastrophes including product tampering, leadership missteps, fighting disinformation, death of a senior executive, and many more. If you want to get a handle on how to prepare and how to act during your next crisis—as any smart company should—keep *The Crisis Casebook* handy."

Ed Barks, author and president of Barks Communications

THE CRISIS CASEBOOK

LESSONS IN CRISIS MANAGEMENT FROM THE WORLD'S LEADING BRANDS

EDWARD SEGAL

First published by John Murray Business in 2025
An imprint of John Murray Press

1

Copyright © Edward Segal 2025

A CIP catalogue record for this title is available from the British Library

Library of Congress Control Number 2024950474

Hardback ISBN 978 1 39982 2 381
ebook ISBN 978 1 39982 2 398

Typeset by KnowledgeWorks Global Ltd.

Printed and bound in Great Britain by Clays Ltd, Elcograf S.p.A.

John Murray Press policy is to use papers that are natural, renewable and recyclable products and made from wood grown in sustainable forests. The logging and manufacturing processes are expected to conform to the environmental regulations of the country of origin.

John Murray Press
Carmelite House
50 Victoria Embankment
London EC4Y 0DZ

John Murray Business
123 S. Broad St., Ste 2750
Philadelphia, PA 19109

https://johnmurraybusiness.com/

John Murray Press, part of Hodder & Stoughton Limited
An Hachette UK company

The authorised representative in the EEA is Hachette Ireland, 8 Castlecourt Centre, Dublin 15, D15 XTP3, Ireland (email: info@hbgi.ie)

To Pamela Kervin Segal:
My favorite editor and proofreader

Contents

It takes 20 years to build a reputation and five minutes to ruin it. If you think about that, you'll do things differently.

Warren Buffett

Never let a good crisis go to waste.

Widely attributed to former British Prime Minister Winston Churchill

Introduction

The advice and examples in *The Crisis Casebook* are based on the hundreds of stories I have written as a Leadership Strategies Senior Contributor for *Forbes.com* and my work as a crisis management consultant.

In addition to sharing my crisis management advice, the chapters that follow feature recommendations and insights from many of the public relations, marketing, branding, and other experts I have interviewed over the years.

As noted in the subtitle, this book is about the lessons in crisis management from the world's leading brands. That's why the chapters are organized alphabetically by brands, instead of by themes or crisis types. The roughly A-to-Z nature of the Contents enables readers to quickly find well-known brands and how they responded to a crisis.

I'm happy to refer readers to *Crisis Ahead*, my previous book about crisis management. There they will find more than 100 types of crises and crisis triggers that are listed *according to the types of crisis instead of by brands*. The crises range from accidents, accounting mistakes and active shooters to viral videos, whistle-blowers, and wildfires.

The hundreds of examples in *The Crisis Casebook* and *Crisis Ahead* have an important message in common. It is easier, faster, and more affordable to learn from the experiences of others than to suffer through a bad situation yourself—only to find out afterward what you should have done.

I am a great believer in crisis management cross-training, which means learning from the crisis management experiences of those who are in different industries and professions. The more business executives know about how others responded to a crisis, the more likely it is that they can find the right approach to managing theirs.

My definition of a crisis is anything that can damage the credibility, image, reputation, bottom line, activities, or future of brands and companies, affect the morale of employees, make it harder to recruit or retain workers, or create a risk of litigation.

Crisis management covers a lot of ground as well. One of the best ways, of course, to manage a crisis is to take steps to prevent it from happening in the first place, or at least mitigate the impact as much as possible.

As I noted in *Crisis Ahead*:

- It's not a matter of if companies will face a crisis but when they will, where it will happen, how bad it will be, and what they will do about it.
- Most organizations do not have the knowledge, skills, or resources to face or recover from a crisis. They do not have a crisis plan in place or, even if they do, have not tested it to see how it would hold up in the real world.
- Hope, luck, delay, denial, or stonewalling are not effective strategies for managing a crisis or trying to avoid one. They usually make matters worse.
- A crisis does not respect national boundaries, calendars, clocks, industries, or professions. It can strike any company, organization, or high-profile individual anytime and anywhere.
- You may need specific skills and resources—such as management, public relations, marketing, advertising, legal, HR, and IT—to help get through a crisis. Depending on the situation, you may have to call on assistance from first responders, law enforcement, healthcare providers, financial experts, consultants, or government agencies.
- A lot can be at stake in a crisis, including the image, reputation, credibility, and future of companies; revenue and profits; the ability to attract and retain employees; and careers.

Variables

No two crisis situations are likely to be the same. Some of those variables include:

- The nature and extent of the crisis. Is it confined to one office or multiple offices and manufacturing facilities?
- Who is affected by the crisis, whether they are employees, customers, stakeholders, or the public.
- The age and size of companies. Older and larger businesses often have more layers of management—and red tape—to navigate when responding to a crisis. Younger and smaller companies, on the other hand, may have fewer experienced executives, but could be nimbler when reacting to a crisis.
- The degree to which companies test their crisis management plans—if they have them—to ensure they will work when needed. The less they practice their plans, the less likely it is that their plans will work when a crisis strikes.
- When and how crisis management teams are appointed, and how well they work together. Waiting until a crisis strikes to appoint a team means they will not have been tested to ensure that they would work well under pressure or that personality and other conflicts could prevent them from working well as a team.

- The resources that organizations need in order to respond to a crisis—and what outside resources they need, and how quickly they can access them. The fewer in-house resources companies have, the more likely it is that they will have to obtain those resources outside of the company—which could take more time.
- Who has the authority to activate the plans, and how quickly team members can be reached. The fewer the levels of red tape—and the sooner that crisis team members can be contacted—the better.

Crisis Management Plans

Corporate executives can be lulled into a false sense of security about their readiness to respond to a crisis by assuming their company needs only one crisis management plan.

Big mistake. That is because, like a suit, one plan will not be a good fit for every crisis a company could face. Indeed, an organization's response to a cyberattack will be different from how it reacts to litigation, strikes, or the death of its CEO.

When a disaster, scandal, or other emergency not accounted for in a basic plan occurs, organizations will waste valuable time scrambling to figure out how to manage it. Even companies in the same industry or profession could face different sets of challenges than their competitors.

Customized crisis plans should include tailored messaging for those impacted by the different emergency situations. Depending on the nature of the company, different plans should be prepared to account for the potential of various crisis scenarios for different areas.

Crisis Leadership

As important as it is to have crisis management plans in place, their execution can quickly go off the rails if the people at the top of the organization chart interfere with established crisis response policies and procedures. A micromanaging CEO, for example, could interject themselves unnecessarily into a company's response and prevent the crisis management team from doing its job.

The leadership styles of CEOs and their staff can be wild cards in how companies and organizations respond to a crisis. Their approaches, philosophies, preferences, and temperaments for managing people and corporate emergencies can help resolve a crisis quickly—or extend and worsen the situation.

Crisis Communication

How leaders communicate during and about a crisis can impact how long a crisis lasts—or can make it worse.

Some of the best practices to follow when communicating about a crisis include:

- Be clear. Use plain and simple language so everyone can understand you.
- Be coherent. Avoid using acronyms, buzzwords, and jargon that are unique to your industry, organization, or profession.
- Be current. Only provide the latest updated information about the crisis.
- Be credible. Cite the sources of your information.
- Be correct. Double check all facts and figures before sharing them with others.

The Source of Leadership

There have been times in history when people have been thrust into incredibly intense crisis situations and surprised the world with their remarkable courage, determination, and leadership. Russia's invasion of Ukraine in 2022 was one of those times. And Ukrainian President Volodymyr Zelensky is one of those people.

His remarkable journey, from a comedian playing the president of his country on a TV show to rallying and leading his people against Russian President Vladimir Putin's unprovoked war, was unusual, to say the least.

But how well Zelensky has met and surpassed the challenges of the escalating crisis has been riveting. To say he has important lessons for all business leaders about communicating and responding to a crisis would be an understatement.

Zelensky demonstrates that "leadership comes from deep within," according to Barbara Bell, a retired US Navy captain and adjunct professor of leadership and ethics at the United States Naval Academy. Author of *Flight Lessons: Navigating Through Life's Turbulence and Learning to Fly High*, she was one of the first women to graduate from the US Naval Academy and the US Naval Test Pilot School. "He drew from well deep within himself, showing the entire world what courage and commitment look like as he leads his country through a crisis like no other."

Building Grit

"'Grit is built through struggle. There's no way around it.' This is one of my personal favorite quotes," says Bell. "The Ukrainian people know this tremendously well. They have been tried and tested over many years, and the hope and prayer is that they will prevail."

Where Leaders Come From

"'Leaders can come from everywhere," Bell believes. "In addition to his courage, Zelensky is a 'man of the people.' Meaning, he knows his people. Beginning as a comedian, he developed a keen awareness of what motivates and inspires people. He is now with the people and continuing to motivate and inspire in the darkest of times."

Free Resources

There are several free resources that companies and organizations can use to help supplement their ability to prepare for and respond to a crisis.

National Risk Index

The Federal Emergency Management Agency (FEMA) announced in 2021 the full application launch of the National Risk Index, a new free online resource that "provides a clear, visual guide to natural hazard risks throughout the United States, and information to help communities to understand and reduce those risks, whether they involve flooding, wildfire, extreme heat, or drought," according to the agency's website.

Business leaders can use the Index to identify natural hazards and risks that could create a crisis for their companies and organizations, update their crisis management plans, and conduct periodic tests and exercises to ensure their plans will work when needed.

In the National Risk Index, natural hazards are represented in terms of Expected Annual Loss, which incorporates data for exposure, annualized frequency, and historic loss ratio. The online mapping application identifies communities most at risk to 18 natural hazards, including coastal flooding, cold waves, hurricanes, ice storms, and wildfires. The application visualizes natural hazard risk metrics and includes data about expected annual losses from natural hazards, social vulnerability, and community resilience.

According to then-FEMA administrator Deanne Criswell in a statement on the agency's website:

> "It is important for people to educate themselves about the severe weather events that can pose a serious threat to their communities ... The National Risk Index is a free tool that allows anyone to take a deeper look at local hazards, and can help inform risk-based decision making, so that people can be as prepared as possible."

Multiple Risk Factors

The Index provides an at-a-glance overview of multiple risk factors, and can be used to help communities:

- Update emergency operations plans.
- Enhance hazard mitigation plans.
- Prioritize and allocate resources.
- Identify the need for more refined risk assessments.
- Encourage community-level risk communication and engagement.
- Educate homeowners and renters.
- Support the development and adoption of enhanced codes and standards.
- Inform long-term community recovery.

Dashboards

The ability to monitor and track various aspects of an organization's activities and operations can provide executives with valuable information and insights that can help prevent a crisis or measure progress in addressing an emergency.

Companies and organizations can use the business version of dashboards to keep an eye on all parts of the enterprise and help spot early issues that could turn into a full-scale crisis that threatens the image, reputation, and future of the organization.

There are plenty of examples of how companies and organizations are using—or plan to use—dashboards.

Measuring and Monitoring Workplace Crises

Work Shield launched a dashboard to help employers quickly identify and respond to harassment issues in the workplace. The reporting platform is accessible anytime and anywhere via phone, computer, or tablet. Employees can report incidents and speak with a legal professional, according to Jared Pope, founder and CEO of the company.

The site enables employers to monitor and track incidents by location, department, and other options and uncover trends for several types of incidents.

Pope notes that up to that point none of its clients has faced charges from the Equal Employment Opportunity Commission and that all harassment-related issues have been resolved in an average of five days, which is 25 days less than the national average.

Keeping on Top of Corporate Hotspots

Auto parts company Meritor built what it called a "war room dashboard" to identify and keep track of hotspots throughout the organization, plus data about the COVID-19 pandemic from Johns Hopkins University. The dashboard was tailored so it could quickly provide managers with frequent updates on the status of the business, their partners, customers, and the supply chain. The dashboard also monitors the availability and use of personal protective equipment at various locations to determine which equipment is needed and if there are any work sites that can share surplus supplies.

Guarding Against Disinformation

In 2021, PR firm Weber Shandwick partnered with AI-driven threat intelligence and detection platform Blackbird.ai to launch an online "Media Security Center."

Understanding Threats

According to Weber Shandwick, "The platform helps organizations understand the information landscape in ways that were never before possible so that analysts and comms teams can better respond to the types of threats that are now omnipresent ..."

Driven by AI

The platform uses AI to generate narratives which are collections of topics, posts, and stories that are relevant to customers. It ranks the narratives with a "Harm Score" which is a composite index that combines various risk factors.

War Rooms

Command centers—also known as war rooms—can play critical roles in managing crises. According to Carla Bevins, an associate teaching professor of business management communication at Carnegie Mellon University's Tepper School of Business, "Companies use war rooms to prepare for worst-case scenarios, improve collaboration during events, and help responders adapt and communicate more effectively during crises." A war room "is a centralized center where information from numerous sources is processed, and open communication creates a clear voice of response." Bevins goes on:

> "Effective crisis communications effort requires coordinated internal collaboration and parallel processing. War rooms create a dynamic environment where these conversations can happen ... Make sure that your war room is well equipped with all the tools you'll need before you need them."

Helping to Build Crisis Management Skills

A war room is most important before a crisis breaks out "because it is in the war room where you rehearse, prepare, and build skills in crisis management," claims Andy Whitehouse, an assistant professor at Columbia University who teaches crisis communications:

> "In my class, I argue that companies should regularly bring together the crisis team in the war room to role-play a crisis—since this is the only way to ensure that the team has the experience, capabilities, and comfort to manage a crisis when it happens. A live crisis in a war room is not the moment to find out that an executive is not ready for game time ... Who should be in the war room? It depends on the scenario. Communications, legal, HR, and operations will almost always be present, but other leaders, such as the chief technology officer or the head of security, might be there for a specific crisis."

"Use War Rooms Judiciously"

Carla Bevins sounds a note of caution:

> "Use war rooms judiciously. If you continue to use a war room when it is not needed, its effectiveness can decline. Crises are inherently stressful events where teams work long hours for many days. As the leader of a war room, lead

by example by remaining calm and collected ... When you act as a role model, you help create a psychologically safe space where team members see they have an open line of communication. This can encourage them to speak up when they become stressed or need support."

War rooms can be useful even when there is no immediate crisis, such as preparing for the threat of an economic-related challenge like inflation and recession.

What Next?

Risk indexes, dashboards, and war rooms are just some of the many tools companies and organizations can use to help measure and respond to crisis situations.

Armed with the crisis management lessons you will learn in the following pages, combined with the resources above, I hope you will feel confident—or more confident—in responding to crisis situations in the days ahead.

CHAPTER 1
Academy of Motion Picture Arts and Sciences

Penalizing Bad Behavior

Holding people accountable for their role in creating a crisis can be a crucial step in ensuring that a similar crisis is not repeated. That accountability can depend on the organization and the nature of the crisis and set an example for others.

For actor Will Smith, who slapped comedian Chris Rock in front of a live international television audience during the 94th Academy Awards in April 2022, accountability took the form of barring him from attending or participating in any Academy events or programs for ten years.

The Academy of Motion Picture Arts and Sciences, which stages the event, reiterated its position about the incident, saying, "We are upset and outraged that [the awards] were overshadowed by the unacceptable and harmful behavior on stage by a nominee. To be clear, we condemn Mr. Smith's actions that transpired [that] night."

Condemning Smith's Actions

The Academy issued this statement: "The academy condemns the actions of Mr. Smith at last night's show. We have officially started a formal review around the incident and will explore further action and consequences in accordance with our bylaws, standards of conduct and California law."

The organization noted that its "response to Will Smith's behavior is a step toward a larger goal of protecting the safety of our performers and guests and restoring trust in the Academy. We also hope this can begin a time of healing and restoration for all involved and impacted."

Smith, who had resigned from the Academy before the announcements, said in a statement, "I accept and respect the Academy's decision."

There had been calls "from industry insiders and moviegoers for Smith's Oscar to be taken back, which the Oscars have no legal authority to claim. To compare, convicted criminals Harvey Weinstein and director Roman Polanski still hold their Oscars following their expulsions," according to *Variety* magazine.

Mitigating Factors

There can be mitigating factors that limit what can be done in response to a crisis.

"The organization didn't have too many other options to impose, especially with Smith's membership now no longer active following his resignation. His resignation and barring from future telecasts does not preclude him from being nominated or even winning future Academy Awards during that time," *Variety* reported.

Smith's resignation means that he is no longer part of the Academy's voting body, but it does not prohibit him from being nominated for his work in the future.

No Consensus

Not everyone agreed with the Academy's decision. Some thought it was too lenient, while others said it was too harsh. John Van Vliet, a member of the Academy, said:

> "Assault is assault. If that had been any 'non-celebrity' charging up onstage to strike a performer, they would probably have been arrested ... Physically striking another performer went far beyond what would be considered tolerable 'antics' and should result in Mr. Smith being removed from the Academy completely."

CHAPTER 2
Adidas

Celebrity Endorsements

Companies seeking to profit from their relationships with celebrities can find themselves in a crisis when celebrities do or say controversial things that tarnish corporate brands, images, and reputations. Because the court of public opinion can render its verdict quickly, corporate executives need to react just as fast to help prevent or mitigate damage to their brands.

One example is Adidas, which sold rapper Kanye West's line of shoes and had a marketing partnership with him for almost a decade. But the singer, who changed his name to Ye, continued to make international headlines with his antisemitic comments and views.

Ye did not apologize or recant, which led Adidas to terminate its partnership with the singer in October 2022.

"Adidas does not tolerate antisemitism and any other sort of hate speech," the company said in a statement. "Ye's recent comments and actions have been unacceptable, hateful and dangerous, and they violate the company's values of diversity and inclusion, mutual respect and fairness."

Other companies, including CAA, the talent agency that represented Ye, also cut ties with the artist.

Slow to Respond

In October 2022, the German footwear giant had said that its partnership was under review, but since it had not issued any updates, it continued to release new Yeezy merchandise, "even as the rapper double[d] down on antisemitic tropes and conspiracy theories," *NPR* reported.

John Goodman of John Goodman PR observes:

> "The only surprise here is that it took Adidas way too long to respond ... This was such an outright [antisemitic] rant that it deserved an immediate response from

the company. Sometimes, it's wise to wait a while before you respond. But this was so blatant and so offensive that Adidas needed to respond much sooner."

The sooner that companies respond to a crisis-causing issue, the better.

A Matter of Timing

Timing is always important when trying to prevent or manage a crisis. Nick Kalm, founder and CEO of Reputation Partners, a national strategic communications and public relations firm, explains:

> "In crisis management, success is defined as not only doing the right thing but doing it at the right time. In this case, Adidas did the right thing by terminating their relationship with Ye, and their statement hit the right notes, but they took too long to do it."

Even if a company is slow to respond to a crisis, there is no reason why it should not have—and follow—a crisis management plan:

> "It was a bit surprising that a consumer-facing company like Adidas was so slow to respond to the crisis, but perhaps it was due to the significant financial charge the company incurred as a result of the separation. In any case, any company with celebrity endorsers must have a crisis plan and scenario-based decision-making completed in advance."

A Risky Strategy

Doing nothing about a crisis and hoping it will disappear sooner rather than later can be a risky strategy. The longer a company waits to act, the worse the situation could become.

Every Situation Is Different

Stacy Elmore, co-founder of The Luxury Pergola, a company that works with social media influencers, takes a measured view:

> "Every situation is different, so there's no one-size-fits-all answer. However, a good rule of thumb is to see what happens ... Sometimes the controversy will blow over and be forgotten within a week or two, in which case you can resume normal operations as usual. But other times, the controversy will continue to be

a topic of conversation (or even grow), and in that case, you'll need to decide whether continuing to work with that celebrity is worth the potential backlash ... Keep in mind that the world doesn't revolve around your brand—bad news for celebrities often means bad news for brands too. And finally, remember that the news cycle moves fast—if you do decide to part ways with a celebrity, don't try to publicly embarrass them. It's always a bad idea to burn bridges," Elmore concluded.

There may be other factors at play when agreeing to work with or end arrangements with celebrities. That's why the more that both parties understand and agree to the basics of their relationship and what each side expects to gain from it, the better. And there could be provisions in the agreement that will govern how controversies involving celebrities will be addressed.

If a company is too slow to react to a crisis, it could be pushed into action by outside forces, such as an immediate and sustained public outcry.

CHAPTER 3
Airbnb

Mass Shootings

Companies and organizations need to act quickly and decisively when a crisis strikes. That's especially true when, despite their best efforts, a crisis they tried to prevent strikes anyway. Airbnb is a case in point.

In 2019, there was a shooting at a large Halloween party at a property rented through Airbnb in Northern California.

ABC News reported:

> "Five partygoers were killed on Halloween night at a house in the affluent town of Orinda, just east of Berkeley, that had been rented through Airbnb. The owner of the home told the *San Francisco Chronicle* that he had rented out the house to a woman who told him she was planning to have a family reunion for about a dozen people ... Instead, authorities said that upwards of 100 partygoers fled the house in panic after shots rang out. One witness told the *Chronicle* that most of the party's attendees were college students."

According to the *BBC*, the incident led Airbnb to ban party houses. CEO Brian Chesky said in a tweet the company would take steps to "combat unauthorized parties and get rid of abusive host and guest conduct."

The series of safety-related actions and policies was designed to help prevent the repeat of a similar crisis.

A Second Mass Shooting

But despite those steps, a second mass shooting at a large party at a different Airbnb rental property in 2022 made national headlines. According to *The Washington Post*, a shooting at an Airbnb in Pittsburgh, Pennsylvania, left two people dead and at least eight injured at a house party that was attended by about 200 people:

> "More than 90 rounds were fired inside the house, prompting some partygoers to jump out of windows, Pittsburgh police chief Scott E. Schubert said at a news

conference Sunday afternoon. Police said the shooting was from a property that had been rented via Airbnb ... It was a very chaotic scene. You had people who were fleeing—you know, just trying to get out of there. Many of the partygoers were underage, and one victim was as young as 14 years old, Schubert said. Police believe there was more than one shooter and do not yet have anyone in custody."

Crisis Management Best Practices

In the aftermath of the country's largest mass shooting at the time, Airbnb appeared to be following several best practices for responding to and managing a crisis.

Issue a Statement

Say something appropriate about the crisis as quickly as possible.

An Airbnb spokesperson said:

> "We share the Pittsburgh community's outrage regarding this tragic gun violence. Our hearts go out to all who were impacted—including loved ones of those who lost their lives, injured victims and neighbors ... Airbnb strictly bans parties, and we condemn the behavior that is alleged to have prompted this criminal gun violence."

Tell People What You Have Done and Will Do

Explain what you have done in response to the crisis.

In its statement, the company explained that:

> "We have reached out to the Pittsburgh Police Department as well as Mayor Gainey's team to offer our support for their investigations, and we hope the people responsible for this bloodshed will be found quickly. The booking guest has been issued a lifetime ban from Airbnb and we will be considering all legal options to hold this person accountable."

Share What You Know

Provide any insights or information about the situation that can help people understand the crisis or what caused it.

Airbnb's spokesperson said, "We can confirm that this was an unauthorized party, thrown without the knowledge or consent of the host," and that the host had clearly stated their policy about parties on the property's listing page. According to their policy, no parties were allowed, and any evidence of parties would result in a $500 fine.

Reiterate Company Policy

If you have policies or procedures in place designed to help prevent the crisis, share them with the public on your website.

The company's website noted:

> "As of Aug. 20, 2020, Airbnb announced a global ban on all parties and events at Airbnb listings, including a cap on occupancy at 16, consistent with our community policies. This party ban applies to all future bookings on Airbnb, and it will remain in effect indefinitely, until further notice."

Don't Assume

Don't assume that people will know or remember the steps you have taken in the past.

Airbnb said in its statement that it has taken several steps to try to prevent parties at rental properties. The measures include:

- Adopting a policy that strictly bans parties.
- Operating a neighborhood support line so neighbors can flag any possible parties in real-time, as well as any listings that they believe to be "party houses."
- A 24/7 safety team that enforces the company's party policies.
- Conducting identity verification and background checks in order to use Airbnb in the US.
- Using safety-focused technology that restricts certain reservations based on risk factors—including reservation attempts for certain local, entire home listings made by guests under the age of 25. Airbnb said: "This technology is aimed at trying to

prevent unauthorized parties and has blocked thousands of distinct reservation attempts in the US."

Taking Legal Action

In 2021, San Francisco-based news and entertainment website *SFist* reported:

"As it has done in similar cases in the past, Airbnb announced ... that it is taking legal action against the guest who threw an unauthorized teenage bash at a rental home in Sunnyvale on August 7 that tragically ended in a fatal shooting ... The guest, who has not been named publicly, has been permanently banned from the Airbnb platform, and the company said it had informed the guest ... of its intent to bring legal action. As *KPIX* reported, the guest is accused of violating the company's Community Standards and Terms of Service and booking a listing under false pretenses."

Advice

- Consult with staff and others to identify the worst-case crisis scenarios that would affect your company. Then take steps to help ensure that those scenarios do not become a reality, or if they do, that you will be ready to respond to them.
- Don't assume that the efforts you made to prevent repeating a crisis will be effective.
- Periodically remind people who could create a crisis for your company about the policies, procedures, and protocols that they must follow.
- On a regular basis, conduct tests and exercises to help guarantee your crisis response plans will work when needed.

CHAPTER 4
Alaska Air, Boeing, and the Federal Aviation Administration

Accidents

The Federal Aviation Administration grounded all Boeing 737 MAX 9 aircraft temporarily in 2024 after the blowout of a cabin panel on one of the brand-new Alaska Airlines planes. The agency's decision provides leaders with an important crisis management lesson: as soon as you know something, do something.

The episode that led to the grounding of the planes "raised troubling new questions about the safety of a workhorse aircraft design dogged by years of problems and multiple deadly crashes," *The New York Times* reported.

Immediate Inspections

"The FAA is requiring immediate inspections of certain Boeing 737 MAX 9 planes before they can return to flight," FAA administrator Mike Whitaker explained. "Safety will continue to drive our decision-making as we assist the NTSB's [National Transportation Safety Board] investigation into Alaska Airlines Flight 1282.

"Alaska had grounded its fleet of Boeing 737 Max 9 aircraft on Friday after one of its planes made an emergency landing at Portland International Airport in Oregon because of a midair pressure problem that passengers said blew out a chunk of the fuselage, or body of the plane," according to *The New York Times.*

Alaska Air

"In a statement, Alaska Air Group CEO Ben Minicucci said the airline's fleet of 65 MAX 9s would be grounded and inspected to ensure safety. He anticipated inspections would be complete in the next few days," *The Seattle Times* reported.

"Each aircraft will be returned to service only after completion of full maintenance and safety inspections," Minicucci explained. "I am personally committed to doing everything we can to conduct this review in a timely and transparent way."

Boeing

"Safety is our top priority, and we deeply regret the impact this event has had on our customers and their passengers. We agree with and fully support the FAA's decision to require immediate inspections of 737-9 airplanes with the same configuration as the affected airplane," Boeing explained on its website.

"In addition, a Boeing technical team is supporting the NTSB's investigation into last night's event. We will remain in close contact with our regulator and customers."

Consequences

Companies and organizations that delay in responding to a potential crisis run the risk of allowing the problem to turn into a full-blown crisis.

That, in turn, can damage the image, reputation, credibility, and bottom line of organizations—and harm the careers of executives.

Precautions

There are several steps corporate executives can take to help ensure they respond quickly to problems and issues that could create a crisis situation.

- **Crisis triggers:** Determine what would cause a crisis for the company and include those crisis triggers in updated crisis management and crisis response plans.
- **Scenarios:** Create scenarios based on the crisis triggers, and practice responding to the scenarios when conducting crisis response drills, exercises, and simulations.
- **Pay attention:** Establish and maintain an early warning system that immediately notifies executives about a possible crisis. This can include monitoring social media platforms for comments or criticisms about the company and its products, services, and activities.
- **Response team:** Appoint a crisis response team before there is a crisis. Without a team in place when a crisis strikes, valuable time will be lost in responding to and managing an unfolding situation.
- **Spokesperson training:** Ensure that the person who would represent the company to the public in a crisis has received spokesperson training or periodic refresher training.

CHAPTER 5
Amazon

Leaked Documents

The release of confidential information about a company's activities, products, services, or employees can create a crisis for organizations by damaging—or further damaging—their credibility, image, and reputation.

When those documents are leaked, it's crisis management best practice for companies to tell their side of the story. Amazon did just that in response to the release of confidential information in 2022 about its high rate of employee attrition and other matters.

The issues raised by the leaked documents cast a spotlight on important aspects of today's workplace and how business leaders respond to them—or should—so that they do not create a crisis for their businesses.

The Documents Paint a Bleak Picture

Engadget was the first to report details about leaked confidential Amazon documents that were prepared in 2022. *Engadget* said the information showed that the online retailer had an annual employee turnover rate of 150 percent—double the industry average—costing the company and its shareholders $8 billion annually.

The materials, "which include several internal research papers, slide decks and spreadsheets, paint a bleak picture of Amazon's ability to retain employees and how the current strategy may be financially harmful to the organization as a whole," according to the news outlet. The documents "also broadly condemn Amazon for not adequately using or tracking data in its efforts to train and promote employees, an ironic shortcoming for a company [that] has a reputation for obsessively harvesting consumer information."

Statement from Amazon

Steve Kelly, an Amazon spokesperson, pointed out:

> "We weren't afforded the opportunity to review the draft documents cited in the *Engadget* article ... That said, they are most certainly early drafts that weren't appropriately refined or vetted, let alone finalized. Basing articles on unverified documents—without knowing when they were written, if they were validated, or if they were later corrected—can be misleading, as is the case with the *Engadget* article."

In a statement, Amazon said:

> "Amazon has a rigorous document review process—oftentimes documents never make it past the draft stage, are rejected due to lack of reliable data, or are modified with corrected information. ... After the *Engadget* article [was] published, we believe we were able to identify all of the leaked documents in question and can confirm that none of them had been fully vetted or approved."

"A Crisis of Culture"

Robert C. Bird, a professor of business law and Eversource Energy Chair in Business Ethics at the University of Connecticut, explains about the cost in human capital:

> "How well Amazon pays relative to the market is certainly a relevant factor, but the mass quitting could originate from a crisis of culture ... If employees do not feel valued or do not envision a long-term future for themselves at Amazon, [and] if jobs are available [elsewhere], they will seek employment elsewhere. Every employee that leaves Amazon takes with him or her valuable firm-specific human capital ... This includes knowledge and experience that is specific to Amazon that will need to be retrained all over again when hiring replacement workers. Amazon will need to conduct some frank introspection in order to determine the underlying causes of the mass employee departures and consider how to restructure their workplace so that employees feel sufficiently valued."

The Bottom Line

Companies should not be shy about touting the positive things they are doing. And when faced with the leak of confidential documents, organizations should—as Amazon did—tell their side of the story.

And the sooner, the better.

Otherwise, what others may have gotten wrong could become conventional wisdom. And the longer that inaccurate or outdated information is left standing, the harder it will be to set the record straight.

CHAPTER 6
American Airlines

Cybersecurity Vulnerabilities

American Airlines is an example of how businesses and organizations are vulnerable to email-based cyberattacks.

In September 2022, American Airlines reported a data breach it had discovered in July. "American Airlines said the successful phishing attack led to the unauthorized access of a limited number of team member mailboxes," according to Malwarebytes Labs.

The company notified customers that "personal information such as an address, phone number, driver's license number, passport number and/or certain medical information may have been accessed by the hacker," *Reuters* explained.

"We regret that this incident occurred and take the security of your personal information very seriously," American Airlines' chief privacy and data protection officer Russell Hubbard said in a letter to consumers, according to the wire service.

A study released in 2022 by Tessian, an email security platform, stated that emails are one of the weakest links in a company's defense against cyberattacks, and cyber thieves appear to be taking advantage of this vulnerability:

> "Organizations send and receive thousands of emails per day, making email a massive vulnerability for the enterprise and opening the door for advanced attacks like spear phishing, impersonation and ransomware ... These types of attacks also ranked as the top email threat that security leaders are most concerned about."

Tessian's "Email Security Report 2022" found that:

- 92 percent of companies experienced a data breach caused by an end-user making a mistake on email—such as sending an email to the wrong person or failing to send the correct attachment.
- Nearly one in five of these attacks was successful; 39 percent of respondents cited the breach of customer data, 34 percent reported financial losses, and 32 percent experienced a ransomware infection.

- Smaller companies were most likely to receive email attacks from threat actors impersonating board members and investors. In contrast, larger companies received emails from threat actors who impersonated employees or company suppliers, reflecting how cybercriminals tailor their scams to make them more believable.

The survey was conducted in September 2022 for Tessian by third-party research house Censuswide, which queried 600 IT and security leaders in organizations across the US, UK, Middle East, and Africa.

Seizing the Corporate Crown Jewels

According to the executive summary of the report:

"Threat actors are attempting to access corporate networks and are leveraging novel exploits to seize a business' crown jewels, namely its data. Email remains a leading initial attack vector ... that does not appear likely to change.

The issue of email as a go-to channel for threat actors is further complicated by the macroeconomic climate throughout the back half of 2022, with fears of a looming recession altering markets, and potentially headcounts moving into the next calendar year.

Typically, malicious actors carry this out by baiting users with social engineering campaigns that can include impersonated pleas from trusted figures of authority or other fraudulent scams or promotions. Regardless, threat actors view the channel as one of the easiest inroads to compromising businesses."

A Costly Crisis

Art Ocain, vice president of service delivery at cybersecurity company Airiam, explains how vulnerable organizations can be to such an attack:

"Just one employee taking the email bait from a phishing attack can bring a successful organization to its knees. Corporate emails, targeted through phishing and weaponized malware, are the main entry point for most breaches ... Hackers are getting more innovative, and many employees unknowingly click a link or open an attachment and let the bad actors into the network."

In addition to the crisis that a data breach can create for a company, the attacks can be costly. According to a report by IBM, the average cost of a data breach in the US was more than $9 million in 2024, more than double the global average.

"The Solution Is Plain and Simple"

David Moody, a senior associate of Schellman, a global cybersecurity assessor, considers a possible solution:

> "When it comes to protecting against phishing attacks, it does seem like some employees always fall for them ... The solution is plain and simple: There is no substitute for training. A common method is to conduct simulated phishing exercises and use that information to identify and provide training for those who need it. There are companies who do this service for organizations and can also provide insight into larger company weaknesses, as well (such as email filtering and management policies)."

Josh Yavor, chief information security officer at Tessian, agrees that prevention is the best approach:

> "Chief information security officers and business leaders need to focus on how they can defend and protect employees both within and, critically, beyond the walls of corporate systems ... On the corporate side, security teams should focus on preventing as many malicious emails from reaching inboxes as possible but anticipating that some will get through."

CHAPTER 7
Apple

Sending the Wrong Message

Getting attention for a company's products is important—but so is sending the *right* message about the products, and why people should buy them. Companies that send the wrong message run the risk of generating the wrong kind of publicity for themselves and creating a crisis for the brands they promote.

Apple learned that crisis management lesson the hard way in 2024 when it advertised its iPads in an online commercial that was quickly dubbed the "crushing creativity" ad.

"It was supposed to be a clever product demonstration for Apple's latest sleek, artificial intelligence-powered iPad Pro," *Adweek* reported. But the brand, typically praised for its advertising, sparked a wave of backlash for a commercial that crushes and destroys creative tools.

Not the Metaphor Apple Wanted

Instead of seeing how an iPad could help them create, most people saw the ad "as [a] metaphor for how Big Tech has cashed in on their work by crushing or co-opting the artistic tools that humanity has used for centuries. The image was especially unnerving at a time when artists fear that generative artificial intelligence, which can write poetry and create movies, might take away their jobs," according to *The New York Times*.

"It's unusual in its cruelty," said Justin Ouellette, a software designer in Portland, Oregon, who does animation work and is a longtime Apple product user. "A lot of people see this as a betrayal of its commitment to human creative expression and a tone deafness to the pressures those artists feel at this time."

Apple's Response

"Creativity is in our DNA at Apple, and it's incredibly important to us to design products that empower creatives all over the world," Apple marketing vice president Tor Myhren told *Ad Age* in a statement. "Our goal is to always celebrate the myriad of ways users express themselves and bring their ideas to life through iPad. We missed the mark with this video, and we're sorry."

Apple's misstep is a lesson for all companies that marketing messages should be in sync with how the brand is perceived by the public and does nothing to harm the reputation of the product—or its company. If not, the result could be a crisis.

Apple was in hot water again a few months later after pulling the "crushing" ad when it ran a 10-minute ad on YouTube that showed how co-workers in Thailand used the company's products to address workplace-related issues.

Critics charged that the ad portrayed an outdated and stereotyped image of Thailand that made the country look as if it were underdeveloped. Apple removed the ad and apologized for it.

"Thai people are deeply unhappy with the advertisement," Thai lawmaker Sattra Sripan said in a statement reported by *Bloomberg*. "I encourage Thai people to stop using Apple products and change to other brands."

Apple pulled the ad.

CHAPTER 8
Astroworld Festival and Travis Scott

Expect the Unexpected

The less that organizations plan for what they consider to be an unexpected crisis, the more likely it is that they will be behind the eight ball when the unthinkable happens.

The Astroworld Festival learned that lesson in 2021 when a Travis Scott concert without any warning suddenly turned into a mass casualty event. The *BBC* reported that, "Ten people died and hundreds of others were injured at the concert in Houston, Texas, after the crowds surged towards the stage."

Pay Attention to Early Warnings

Ten days before the event, the festival's head of safety raised a concern about the number of people who would be near the stage. "I feel like there is no way we are going to fit 50k in front of that stage," Seyth Boardman wrote to the Texas festival's operations director, according to the *BBC*.

The New York Post reported that, "Houston Police Chief Troy Finner visited Travis Scott in his trailer to voice his concerns about 'public safety' ahead of the deadly Astroworld concert, the chief announced ..."

Finner, who knows the rapper and songwriter personally, explained in a statement on Twitter:

> "I met with Travis Scott and his head of security for a few moments last Friday prior to the main event. I expressed my concerns regarding public safety and that in my 31 years of law enforcement experience I have never seen a time with more challenges facing citizens of all ages, to include a global pandemic and social tension throughout the nation."

When You Know Something, Do Something

Scott continued to perform for almost 40 minutes after a "mass casualty incident" had been declared at the Astroworld Festival, according to an *ABC-TV* news station.

Your Words Can Come Back to Haunt You

Kojenwa Moitt teaches public relations, marketing, and branding at the Parsons School of Design in New York and is CEO of Zebra Public Relations. She notes:

> "Travis unfortunately has been associated with telling his fans to create mosh pits and rush the stage and fans will, just to get closer to the celebrity. When fans who feel obsessed rush the stage, it creates the kind of damage P Diddy experienced once at one of his concerts."

Have a Crisis Management Plan for Every Scenario

"The security and emergency response plan prepared by Astroworld organizers ahead of the festival outlines scenarios ranging from bomb threats and active shooters to lightning, tornadoes and even an earthquake," *KHOU-TV* reported.

But the 56-page document never once mentions crowd surge.

"Nothing about crowd emergencies, nothing about crowd density, crowd collapse, crowd crush," says Paul Wertheimer, a nationally recognized crowd safety expert and founder of Crowd Management Strategies. "And yet it's a concert and festival with standing room environment, and ... they don't even mention that as one of the emergencies," the news organization said.

Tell People How You Feel About What Happened

According to *CNN*, Scott took to social media over the weekend and wrote, "I'm absolutely devastated by what took place last night. My prayers go out to the families and all those impacted by what happened at Astroworld Festival."

Nick Kalm, founder and CEO of Reputation Partners, a national strategic communications firm, observes:

> "Travis Scott was right to immediately express what appeared to be genuine sympathy for the victims and cancel his upcoming appearances."

Going a Step Further?

Speed matters when saying something about a crisis—but so does saying the right thing.

Kalm notes:

> "[As] evidence of his past [encouragement of] unruly behavior at his concerts has come to light, he should have added to his statement with remorse and regret for those actions. If he wanted to go above and beyond, he could offer financial support to the victims' families, but his attorneys are likely to counsel against that given the inevitable wrongful death legal claims headed his way."

In addition to expressing remorse and regret about a crisis situation, conveying a sense of empathy can be just as important.

Moitt explains:

> "Travis revealed a lot of empathy, and this is the correct response when dealing with tragedy and [fatalities]. By connecting immediately afterwards to his fans on social media he was able to convey that he was distraught. Also, by canceling a future appearance in Las Vegas, it would seem that his heart and intention were in the right place."

Do What You Can Afterwards

Refunds

USA Today reported that festival organizers issued full refunds to all those who bought tickets for Astroworld following the tragic turn of the Houston concert that left 10 dead and many others injured.

Organizer Scoremore issued a statement on Twitter offering its condolences and providing an update on the incident. "Full refunds are being offered for all those who purchased tickets," Scoremore said in its tweeted statement about the steps it was taking along with events company Live Nation and the Astroworld Festival team.

Funerals and Mental Health Services

CNN reported that Scott would cover all funeral costs for the victims who died at his Astroworld Festival, according to a statement released by a representative for the rapper and producer. The Houston-born artist said he would partner with the mental health platform BetterHelp to provide free mental health services to all those affected by the tragedy.

Expect Blowback

The Daily Beast wrote:

"... disgusted that Scott's Spotify monthly listeners had increased by nearly 200,000 between the end of October and the tragic events on Friday night in Houston, some users have encouraged others to boycott his music, selecting an option on his Spotify artist profile that will block the play of all of his songs for that user.

The hope is that at the very least the 30-year-old won't profit from his newly released songs 'Escape Plan' and 'Mafia,' and perhaps urge Spotify to reconsider having the artist's photo featured on its popular playlists Rap Caviar and New Music Friday."

CHAPTER 9
Audi and Wheel of Fortune

Do the Right Thing

Sometimes companies need help from an outside source to do the right thing about a self-inflicted controversy. For gameshow *Wheel of Fortune*, the solution to its corporate emergency was the crisis management version of roadside assistance.

Fans of the show—which attracts millions of viewers each week—were outraged in 2022 when a contestant did not win an Audi Q3 because of a technicality.

Taking Too Much Time

As recounted by *Good Housekeeping* it all began when contestant Charlene Rubush "entered the bonus round after winning $16,500. During the 'What Are You Doing?' category, Charlene's initial guess was 'choosing the right card.' Quickly, Charlene paused and realized the one-word difference and changed her guess to 'choosing the right word.'

"We'll allow for a little pause, but not four or five seconds. I'm sorry. You did a good job in getting it, but we can't give you the prize, and it was the Audi," said Pat Sajak, the show's host.

Viewers React

Sajak's decision generated national headlines such as "*Wheel of Fortune* Contestant Loses New Car With Right Answer "on *CNN's* website, and criticism from viewers."

CBS News reported that, "*Wheel of Fortune* fans watching the episode immediately protested, saying Rubush had been robbed. Video snippets of the show were soon posted on social media as people vented their disapproval."

According to *Newsweek*, "Viewers took to Twitter to express their dissatisfaction at the decision, with former *Jeopardy!* champ Alex Jacob tweeting: 'Come on @ WheelofFortune, the woman literally chose the right word. Give her the car.'

'Wheel of Fortune, you just lost a viewer,' Twitter user @TalinOrfaliGhaz wrote. 'I am choosing the right word to never watch this show again.'

Audi to the Rescue

Fortunately for the game show and Rubush, Audi stepped up and did the right thing. *CBS News* reported, "The company announced on Wednesday that it would give Rubush the same model car she attempted to win on *Wheel of Fortune*."

"You're a winner in our eyes Charlene," the company tweeted. "Now, let's get you a prize. Time to #GiveHerTheQ3."

Audi confirmed the car giveaway in a statement to *Newsweek*, saying the car would be gifted to Rubush.

"[We] saw Charlene's *Wheel of Fortune* episode on Monday and were collectively disappointed that she missed out on the opportunity to take home an Audi Q3 due to a technicality," the company said.

Audi announced on Twitter that Rubush had received her Q3.

Advice

- Don't wait to do the right thing about a crisis—especially the one you created.
- Find ways to do the right thing—even if you must bend the rules a bit to make it happen—but only if it is appropriate and possible to do so.
- Consider the potential consequences of every decision you make about dealing with a crisis. Will it make things better—or worse? If it makes things worse, will it be worth the price?
- Before you are confronted by a crisis, decide if, how, or when your organization would bend to the pressure imposed by others to address or resolve a crisis.
- After every crisis, carefully review any policies, procedures, or protocols that may have caused or contributed to it and take steps to prevent the same crisis from happening again.

CHAPTER 10
Aunt Jemima and Uncle Ben's

Offensive Product Names

Product names can be a double-edged sword for companies. The right name can create a memorable identity that helps ensure that the product is easier for consumers to remember. But an inappropriate name could offend consumers, generate negative publicity, and create a crisis for companies.

In 2020, Mars changed the name of its Uncle Ben's rice to Ben's Original and a year later PepsiCo changed the name of its 130-year-old Aunt Jemima pancake and syrup products to Pearl Milling Company.

The name changes followed years of allegations that the original brand names and their images had racist connotations. When the two companies dropped the names, they also eliminated the images on the packages that people had found offensive.

As with any crisis, it's important to eliminate the cause as soon as possible. And if you can stop an issue from turning into a crisis in the first place, so much the better. There are best practices that companies can follow to help ensure the names they select for their products do not lead to harmful headlines and crisis situations.

"The best brands start with core values that form a strong moral compass and guide what they look and sound like in the market, but they are also highly responsive to the constantly changing dynamics of what the world needs right now," says Jack Spaulding, executive director of strategy at Planit, a marketing and communications firm. He advises Fortune 500 brands, small businesses, and nonprofits on how to build lasting brands that connect with their audiences:

> "To avoid diagnosis as a 'terminal brand,' organizations should conduct a brand audit at least once a year. This audit should help assess what your brand stands for, how well its current image reflects the organization's values, and how effectively your brand is connecting (or not) with your audiences. Collect input from staff, customers, key stakeholders, and even public opinion to gauge hotspots that may be of concern and provide awareness beyond your own line of sight ... As soon as you discover misalignment, plan for change. Walking away from an existing name

or brand identity is never easy, especially if it has built up valuable equity and some customers are still happily buying. But the sooner organizations recognize a problem, the better."

Don't Ignore the Crisis

Spaulding emphasizes the importance of tackling the issue head on:

"Discovering an identity crisis is difficult, but ignoring it is fatal. To their credit, brands like Aunt Jemima, Uncle Ben's, and the Washington Redskins realized they were facing challenges. Unfortunately, each of them waited exceptionally long (decades, even) to take action after first realizing the offense, allowing consumers to build negative perceptions and ultimately demand change ... Of course, a brand would rather drive their evolution from within than have it controlled for them. Had these companies audited their brands more regularly, they might have been better prepared to change with the times on their own terms—creating untold upside value instead of the opposite."

What to Avoid

Luc Wathieu is a professor of marketing at Georgetown University's McDonough School of Business, and an expert in consumer behavior, branding, and marketing. He recommends that, "Generally, brands should stay away from adopting a name because of connotations that might change or evolve."

Do Your Research

Niles Koenigsberg, a digital marketing specialist at Real Fig Advertising + Marketing, underlines the importance of research:

"As you develop new products, logos, and brands, you must take the time to consider those images and names from multiple angles ... Do your due diligence and conduct some historical research on those images or names. A particular name could sound harmless at first, but a little bit of digging could reveal a deeper issue that your brand may want to avoid."

Listen

"Being tone-deaf is no excuse for organizations to create or retain overtly offensive names or branding. Such actions leave them exposed to backlash that affects revenue and brand image," says Denise Graziano, who is a strategic advisor and expert in organizational transformation and growth, and CEO of Graziano Associates. She goes on:

> "However, in today's hypersensitive environment, the definition of 'offensive' can be a moving target. The worst thing companies can do is make snap judgments and actions about their brands. When companies bend to every outside expectation, it can erode trust from customers, employees, and investors."

Take the Initiative

Real Fig's Koenigsberg emphasizes the value of immediate action:

> "Companies shouldn't wait for the bad PR to start pouring in over social media before changing their images or names. Instead, the companies should take the initiative to examine the history of their brands in tandem with the cultural and societal histories of our country and consider whether or not it would be appropriate to adjust their branding ... As an increasing number of brands and organizations are making the decision to change their branding and make it less offensive, it has become clear that most companies are acting reactively and are suffering for it. We believe it is far wiser to get ahead of the storm and be proactive in your branding decisions."

Graziano recommends that when changing the names of products, you explain what you did—and why:

> "... when there is a clear need to pull a brand or name, organizations should use active language such as 'these are the actions we have taken, and this is why ...' In this way, they retain control of the announcement instead of becoming a cancel culture news story."

Advice

- Keep up with the latest trends, developments, and consumer sensitivities.
- Conduct annual reality checks to determine how well—or poorly—your brand reflects the priorities and values of your company, consumers, and society.
- Don't wait to change or modify aspects of the brand that are out of sync. The longer you wait, the more likely it is that the misalignment could create a crisis.

CHAPTER 11
Lloyd Austin, Scott Kirby, and Angela Merkel

Admit When You're Wrong

Lloyd Austin

Secretary of Defense Lloyd Austin had to apologize in 2024 for his delayed disclosure to President Joe Biden and the public about his prostate surgery. It is an example for business executives about the importance of admitting when they've done or said something wrong.

Austin told a press conference at the Pentagon:

> "I should have told the President about my cancer diagnosis, I should have also told my team and the American public and I take full responsibility. I apologize to my teammates and to the American people ... We did not handle this right, and I did not handle this right."

Seven Best Practices

The longer executives wait to publicly express remorse about their actions or words, the longer they will be digging themselves into a deeper hole that could help lengthen or worsen the situation.

The best practices for business leaders to follow when they admit they're wrong are:

- Don't delay. The sooner an apology is issued, the better.
- Take full responsibility, and don't make any excuses.
- Be sincere in what you say and how you say it.
- Use all available communication channels to share the apology with the public and stakeholders.
- Explain your actions and the circumstances surrounding the issues that were involved.
- Discuss the steps that will be taken to help guard against similar transgressions.

- Be open and transparent about answering questions about the apology, and the circumstances that led up to it.

There are plenty of other remorse-related examples in the corporate world and political worlds from which business leaders can learn.

Angela Merkel

Former German chancellor Angela Merkel apologized in 2021 for a decision related to the measures she enforced around COVID-19.

"This apology was a rare instance where she admitted a misstep in her handling of the pandemic. She expressed this apology publicly, demonstrating her willingness to be accountable for her decisions," Christine Haas, CEO and founder of Christine Haas Media, recalls.

Scott Kirby

In July 2023, United Airlines CEO Scott Kirby faced significant backlash when he flew on a private jet while thousands of United flights were being canceled.

"Kirby publicly admitted his mistake, saying that his decision was 'wrong' and 'insensitive' towards customers who were struggling to get home and United team members who worked tirelessly to fix the situation. He extended an apology to both customers and team members for his actions," observes Nikki Jain, CEO and founder of The Sprout PR.

Actions Have Consequences

"Leaders are always under scrutiny and their actions have widespread consequences. Effective crisis management involves transparent communication, accountability, and a clear path towards rectification and improvement," Jain concludes.

CHAPTER 12
Bed Bath & Beyond

The Death of a Top Corporate Executive

The sudden death of top corporate officials, which can create a crisis for companies and organizations, underscores the need for succession plans, policies, and procedures and the importance of accounting for such events in crisis management plans.

The death of Bed Bath & Beyond CFO Gustavo Arnal in 2022 created a crisis situation for the company.

"The chief financial officer fell to his death from New York's Tribeca skyscraper known as the 'Jenga' tower," *Reuters* reported.

Trimming Corporate Costs

The death of Arnal, 52, came "days after the retail chain announced it would close about 150 of its more than 700 namesake stores and lay off about 20% of its 32,000 employees after its stock fell more than 21% last Wednesday, and 65% in the past year, according to The *Associated Press*," *NBC News* said.

"The home-goods seller is attempting to trim costs and raise money as it tries to correct recent operating missteps and navigate a challenging economic environment. It has been burning through cash reserves for several quarters, and a shopper exodus has shaken investor and vendor confidence," according to the *Wall Street Journal*.

"A More Proactive Approach Is Key"

Catherine Rymsha, a visiting lecturer in management at the University of Massachusetts Lowell, has seen the results of failing to prepare for the future:

> "One company I work with used to plan execs only for emergencies, without much thought for preparedness of successors ... While having an emergency plan is helpful, taking a more proactive approach is key in naming successors annually and developing them routinely ... as well as the people who could

succeed them ... Some companies don't even tell successors they are successors, which can drive people out when they don't see career growth. When a high-level executive passes suddenly, it makes the practice even more valuable. To backfill the role, it puts pressure on HR and senior leaders to fill the role quickly. But this could turn into a nightmare scenario if they fill the role with an unfit candidate."

Act Quickly

Charity Lacey, principal at you+me marketing, explains the importance of acting quickly:

"For organizations that don't have a succession process in place and lose a key team member, engaging your communications team immediately, and knowing their core competencies, are paramount. It is also important to understand which external stakeholders need to be informed ... It's vitally important that organizations understand that there may be circumstances where a key executive may pass unexpectedly—even if they are in good health today. If the coronavirus taught us anything, it is to expect the unexpected. The time to plan for a crisis is before you're in a crisis ... This might include internal teams, partners, vendors, customers, investors or other financial stakeholders, analysts, and media. Which audiences need to know sooner than others and ensuring that the information is shared in a timely manner while being respectful of the family's wishes should be the first step in developing a program."

No Good Reason

Deloitte emphasizes how there are no good reasons not to embrace succession planning:

"There isn't a good reason to justify the common oversight of not planning for business succession. Some business leaders are too caught up in the challenges of the present. Some have a subconscious aversion to the reality that they won't be around forever or assume succession will work itself out naturally ... Others are aware of the task's true complexity and find it overwhelming. Ultimately, however, the reasons people avoid succession planning aren't as important as the reasons they should embrace it."

Preoccupied with Other Issues

A post on the Harvard Law School forum on corporate governance sounds the wake-up call:

> "Understandably, many companies have been preoccupied with the major economic disruption in the market and may not have invested the time or leveraged the expertise of their board members to focus on effective CEO succession planning ... If you're not thinking about this topic now, though, you may be in need of a wake-up call, especially in today's competitive labor market. All signs point to a hiring desert for companies that are unprepared. Some companies are late to the game—but it's not too late. Boards can act now to ensure their plans are ready to meet the challenges of the future."

Corporate Activism

The actions and positions that companies take on hot-button political issues—also known as corporate activism—run the risk of creating negative publicity and blowback for the brands on social media.

That was the case for ice-cream maker Ben & Jerry's when it tweeted in 2023 that it was "high time we recognize that the US exists on stolen Indigenous land and commit to returning it," and that we should start with Mount Rushmore, political website *The Hill* reported. "The ice cream company said in a post on its website that the parades, barbecues and fireworks displays typical of the [Fourth of July] holiday can 'distract' from the 'essential truth' of the birth of the United States—that it was founded by taking land from Indigenous populations."

While the company sparked outrage on social media with the Independence Day Twitter post, the Vermont ice-cream maker is no stranger to criticism over its stances on divisive issues.

Earlier in 2023, Ben & Jerry's fended off calls for a boycott after co-founder Ben Cohen voiced his opposition to the US military providing aid to Ukraine. Scrutiny had continued to escalate over the company's support of the LGBTQ+ community and the "Black Lives Matter" movement, among other polarizing issues, *Newsweek* reported.

Ben & Jerry's approach to activism can be instructive for corporate leaders across the political spectrum who want their companies to have an impact on hot-button issues. Executives should be mindful, however, of how customers and members of the public, who may not agree with that activism, will respond to those efforts.

State Corporate Values

Before going down the activism road, it's important to clearly state—internally and externally—the values and beliefs of the organization.

"We believe that ice cream can change the world," according to Ben & Jerry's website. "We have a progressive, nonpartisan social mission that seeks to meet human needs and eliminate injustices in our local, national, and international communities by integrating these concerns in our day-to-day business activities."

Connect with Audiences

Depending on the nature and purpose of the business, corporate executives should identify when and how they will connect with the public.

Tenyse Williams, an adjunct digital marketing instructor at Columbia University, George Washington University, and University of Central Florida, explains:

> "Ben & Jerry's doesn't just sell ice cream; it serves up a scoop of activism with every cone; connecting with their audience on a profoundly deeper level than mere consumption ... Their strategy is a masterclass for business leaders on how to create a community with their customers by crafting experiences that resonate on a personal level. This results in turning everyday transactions into meaningful ones. Such a strategy doesn't just boost brand loyalty and customer engagement—it turns occasional buyers into lifelong fans, which is a key driver of profitability."

Be Committed and Authentic

Consistency, determination, and persistence are keys in helping to ensure the success of corporate activism.

Tara Furiani, CEO of Not the HR Lady, underlines the importance of authenticity:

> "Ben & Jerry's doesn't do performative activism. Every campaign, every message, and every pint sold is a testament to their unwavering commitment to social justice ... Ben & Jerry's teaches that authenticity cannot be an afterthought or a marketing ploy; it must be the core ingredient of your brand. As leaders, our challenge is to embed this authenticity into the fabric of our companies, ensuring that our actions always align with our words."

Exercise Leverage

"Political and social activism relies on the personal charisma of the activist, and both Ben and Jerry leveraged their own charm to great effect in promoting their company and its values," Robert C. Bird, a professor of business law and Eversource Energy Chair in Business Ethics at the University of Connecticut, explains.

Recognize Limitations

Corporate activism campaigns usually do not last forever, and there can be built-in limitations as to how long they can or should last. Bird goes on:

> "When a brand is sold to a company, the social and political values of the founders only remain for so long. Eventually the enterprise becomes culturally integrated into the larger company and loses some of the distinction that made Ben & Jerry's ice-cream company unique."

CHAPTER 14
Joe Biden

Know When to Go

President Joe Biden's surprise announcement in July 2024 that he would "step aside" and no longer seek re-election—and his endorsement of Vice President Kamala Harris to succeed him—underscored critical issues about whether and when corporate executives should resign or retire during or after a crisis.

The answers can depend on different factors and variables.

Performance-Driven

Biden's disastrous debate performance in June 2024 sparked renewed concerns that quickly turned into alarm about his cognitive ability and communication skills.

The editorial board of *The New York Times* said Biden should leave the race for the White House, noting that:

> "The president appeared on Thursday night as the shadow of a great public servant. He struggled to explain what he would accomplish in a second term. He struggled to respond to Mr. Trump's provocations. He struggled to hold Mr. Trump accountable for his lies, his failures and his chilling plans. More than once, he struggled to make it to the end of a sentence."

In the Business World

In the business world, a similar performance by a CEO at a shareholder or board meeting would likely spur calls that he or she immediately seek medical attention, take a leave of absence, or step down. Their reluctance or refusal to leave would automatically put the executive into a defensive situation, which is never a good place to be. And it could strengthen arguments as to why they should step down immediately.

Being self-aware could help an executive avoid an uncomfortable situation, especially if their performance or interest in doing the job fades, or if their mental or physical health declines.

Darcy Eikenberg, a leadership and executive coach, explains:

> "No matter what our age, smart organizations know they're at risk if one person holds all the knowledge cards ... Requiring successor conversations and backup plans is an essential business process for every person, but it's magnified for employees over 60."

Protest-Driven

It is not unusual for boards of directors to ask or pressure senior executives to step down because of their role in creating or perpetuating a crisis.

Think back to 2023 when, in the aftermath of campus protests and of headline-making testimony before a congressional committee, the president of the University of Pennsylvania resigned. (See related story in Chapter 25.) She stepped down "amid pressure from donors and criticism over testimony at a congressional hearing where she was unable to say under repeated questioning that calls on campus for the genocide of Jews would violate the school's conduct policy," the *Associated Press* reported.

Company officials who immediately submit their resignation after a crisis can help their organizations move on. But executives who insist on staying—even in the face of growing internal or public pressure that they leave—run the risk of making a bad situation worse by extending or adding a new aspect to the crisis.

Restoring Confidence

"Biden's [earlier] decision to stay in the 2024 race, despite calls for him to step down, mirrors corporate scenarios where CEOs faced immense pressure but chose to remain," Lakesha Cole, founder and principal publicist at she PR, says. She comments:

> "Boeing CEO Dennis Muilenburg was ultimately ousted as Boeing CEO after a tumultuous period marked by two fatal 737 Max crashes, production delays, and numerous issues with the aircraft [see related story in Chapter 4] ... The intense pressure from stakeholders, regulators, and the public led to his resignation, deemed necessary to restore confidence and allow Boeing to address the significant challenges in getting its crucial product back in the air."

Pressure from Stakeholders

Christine Haas, CEO and founder of Christine Haas Media, recalls how Volkswagen CEO Martin Winterkorn initially refused to step down despite the massive fallout and pressure from various stakeholders because of the company's emissions scandal in 2015:

> "His decision to stay on was seen as a move to stabilize the company during the crisis. However, as the scandal deepened and the company's credibility was severely impacted, Winterkorn eventually resigned, recognizing that his departure was necessary to restore trust and enable the company to move forward with a new strategy and leadership."

Paving the Way for New Leadership

Haas also notes how Travis Kalanick, the CEO of Uber, faced immense pressure to resign in 2017 following a series of scandals, including allegations of a toxic work culture and regulatory issues. Despite his significant role in building Uber, "Kalanick stepped down, allowing the company to bring in new leadership under Dara Khosrowshahi, who focused on stabilizing the company and improving its public image."

For President Biden, his initial decision to remain in the race underscored his commitment to his agenda "and his belief in his ability to lead. However, it also raise[d] questions about the broader implications for party unity and electoral success, much like how corporate leaders must weigh their personal leadership against the long-term health of their organizations," Haas says.

Responding to Growing Backlash

The resignation in 2024 of Harvard president Claudine Gay was a rare exception to the familiar and predictable script that often plays out during or after a crisis and reflects the impact of a confluence of factors.

The announcement of her sudden resignation was precipitated by not one but two different crises: the backlash over her comments before a House committee that held a hearing about antisemitism and new allegations of plagiarism.

Gay's resignation was unusual for four reasons.

- **Time:** The amount of time that elapsed after her headline-making remarks to the congressional panel. By contrast, Liz Magill, president of the University of Pennsylvania, resigned just days after making similar controversial comments to the House committee.
- **Parallel controversy:** The growing impact of a parallel but unrelated controversy: allegations of plagiarism. "Harvard said it first learned about allegations of plagiarism against Gay in October and that the Harvard Corporation, the school's 12-member governing board, engaged three political scientists from outside the university to carry out their own investigation. The school has declined to identify them or release their review," according to *the Wall Street Journal.*
- **Political opposition:** The crises generated fierce political opposition to her tenure. "Republican lawmakers welcomed Harvard University president Claudine Gay's resignation after weeks of calling for her to step down over her response to antisemitism on campus—and her testimony on the topic at a fiery House hearing," according to *Politico.*
- **Length of tenure:** Gay had been in her position for only six months.

Gay's Statement

Gay wrote in a letter to the Harvard community:

> "It is with a heavy heart but a deep love for Harvard that I write to share that I will be stepping down as president. After consultation with members of the Corporation, it has become clear that it is in the best interests of Harvard for me to resign so that our community can navigate this moment of extraordinary challenge with a focus on the institution rather than any individual."

Gay announced in her letter she would return to a faculty position "and to the scholarship and teaching that are the lifeblood of what we do," according to *CNN.*

"Professional Attacks"

"The professional attacks against her included accusations that on dozens of occasions, she plagiarized other academics in several published papers and her Ph.D. dissertation," *the Wall Street Journal* reported. "The Harvard Corporation, the university's top governing board, said in December that reviews of her work uncovered some instances of 'inadequate citation,' but that the omissions didn't meet the bar of outright research misconduct."

Crisis Issues

When navigating through or after a crisis, corporate boards of directors should keep the following points in mind.

Investigations

- Who will examine the cause of the crisis, and how will they be selected?
- How and when will the results be announced?

Additional Controversies

- Are there controversies or scandals that have or could come to light?
- If and when they become public, how will they be handled?
- How could the other controversies impact the current crisis?

Crisis Response Plan

- Does the organization have a crisis management plan?
- If so, what guidance does it provide for responding to current or new crisis situations?

Next Steps

- What actions should be taken to help guard against similar crises in the future?

"It's Never Easy"

It's never easy for senior executives in or outside of government to decide whether to stay or go during a crisis—or wait to be pushed.

A lot can be at stake for their legacies—and for the future of those for whom they work.

CHAPTER 15
Big Pharma

Recovering from a Crisis

There was a silver lining to the dark cloud of COVID-19: the pharmaceutical industry showed business leaders how companies and organizations can recover from crisis situations.

"The Great Awakening," a report about a national survey conducted by The Harris Poll, observed that:

> "In previous crises, business was viewed as part of the problem. In [the coronavirus] crisis, business is clearly regarded as part of the solution. Corporate reputations surged across a variety of sectors, even in industries traditionally unpopular with consumers ... What's clear, however, is that the traditional drivers of corporate reputation—high-quality products and services and delivering solid business results—are now simply the price of entry."

Character and Trust Count

According to "The Great Awakening," what differentiates companies and reputations today is a company's character, all underpinned by trust. The report pointed out that:

- Prior to COVID-19, only one-third (32 percent) of Americans had a positive opinion of the pharmaceutical industry.
- After vaccines brought the end of the pandemic within reach, the number of Americans with a positive opinion nearly doubled to 62 percent.
- Just less than half (44 percent) of Americans say their opinion of the industry has improved since the start of the pandemic—because of the actions the pharma industry has taken.

Laura Guitar, who leads rbb Communications' Reputation & Risk Advisors, points out that:

"One key reason that business is enjoying a boost in reputation has much to do with the government's failure in the early stages of the pandemic response, creating a crisis of convergence in which mishandling of a crisis of coincidence bled into a crisis of confidence."

Looking for Answers

Guitar goes on:

"When government fails, people look to business for answers to society's issues. In response—and in conjunction with the social justice movement last summer—many companies chose to champion purpose and values. By doing so, those companies have been able to emerge from the pandemic's crisis of coincidence in a position of strength. But holding on to that position will take intention and care."

Reputation Versus Branding

Caroline Sapriel is founder and managing partner of CS&A International, 30-year-old crisis resiliency firm that counsels multinational clients across industry sectors around the world. She offers the following advice:

"Reputation is what others think/say, not what organizations say about themselves, that's branding. Reputation is granted by stakeholders, not acquired by the organization. Organizations that can demonstrate consistent and sustained action to 'fix' the problem(s) are the ones most likely to not only recover but also emerge stronger from crises."

Success Factors

Crisis management expert Martha Holler, founder of Shine PR, observes that three things stand out about pharma's actions during the pandemic:

- **Priorities:** "They put people before profits. When brands align with the consumer and are seen acting, authentically, in consumers' best interests, then brand love and profits follow."
- **Results:** "They underpromised and overdelivered. It was a race against the clock to develop a viable vaccine and slow the spread of this deadly disease. With internal alignment of resources and a clear focus on a singular goal, pharmaceutical

companies achieved what did not seem possible—safe and effective vaccines within six months."

- **Visibility:** "They kept senior executives visible and drove the narrative. Oftentimes in a crisis, organizations circle the wagons, and information is hard to come by. This leaves consumers, media, critics, regulators all wondering what they are hiding. This was not the case here."

Michael Toebe, a trust and reputation risk management and executive communications specialist at Reputation Intelligence-Reputation Quality, observes that:

"The pharma industry benefitted greatly by having a crisis develop that happened to be in their scope of competence and expertise. It was imminently qualified to respond. Its reputation at the time was being heavily scrutinized and criticized ... Being able to put their intellectual and financial resources to use to develop a vaccine in the midst of a global pandemic was a tremendous opportunity to restore, or some might say reconstruct, reputation. It was granted the ability to change perception, judgment, and a negative narrative."

Based on the success of pharma and other industries, it is possible for companies and organizations to bounce back from a disaster, scandal, or other corporate emergencies.

Commitment

Scott Sobel, a crisis, media, and litigation communications counselor at kglobal, advises:

"It is no surprise that pharma's credibility has grown incredibly [by] developing COVID-19 vaccines in record time ... Pharma and all businesses with reputation challenges can never sit back on their laurels. Those businesses need to continue to communicate past and future successes."

Toebe says that business leaders can learn from pharma's success by:

- Clearly, accurately, promptly, and fully recognizing the opportunity or opportunities that present themselves to solve big problems that are likely right in front of you.
- Then humbly and confidently declare your intention to address it for the right reason—to do "right" for others.

Transparency

Christina Eyuboglu, a public relations and crisis communications consultant, believes that:

> "There's a lot to be learned from companies that are helping us climb out of this pandemic and a lot of different forces at play that have created a more favorable reputation for previously low-confidence industries/companies ... Chief among them is transparency. There was a lot of open information from several of the companies developing the vaccine from early on until today. This information wasn't communicated through a board of directors meeting or company stakeholder meeting but went directly to the press [so it would go] directly to the consumers."

Connecting

Sobel emphasizes the importance of a personal touch:

> "Effective crisis management, mitigation, and rebuilding reputation are dependent on connecting with target audiences on a personal trust level ... You have to personalize clients, make corporations present as personal, caring, and responsible entities with the same interests as the target audiences."

CHAPTER 16
Buckingham Palace and the Duke and Duchess of Sussex

Tell Your Side of the Story

Oprah Winfrey's interview in 2021 with the Duke and Duchess of Sussex was must-see TV for many people who have a role in preventing, responding, managing, communicating, or trying to recover from crisis situations. No matter what business or profession you are in, it is always possible to learn from the successes and mistakes of how others are handling their own crisis situations.

It's worth remembering that the British monarchy is a multi-billion-dollar business. Family feud or not, a crisis is a crisis—and any crisis has the potential to damage the brand, image, reputation, and bottom line of an organization.

A basic rule in crisis communication is to tell your side of the story the best and most effective way you can, with as few filters as possible. You'll have more credibility if you tell your side of the story yourself, instead of waiting for others to do it for you. And the sooner the better.

The two royals did not appear to hold anything back in the interview with Oprah and did and said what was necessary to tell their side of the crisis.

- Harry and Meghan agreed to be interviewed by Oprah, who has a loyal following of millions of people around the world.
- They made their points with stories, anecdotes, and occasional humor.
- The couple came across as credible, open, and honest, with nothing to hide.
- Rather than say "no comment" to two questions they did not want to answer, they explained *why* they did not want to respond to the questions.

Spin Control

It is unusual for both sides in a crisis to do their best to level allegations and counter accusations against each other. The charges and countercharges were flying in the days leading up to the broadcast interview. As reported by *The New York Times*: "The couple's lawyers accused the royal family and its staff of malice and deception, telling *The Times* of London that the newspaper was 'being used by Buckingham Palace to peddle a wholly false narrative.'"

Through a spokesman, Meghan and Harry decried the stories as "distorted several-years-old accusations" packaged together as part of a "smear campaign" intended to harm their reputations ahead of their interview with Oprah.

After the allegations were published, Buckingham Palace issued a statement expressing concern and announcing plans to look into the matter: "Accordingly, our HR team will look into the circumstances outlined in the article. Members of staff involved at the time, including those who have left the Household, will be invited to participate to see if lessons can be learned," according to *The New York Times*.

Christina Eyuboglu, a public relations and crisis management consultant, points out that:

> "They began the statement by offering sadness for the challenges the Sussexes faced. They acknowledged that the issue of race was 'concerning.' Would I have used a stronger word there? Yes. How about 'upsetting, horrifying, shocking' to name a few. Where they pivoted and lost the spirit of the message was when they said that 'some recollections may vary.' This is tantamount to 'sorry you feel that way.'
>
> They get a few points for saying that these issues will be addressed by the family ... until they said 'privately.' While I would have preferred a list of concrete actions and a timeline, they are asserting this is an internal family issue, versus a corporate one. Troubling, considering this family operates as a 'business' most of the time, and a 'family' when it's convenient.
>
> You can't have it both ways. Signing off by saying that 'Harry, Meghan, and Archie will always be much-loved family members' shows that they are open for reconciliation and that the family will remain intact. Oh great, clearly it's kumbaya from here!"

Keep Calm and Carry On

Crisis situations have the potential to engulf organizations and distract CEOs from the day-to-day business of running their companies.

For her part, the Queen seemed determined not to let the family drama distract her from her official duties and obligations. As reported by *Harper's Bazaar*, hours before the interview with Harry and Meghan was scheduled to air, the Queen "... delivered a passionate speech on 'selfless dedication to duty.'"

CHAPTER 17
Burger King and Dollar General

Rage-Quitting

All publicity is not good publicity. A Burger King restaurant in Lincoln, Nebraska, found itself the center of unwanted national attention in 2021 when all of its employees resigned, proclaiming on the sign outside the eatery that, "We all quit. Sorry for the inconvenience."

According to *The Washington Post*:

> "The candid note ... was the employees' way of expressing in no uncertain terms that they had had enough—enough of management, enough of understaffing and enough of the scorching-hot kitchen that at one point allegedly hospitalized a worker with dehydration."

Not the First Time

Business Insider Australia reported that so-called rage-quitting is:

> "... as old as work itself. Some people prefer to end things with a bang, not a whimper. So things like bridge-burning, walking off [without] a two weeks' notice, or even making a scene are nothing new when leaving a workplace. But the American workforce seems to be primed for rage-quitting at the moment—especially hourly workers in low-wage occupations like retail, which make up a giant portion of the *workforce*. In fact, hourly workers made up 58.1% of the U.S. workforce in 2019, according to the Bureau of Labor Statistics."

The report goes on to say how in 2021 several Dollar General employees at a store in Maine:

> "... walked off the job after posting notes decrying the company's work culture and pay. Similar incidents have occurred at Chipotle, Hardee's, and Wendy's around the country. Meanwhile, employers are complaining of a tight labor market, in some cases accusing unemployment benefits of luring potential workers away."

Advice

There are several important steps corporate executives can take when they find that their companies and organizations are, for whatever reason, in the harsh glare of the public spotlight.

Tell What You Are Doing About the Crisis

A spokesperson for Burger King told *NBC's Today Show* that, "The work experience described at this location is not in line with our brand values." The restaurant's franchisee is investigating the situation to prevent similar incidents, the spokesperson added, as reported by *The Washington Post*.

Use All Communication Tools at Your Disposal

In telling your side of the story, use all communication methods available to reach all your stakeholders and other audiences. Burger King did not appear to do that in this case—they made no mention of the incident on the press page of their website, which did not appear to have been updated in more than three years.

Respond to Press Inquiries

Immediately respond to all requests for information or comments from legitimate news organizations and news outlets that are followed by your stakeholders and other audiences. In its story, *The Washington Post* noted that, "A spokesperson for Burger King ... did not respond to a request for comment."

Recommendations

- Address the issue that caused the bad publicity to help guarantee that it is not repeated.
- Be careful what you say though—anything you say to employees could be leaked to the media or posted on social media.
- Apologize to those who were affected by the incident.

- Include in your crisis management plan provisions for responding to any episodes of rage-quitting at your organization if or when they occur or any other unexpected event that could generate bad publicity.
- The next time your company holds practice sessions to ensure the crisis management plan will work when needed, include scenarios that involve rage-quitting and other events that would create negative news coverage for your organization.

CHAPTER 18
California Pizza Kitchen

Turn Lemons into Lemonade

Paying close attention to the allegations, charges, and criticisms that customers make on social media about your company or organization can be an important way to help head off a potential crisis and prevent a bad situation from becoming worse.

It's not often, however, that a company can pivot quickly and turn an unhappy customer into favorable publicity and a national sales promotion.

But that's what the California Pizza Kitchen restaurant did.

A Delivery Order Mistake

A TikTok user named Riley posted a video in July 2024 to complain that the company made a mistake when it fulfilled a delivery order she placed for macaroni and cheese, according to the *Today Show*:

> "I'm having the worst week of my life," Riley said in her video, because "my boyfriend and I broke up, so I ordered mac and cheese from California Pizza Kitchen, and they just sent me cheese. Just cheese, no mac."

The customer flagged the mistake to the restaurant, but to no avail. "Riley says she called the restaurant, and two separate people told her she ordered incorrectly—she can see on her receipt that she did order a side of Mac N Cheese," the *Today Show* reported.

Riley's video was seen more than 3.4 million times and generated thousands of comments, according to *PR News*.

Admitting They Were Wrong

In response to her complaint, the restaurant chain posted a video on TikTok admitting that it got her order wrong and announced a national promotion to encourage people to order its mac and cheese. That video was seen by more than 10 million people, according to *Media Post*.

"Hello everyone, Chef Paul here," Paul Pszybylski, CPK's vice president of culinary innovation, said in the video, according to *KTLA-TV.* "I heard there's been a little bit of confusion on how to properly make our mac and cheese, so I thought I'd send this video out nationwide to make sure everybody knew the proper steps."

That's when the company turned its mistake into a national headline-making sales promotion.

"Since, recently, we gave one of our guests only half a mac and cheese, we're gonna give *all* of our guests half off mac and cheese starting today through the rest of the month," he announced.

Making Things Right

The company sent Riley a second delivery: a basket with a note, a certificate granting the customer free mac and cheese for a year, another certificate for free pizza for a year that was hidden in a pizza box—and a bunch of uncooked pasta, *USA Today* reported.

Why did the company go to such lengths?

California Pizza Kitchen wanted to "make things right with her and then use it as an opportunity to remind everyone what matters to us," Dawn Keller, chief marketing officer, told *USA Today.*

Surprised by Reactions

"Honestly, we had no idea [that its video] would go viral—we've been blown [away] by the response," Keller commented. "We appreciated that (she) had a sense of humor about it all, so we responded with something light-hearted that would make her day and maybe bring a bit of joy to all our fans as well," the newspaper reported.

The Benefits of Social Listening

All organizations could benefit from social listening the same way that the national restaurant chain did. According to social and internet data analysis company Social Intelligence Lab:

"Social listening is the process of tracking mentions of a brand, product, or competitor online. That can mean tracking direct mentions of a brand or product for the purpose of measuring customer feedback or it can be watching the conversation for discussion around a topic."

As California Pizza Kitchen demonstrated so well, monitoring what customers are saying or showing about your company on social media—and reacting quickly to what you hear or see—can be an effective way to help prevent a bad situation from turning worse—or into a full-blown crisis situation.

CHAPTER 19
Carvana

Firing People Via Zoom

It is not unusual for companies to reduce their workforce in response to crises—industry upheavals, revenue shortfalls, or global pandemics—but if employers decide to fire people en masse on Zoom (or use other impersonal approaches), they can create a second crisis that makes a tough situation much, much worse.

Take what happened at Carvana, an online used car dealer which laid off 2,500 people in 2022, many of them over Zoom.

"An email from Carvana CEO Ernie Garcia, titled 'Today is a hard day,' cites economic headwinds including higher financing costs and delayed car purchasing. He says the company 'failed to accurately predict how this would all play out and the impact it would have on our business,'" *CNBC* reported.

In an email to *CBS MoneyWatch*, Carvana said it had "as many conversations as we could in person, and where in-person was not possible, we spoke to our team members over Zoom." The spokesperson added, "Not all of the conversations were through Zoom."

Quick Blowback

Reaction on social media was swift and critical, with people expressing their anger on how they were let go and how the online session was conducted. This response on Twitter (now X) was typical: "Part of [Carvana's] principles is 'we are all in this together' and I don't believe that at all. Carvana, next time you need to lay people off do it in a more organized way than what happened today because honestly, that was ridiculous."

"They were doing mass layoffs in these Zoom calls," Leigh Frantz, 26, of North Liberty, Iowa, told *CBS MoneyWatch*. She said that a woman read from a prewritten script to inform them that they had lost their jobs. Workers weren't allowed to ask questions on the Zoom call. "It was so disrespectful."

The remote firings have been seen as a cold, impersonal, and detached way to lay off people.

Challenges and Issues

Using Zoom and similar services can create a second crisis for organizations.

Depending on how workers are notified and what is said on video calls, fired employees could respond by placing businesses on the defensive and damaging the credibility, image, and reputation of CEOs and organizations.

Videos can take on a life of their own when recorded by employees and shared on social media. And they could be edited in such a way as to put the company in a bad light and on the defensive. And if a fired employee files a lawsuit against the company, it's possible that the video could become part of the legal proceedings.

Leaked copies of any recorded video calls about the layoffs can add fuel to the fire and help lengthen the crisis or make it worse. "Leaked video from a second meeting that Better.com held minutes after the now-infamous Zoom call in December when it terminated 900 employees provides stunning new insight into the level of mismanagement that went into perhaps the most bungled corporate downsizing in recent memory," *Fast Company* reported.

A third crisis could be created by the videos because of the impact they can have on company morale and the ability to retain or recruit employees.

Advice

Beware

- Employees could immediately post copies of the video on social media platforms.
- Do not say anything on the call that you would not want to be reported by news organizations.

Be Clear

- Take steps to ensure that the reasons for the layoffs are clearly understood by all those who are affected by the reduction of your workforce or who may learn about it later.
- This includes posting an official statement from the company on its website, social media platforms, and emails, distributing a press release, and posting a video from a corporate spokesperson on YouTube.

Be Prepared

- Be ready to immediately respond to any blowback about the video or why employees were fired.
- Prepare in advance key messages about the firings to use when responding to calls from the media, messages from remaining employees, and criticism on social media.
- Conduct media training sessions before the video calls to ensure you are ready to respond to questions from reporters.

Be Available

- Make yourself available to answer questions people and news organizations may have about the layoffs and respond quickly to their inquiries.
- Immediately respond to any allegations or charges about the reasons for the layoffs.

Seek Counsel

- Seek advice or counsel from your internal or external PR and legal teams about potential issues related to firing people via video that may be unique to your company, organization, industry, or location.
- The more you know about potential problems that can cause or exacerbate a layoff-related crisis for your company, the better.

CHAPTER 20
Catherine, Princess of Wales
(Kate Middleton)

Doctored Photos

It can be very tempting for people to experiment with technologies to see how they can be used. But even with the best intentions and for the best purposes, how people use technology could create a controversy or crisis. Just ask one of the members of the British royal family.

Catherine, Princess of Wales, apologized in early March 2024 for doctoring a photo of herself and her children published by several news organizations. The *Associated Press* reported:

> "The first official photo of Kate, the Princess of Wales, since she underwent abdominal surgery nearly two months ago was pulled from circulation by The *Associated Press* and several other news organizations because the image appeared to have been manipulated.
>
> Kensington Palace had issued the image [on March 10] as speculation swirled on social media about the whereabouts of the oft-photographed princess who hadn't been seen in public since December."

Then came word that she altered an earlier image of the royal family.

"Reigniting a Storm of Speculation"

"The decision to recall the photo [that was distributed earlier this month] reignited a storm of speculation about Catherine, who has not been seen in public since she had abdominal surgery two months ago. In her statement, the 42-year-old princess chalked up the alteration to a photographer's innocent desire to retouch the image," *The New York Times* wrote.

"Like many amateur photographers, I do occasionally experiment with editing," Middleton wrote in a post on social media. "I wanted to express my apologies for any confusion the family photograph we shared yesterday caused," she was quoted as saying in that newspaper.

Signs of Editing

"Acknowledgement of the doctored photo came after several news agencies retracted it. The *Associated Press*, for instance, noted the odd "alignment of Princess Charlotte's left hand with the sleeve of her sweater" and stated, "At closer inspection it appears that the source has manipulated the image," according to *NPR*.

Adding Fuel to the Fire

Jonathan Hemus, managing director and crisis management consultant at Insignia, advises the following:

> "In a crisis, retaining trust is critical; anything which undermines your credibility will make protecting your reputation even harder ... As such, Catherine's doctoring of the photo—innocuous or not—has added fuel to the fire rather than dampening it down. The only viable course of action now is to be more open and proactive with communication, to re-establish Catherine and William as the source of truth."

"A Very Good Move"

Catherine's apology and explanation "that she edited them as an amateur photographer was a very good move," Rhea Freeman, a public relations, marketing and social media consultant in the UK, comments: "Staying silent on this occasion, in my opinion, would have given the story a longer life, but admitting the oversight, I believe, was the correct action and should help to manage the story and its lifespan."

Not the First Time

It later turned out that this was not the first time that a member of the royal family had manipulated an image that was distributed to news organizations.

On March 19, 2024, "Getty Images placed an editorial advisory on a second photo taken by Catherine, of Queen Elizabeth II surrounded by her grandchildren and great-grandchildren, saying the image had been altered before it was released by the palace," according to *The New York Times*.

The news agency explained in a statement that "in accordance with its editorial policy it has placed an editor's note on a handout image stating the image has been digitally enhanced at source."

Raising Red Flags

Companies that are discovered to have done something wrong or illegal in the past should not be surprised when news outlets dig deeper in an effort to find other issues that had gone unnoticed.

If and when those issues are discovered, news about them can raise new questions and concerns, and rekindle media and public scrutiny of the organizations.

How to Be Proactive

Reports about the two incidents are timely reminders for leaders of companies and organizations about the dangers of altering photos that can deceive the public, and how they might impact their image, reputation, and credibility.

Policies

Organizations may want to consider:

- Adopting policies that prohibit the use of altered images and videos.
- Taking steps to ensure that all employees and independent contractors are aware of the policies.
- Implementing protocols to guarantee that all images and videos that are distributed by or on behalf of the company are accurate and unaltered.

Procedures

To guard against the impact this form of disinformation can have on businesses:

- Be proactive. As soon as you learn about the doctored image, notify clients, customers, and the public about it.
- Don't wait. The longer you wait to react to the deepfake, the more likely it is that people will assume that it is legitimate.

- Contact the social media platform where it appears and ask that it be removed at once. Such images may violate the platform's terms of service.
- Account for deepfakes in crisis management and crisis communication plans.
- Practice responding to different deepfake crisis scenarios in corporate exercises and simulations to ensure that the plans will work when needed.

CHAPTER 21
Centers for Disease Control and Prevention

Admit Your Mistakes

A best practice for managing the recovery from a crisis is to admit when you've made mistakes.

That's exactly what Dr. Rochelle Walensky, who was then the director of the Centers for Disease Control and Prevention, did when she announced plans to reorganize the federal agency in April 2022. "To be frank, we are responsible for some pretty dramatic, pretty public mistakes, from testing to data to communications," she said in a video distributed to the agency's roughly 11,000 employees, *The New York Times* reported.

Crisis management and public relations experts weighed in with their observations of what the CDC got right—and wrong—in responding to the COVID-19 pandemic.

Admit Your Mistakes

Andrea B. Clement, a media relations and communication expert and founder of Clem. co, observes:

> "It's remarkable for a huge government organization such as the CDC to admit to failures on this level or on this scale, and I think that Walensky's public statement and the CDC's current stance is commendable. I think that this shake-up is necessary to fully restore credibility and the public's trust, and to ensure a more effective and efficient response to future health crises. In my opinion and experience, the key takeaway and lesson here for leaders is the importance of accountability and transparency in communication and crisis response, as well as consistency."

"Show Accountability"

Clement also underlines the importance of owning your mistakes:

"Another takeaway from the CDC shake-up is that to recover from mistakes or missteps made in the public arena, your organization must show accountability ... [S]how that you are going to make it right—that you're going to implement the necessary changes to alleviate issues in the future. If you make mistakes in the public eye, you've got to acknowledge it and show that you're making positive changes to fix internal issues in order to rebuild trust among your audience and clients."

Speed Matters

Danielle Grossman, a senior media consultant at Sevans PR, comments on the importance of planning for a communications crisis strategy:

"Having a team dedicated to communicating with the public is a crucial part of managing a crisis, especially during a global pandemic. The most effective leaders understand the importance of addressing the crisis immediately rather than waiting until the crisis is over. Yes, this was an overwhelming and unprecedented situation, but taking a more proactive approach to disseminating information would have been more effective.

Even though the CDC has admitted to its shortcomings, it's a little too late. Business leaders should take their situation into consideration when planning their own crisis communications strategy. Responding quickly and taking responsibility is an important part of dealing with any crisis, especially one of this magnitude."

The CDC and the government in general "are not built for speed, and this [reorganization] will fall flat if swift, meaningful, and visible change does not occur," observes Denise Graziano, strategic advisor and expert in organizational transformation and growth, and CEO of Graziano Associates.

Avoid Contradictory Messaging

Clement emphasizes the importance of clear messaging:

"Contradictory messaging is not only confusing, it erodes trust over time if it continues. I think perhaps it would have been more effective messaging at the time if the CDC had not been so quick to definitively discount masks as a preventive resource, for example ... When company messages are contradictory or in sharp contrast to prior messaging, it makes your company appear very disorganized and could even make your audience of employees/clients/followers feel as though the people in charge don't know what they're doing."

Earn and Maintain Trust

Graziano agrees, advocating clarity and transparency in communication:

> "When it comes to matters of crisis, health or otherwise, transparency, clarity of communication, accountability, speed, and accuracy are necessary to earn and maintain trust ... this announcement will be meaningless unless tangible improvements are made."

Explain Changes

David Thomson, president of the Thomson Communications public relations firm, highlights some of the lessons to be learned from the CDC response:

> "Explain what changes the organization is going to make to show that it learned from [its] mistakes and how it is preparing to do better in the future.
>
> Walensky highlighted some major changes for the CDC that include hiring more staff for a team that responds to public health emergencies, releasing data and scientific findings more quickly, and to ensure the CDC's messaging is in 'plain language'.
>
> In terms of following the guidelines to best manage a public crisis, the CDC said all the right things. Now it is time for them to walk the talk and prove that they truly learned from their mistakes and don't repeat them going forward."

CHAPTER 22
Cinnamon Toast Crunch

Product Tampering

General Mills is one of a long line of businesses to deal with allegations there was something wrong with one of its products. As reported by *The New York Times* in 2021, a man claimed he found shrimp tails in a box of the company's Cinnamon Toast Crunch cereal.

'While we are still investigating this matter, we can say with confidence that this did not occur at our facility," Mike Siemienas, a spokesperson for General Mills, said:

> "We are waiting for the consumer to send us the package to investigate further. Any consumers who notice their cereal box or bag has been tampered with, such as the clear tape that was found in this case, should contact us."

Headline-making accusations that products are contaminated, have been tampered with, or are unsafe can immediately create a crisis for the companies that make them, the retail outlets that sell them, and the people who endorse and buy them.

What's at Stake

How organizations respond to any product safety issues can determine how well or poorly a crisis is handled, how quickly the situation is resolved, and the damage to the image, reputation, and bottom line of a business.

How they treat safety issues can also reflect how they treat consumers.

The speed at which companies respond to crisis situations can be a matter of life and death. Having a crisis plan in place—and testing it at least once a year against various worst-case crisis scenarios—can help ensure business leaders are as prepared as possible for any crisis.

Learning from Others

Rob Britton, principal of RealWorld Leadership who teaches crisis management as an adjunct professor at Georgetown University, wishes that manufacturers of all kinds—from food to automobiles—borrowed from the best practices of operating companies like airlines. Britton, who was part of the leadership team at American Airlines that rebuilt the brand after 9/11, explains:

> "Airlines and other transport companies prepare crisis-response plans across a wide range of scenarios, then exercise them regularly to improve performance when a real crisis happens. It's clear from General Mills' clumsy handling of this week's cereal-contamination allegation that they don't do that."

Britton adds that another best practice is to assess performance after the crisis abates and use that learning to improve response plans. "Feedback loops are essential to effective crisis management."

Speed Versus Responsiveness

Don't confuse speed with responsiveness. A canned or automated reply to the concerns of customers can be mistaken for brushing off.

Laura Meyers, director of corporate communications for accounting and advisory firm The Bonadio Group, sees the situation involving Cinnamon Toast Crunch as "more of a lesson in crisis response and reputation management in a digital world than it is in food safety-specific communication." She comments that:

> "... the debacle highlights significant, yet common, missteps companies take when dealing with consumer complaints online. We've seen it time and again—someone will send out a negative Tweet about a company, the brand will reply, and the world will ask, 'Who OK-ed that response?' Despite years of seeing the repercussions, brands continue to make mistakes when it comes to addressing and resolving claims."

Meyers notes that the cereal maker responded to the consumer's concerns on Twitter via public reply, which allowed "... their conversation to be viewed and reacted to by the entire Twitter-sphere." In addition, she says the company indicated the consumer "... was mistaken and had no grounds for the complaint."

Advice

Meyers recommends keeping the following advice in mind:

- **Move fast:** Act quickly but gather as many details as possible before responding.
- **Go offline:** Always try to bring the conversation offline, or at the very least, bring it to a private forum. It's important to move conversations away from the public eye, not for the sake of secrecy but to allow for detailed information gathering and discussion of next steps. It's much easier to have these resulting conversations via phone rather than on social media. Note: even if a conversation is brought to a direct message, remember that everything is screen shot-able.
- **Don't minimize:** Avoid minimizing or dismissing claims made by consumers. We've come a long way from "the customer is always right" but that's not to say brands should come across as dismissive.
- **Be proactive:** The sooner companies are made aware of an issue that could turn into a crisis, the better. One way to do that is to invest the resources and staff time to monitor all aspects of the online world. Even the smallest chatter on the internet about an issue runs the risk of taking on a life of its own. You never know when a seemingly isolated post can spark a raging wildfire on the internet.

Incorporating worst-case scenarios when testing crisis response plans is a good way to help gauge the ability and speed of crisis management teams in detecting and addressing complaints by customers and the public.

CHAPTER 23
CNN

Leadership Missteps

CNN, which usually reports the news about crises, went through a crisis itself.

"Chris Licht, the embattled chief executive and chairman of *CNN*, whose brief one-year tenure at the network was stained by a series of severe missteps, departed the company ..." the news organization reported in 2023.

"I met with Chris, and he will be leaving *CNN*," David Zaslav, the chief executive of parent company Warner Bros. Discovery, told *CNN* employees at the start of the network's daily editorial meeting, according to the network.

Licht's brief and rocky tenure at the news outlet provides several lessons for corporate leaders about avoiding and responding to a crisis.

Don't Make Yourself the Story

Debra Caruso Marrone, president of DJC Communications, a public relations and crisis management firm, comments on Licht's fundamental error:

> "As Licht said in his response to [an article about his leadership style in *Atlantic*], a leader should never make himself the story. Unfortunately, that's what he did ... Having read the entire *Atlantic* article (as long as it was), Licht poured his heart out to reporter Tim Alberta and allowed Alberta too much access to his private thoughts and even his close relationships with people like his personal trainer."

Apologize Quickly

After the article was published, Licht apologized for creating a distraction for his company and its journalists, saying, "*CNN* is not about me. I should not be in the news unless it's taking arrows for you."

Internal Followers and Supporters

Laurie R. Barkman, CEO of Business Transition Sherpa, observes:

> "Perhaps Licht did not do enough to build internal followers and supporters. Unlike former *CNN* president Jeffrey Zucker, who [had] an office on a *CNN* newsroom floor, Licht separated himself from the network's journalists.
>
> Was this foreshadowing for the figurative separation Licht would experience with key journalists? Anchor Christiane Amanpour, among others, voiced discontent in some of Licht's programming decisions. It is common practice for new CEOs to hire executives with whom they have worked previously. These are trusted, tested relationships that can add value to a new leadership team.
>
> The challenge is if you don't invest enough in the troops who you need to follow you into battle."

Take Time to Make Changes

For any "new leader, particularly one succeeding a popular predecessor ... become a member of a tribe before you try to lead it," says Ephraim Schachter, a leadership strategist and C-suite coach. He adds:

> "Rather than building rapport, trust, and relationship capital with his new company, Licht is reported to have criticized their work, telling them that *CNN* had lost its way. He physically separated himself, having little contact with staff, even moving offices to a separate floor. This is a recipe for inviting contempt, not building loyalty."

When Everything Is Changing, You Can't Change Everything

Barkman describes how Licht:

> "... entered the company with a mandate for change. In his first six months, he conducted a company-wide business review that led to a series of sweeping changes.

Many changes were met with skepticism and challenges, such as shuttering the *CNN+* streaming service (originally hailed as a future growth platform for the company). He also fired key *CNN* journalists, including Brian Stelter, the network's chief media correspondent and anchor of *Reliable Sources.* While many of these changes may have helped the financials, they likely created a foundational shift in the psyche of the staff."

Don't Let a Crisis Simmer

A crisis can only get worse over time, not better.

Once they know there is a problem—or that a problem is being caused by an employee or top executive—the board of directors or other appropriate corporate leaders should not wait to take decisive action.

CNN's parent company apparently did the right things, for the right reason, and at the right time. It quickly sought to put the story behind them as soon as possible. Otherwise, the story could have dragged on and impacted the ability to keep and attract advertisers and affected the company's stock price.

Andy Barr, CEO and founder of the 10 Yetis digital marketing agency, said in a statement from his company:

"Warner Bros. Discovery has followed the crisis communication playbook to the letter by trying to move fast and get ahead of the story.

Licht could have been left to limp on through his tenure as CEO of *CNN*, and the story would have dragged out. This would have attracted advertiser and shareholder unrest and eventually led to a share price fall, but the fast-paced nature of the decision should now give investors greater faith in the future direction of the company.

This is a great example of decisive leadership by Warner Bros. Discovery, but also another reason why CEOs need to remember that the truth always comes out, especially around emotive subjects such as politics. It will inevitably come out faster if you lose the faith of the workforce in your first few activities, actions, and statements."

Take Responsibility

"For a number of reasons, things didn't work out, and that's unfortunate," David Zaslav told *CNN* staffers. "It's really unfortunate. And ultimately, that's on me. And I take full responsibility for that," *Forbes* reported.

An Apology May Not Be Enough

Saying you are sorry for the actions or words that caused a crisis may not always be sufficient.

That certainly proved to be the case with Licht.

CHAPTER 24
Colonial Pipeline

Preparations and Backup Plans

The ransomware attack on Colonial Pipeline in May 2021 created a crisis for the company and the country and provided important lessons on how to respond and manage crisis situations.

The headline-making attack led the company to shut down its 5,500 miles of pipelines that, as reported by *The Washington Post*, "carry fuel from refineries on the Gulf Coast to customers in the southern and eastern United States. It says it transports 45% of the fuel consumed on the East Coast, reaching 50 million Americans."

Making a Difficult Decision

Joseph Blount, CEO of Colonial Pipeline Co., told the *Wall Street Journal* "that he authorized the ransom payment of $4.4 million because executives were unsure how badly the cyberattack had breached its systems, and consequently, how long it would take to bring the pipeline back."

'I know that's a highly controversial decision,' Mr. Blount said in his first public remarks since the crippling hack. 'I didn't make it lightly. I will admit that I wasn't comfortable seeing money go out the door to people like this. But it was the right thing to do for the country.'

Cyberattack Reality Check

This cyberattack underscored important realities:

- **Vulnerability**: Every company is vulnerable to an attack.
- **Sophistication**: Cyber thieves are getting more sophisticated.
- **Preparation**: Don't wait to help prevent or mitigate ransomware and other attacks.
- **Threats**: Business leaders need to be aware of possible internal cyber threats.

- **Warnings:** You should pay attention to news reports and government warnings about the latest threats and respond accordingly. You don't want to be the last one to know.
- **Plans:** Corporate crisis management plans should be reviewed, updated, and tested regularly to ensure that companies are prepared for the latest cyber-related threats.
- **Consequences:** The failure to prepare for or properly respond to cyberattacks can damage the image and reputation of companies and could result in fines or penalties by regulators.

Human Error

According to IBM's Cyber Security Index Report, human error was a major contributing error in 95 percent of all cyber breaches.

Heather Stratford, founder of Drip7, a cybersecurity education platform, observes:

> "The 'person' is what needs to be 'fixed' or focused on when it comes to cyber-security awareness, and this change generally does not happen overnight. Changing behavior is built on small incremental improvements, which over time tighten the control limits to improve behavior and minimize risk."

Training Takes Time

Stratford goes on:

> "It is impossible to lose 30 pounds by going to the gym for an hour in January. Likewise, training employees once a year to improve critical behavior is not achievable through annual check-box training. The only way to make a difference in the current cybersecurity epidemic is to increase the focus on the people of an organization, not just the systems in place."

Just as important as the lessons that have been learned since the Colonial Pipeline attack are the steps business leaders can take now to help protect their organizations from future attacks.

Advice

Plan

Because of the Colonial Pipeline ransomware attack, "making sure businesses have and continue to improve processes and procedures has been a huge learning lesson for business leaders," advises Bryan Hornung, founder of Xact IT Solutions, a cybersecurity firm and a co-author of books about cybersecurity, including *Adapt and Overcome* and *Under Attack*. "Specifically, having a proper offboarding plan for terminated employees that involves IT is critical. This is also why business continuity and incident response planning [are] critical and should be part of every organization's business plan."

Strive for Cyber Resiliency

Hornung emphasizes the importance of cyber resilience:

"All companies should be striving for cyber resiliency by identifying assets, putting a plan in place to protect those assets, implementing the tools to detect if those assets have been breached, developing a written plan to respond so everyone knows what to do, and executing a recovery that, if developed correctly, will make the event easier to get through.

Without it, you are prone to mistakes, missteps, and human error, which leads to longer recovery times and a larger loss of revenue. It's always less expensive to take care of things on the left side of 'the boom' than on the right side after an event.

Your network security is a team sport and swift public disclosure is better than keeping things within your own silo. Historically business treats cyber events with secrecy, and it's common for [them] to keep things like ransomware attacks hidden from the public. This is just how the hackers like it and is proving to be a counterproductive decision in hindsight."

Assume Nothing

Hornung also points out that:

"The tools, hardware, and software you buy from reputable manufacturers can have undiscovered vulnerabilities in nearly every product. All technology will have undiscovered vulnerabilities, and that is an aspect of cybersecurity many people don't understand yet.

With any cyberattack, the first thing you want to do is isolate the problem by disconnecting it from the internet. Once this is done, the team will need to determine if data was exfiltrated and what leverage they have to reduce the ransom demand, if at all. Once they decide to pay the ransom or not, Colonial is still looking at a heavy investment for new infrastructure because you can't rebuild on the same network that was infected. You're starting over.

Incident response planning is critical and should be part of every organization's business plan. All companies should be striving for cyber resiliency by:

- Identifying assets.
- Putting a plan in place to protect those assets.
- Implementing the tools to detect if those assets have been breached, developing a written plan to respond so everyone knows what to do.
- Executing a recovery that, if developed correctly, will make the event easier to get through."

Go on the Offensive

Curt Aubley, managing director at Deloitte Risk & Financial Advisory specializing in cyber threat detection and response, cautions:

"We've seen that adversaries continue to change their tools, techniques, and processes ... but organizations are not as mature against these new attacks as they perceive they are. And, in many cases, the industry has not fully embraced cybersecurity intelligence programs to advance against new attack approaches.

Companies need to go on the offense and use proactive threat hunting, machine learning, and self-healing systems. Further, we still see the need for companies to address longer-term resiliency planning as well, which includes integrated IT and OT cyber-threat management, Zero Trust adoption, and focus on secure supply chain practices."

Ensure Controls Are in Place

Jason Rebholz is the chief information security officer at Corvus Insurance, an insurance technology company. He counsels that organizations "must take steps to ensure preventative security controls are in place. More importantly, they should ensure that there are processes and technologies in place to establish resilience in the event of an attack."

Mike Campbell, CEO of Fusion Risk Management, says:

"One aspect that is often overlooked is operational resilience, which goes hand in hand with crisis situations. As we see in the shutdown of Colonial Pipeline, preparedness and backup plans must be built into every facet of third-party management.

The pandemic demonstrated resilience is not just about a product but the entire reliance on an infrastructure of stability and reliability. Preparedness involves considering what other alternatives or resources are at your disposal."

CHAPTER 25
Columbia University

Responding to Protests

How university officials responded to student protests on campuses across the country in 2024 provided business leaders with timely lessons about preventing and managing crisis situations at their organizations.

Establish Boundaries

Ray Hennessey, executive partner and CEO of Vocatus, a marketing and messaging consulting firm, explains how those university presidents:

"... who set clear boundaries about what behavior was acceptable [on campus], and then followed through with enforcing those boundaries, largely were able to handle themselves well reputationally ... We saw that best at schools like the University of Florida. On the flip side, presidents who vacillated or sent mixed messages, like at Columbia, found themselves facing criticism on all sides."

Set Expectations

The different ways universities responded to the protests were "a pretty good lesson in the importance of clear communication and then strong follow-up," Hennessey observes. "Executives know they have to clearly set expectations and then follow through. It is hard to criticize any leader, college president or otherwise, when they articulate a plan and then hold stakeholders accountable for meeting their expectations."

Sync Words with Actions

"Columbia's President Minouche Shafik faced backlash during a House committee hearing when members challenged her decisions, remarking that her rhetoric did not match the events on campus. Upon returning to campus, Shafik called police who arrested more than 100 protesters," Lesli Franco, vice president of O'Connell & Goldberg, a public relations firm, points out.

Shafik, who announced in an email in August 2024 that she was stepping down, had held the job for 13 months. She wrote that she had time over the summer to reflect and decided it would be best for Columbia if she moved on, *NPR* reported. She wrote:

> "I have had the honor and privilege to lead this incredible institution, and I believe that—working together—we have made progress in a number of important areas. However, it has also been a period of turmoil where it has been difficult to overcome divergent views across our community. This period has taken a considerable toll on my family, as it has for others in our community.
>
> It has been distressing—for the community, for me as president, and on a personal level—to find myself, colleagues, and students the subject of threats and abuse. As President Lincoln said, 'A house divided against itself cannot stand'— we must do all we can to resist the forces of polarization in our community."

Remember Your Stakeholders

Dustin Siggins, a business writer and founder of publicity firm Proven Media Solutions, highlights the various stakeholders who need to be considered:

> "Because they're non-profits, we often forget that universities have many stakeholders beyond students, alumni, and faculty. Those stakeholders include taxpayers and parents who watched their money be used to host chaotic and often violent protests.
>
> Many university presidents forgot to keep these stakeholders in mind when they responded poorly to the chaotic, often violent, campus protests in the recent school year, and negative media coverage and canceled graduations were the result."

Be Forceful

Vocatus's Hennessey makes the following observation:

> "The biggest differentiator between which college presidents faced criticism and which ones didn't was in how forceful they were in responding and communicating their response to the college protests.

Businesses can learn a simple lesson from how university presidents failed to lead during these crises: always be ready to develop, present, execute, and promote effective plans of action during times of chaos. Otherwise, you look as unnecessarily incompetent as many of these campus protests."

Be Decisive

Be decisive in a crisis. Waffling sends the wrong message to all parties. Use strong, clear, and concise language that everyone can understand.

CHAPTER 26
CrowdStrike

IT Shutdowns

Corporate dependence on technology often comes with built-in risks for crisis situations when the technology—for whatever reason—fails.

A global IT shutdown in 2024 was just one example.

"A global technology outage caused by a faulty software update grounded flights, knocked media outlets offline, and disrupted hospitals, small businesses and government offices, highlighting the fragility of a digitized world dependent on just a handful of providers," the *Associated Press* reported. "At the heart of the massive disruption is CrowdStrike, a cybersecurity firm that provides software to thousands of companies worldwide."

CrowdStrike Is "Deeply Sorry"

"The issue has been identified, isolated and a fix has been deployed," CrowdStrike said in an update on its website:

> "We are referring customers to the support portal for the latest updates and will continue to provide complete and continuous public updates on our blog.
>
> We understand the gravity of the situation and are deeply sorry for the inconvenience and disruption. We are working with all impacted customers to ensure that systems are back up and they can deliver the services their customers are counting on."

"A Massive Headache"

Jake Holyoak, a digital public relations expert, observes:

> "The global IT outage is a massive headache for all the companies involved, and the impact on their image, credibility, and reputation is significant ... When systems go down, especially on a global scale, it shakes customer confidence and raises questions about a company's reliability and preparedness."

Silver Linings

If there are silver linings that can be found in the crisis, they are the crisis management lessons that business leaders should take to heart as their companies recover from the outage—and start preparing for the *next* crisis.

"Act Swiftly"

Holyoak goes on:

> "From a PR [standpoint], the companies affected need to act swiftly and transparently. Immediate, honest communication is crucial here. They should provide clear updates about what happened, what they're doing to fix it, and how they're preventing future incidents. The key is to show they're in control and taking responsibility.

> For leaders, this outage [was] a wake-up call. It highlight[ed] the importance of robust IT infrastructure and disaster recovery plans. Companies should invest in better cybersecurity measures and regular system audits. Additionally, having a solid crisis management plan in place is non-negotiable. This means not only technical solutions but also prepared communication strategies to keep all stakeholders informed."

The Need for Redundancy

"The global tech outage demonstrated why organizations must have reliable and redundant methods to communicate both internally and externally during a crisis," John Yarbrough, senior vice president of corporate marketing at Alert Media, advises:

> "When default methods of communicating with employees, customers, and partners are compromised, the immediate impact is confusion and mistrust in management. By failing to communicate early and often, brands lose the ability to control the narrative as employees and customers inevitably look elsewhere for insight into what's going on and when the situation will be resolved."

Provide Reassurance and Details

Lindsey Chastain, founder and CEO of The Writing Detective, emphasizes the importance of specific details in communications:

"While the initial transparency about the global disruption was a good start, additional reassurance and specific details are still needed ... At this stage, tech leadership should be providing regular service status updates across multiple channels—on social media, on their websites, via press releases, etc. Even if the updates simply acknowledge teams are still investigating, that shows customers they have top-of-mind awareness and are committed to fixing things."

Demonstrate Resolve

Chastain goes on:

"The companies should also have their highest-visibility executives like CEOs or CTOs directly addressing customers and employees to demonstrate their seriousness in resolving the issues at senior levels.

Consumer trust has eroded to the point where transparency about failings and crystal-clear explanations of improvements being made are the only paths forward. Promises won't cut it—tangible technical changes, failover testing results, infrastructure investments must be put forth and progress measured."

Be Available

Charlie O'Toole, senior account manager at SourceCode Communications in the UK, recommends that companies should:

"... acknowledge the disruption, explain what went wrong in plain terms and, this is the part most brands get wrong, explain exactly what you're going to do to ease that disruption for your customers.

That means being available, being honest, and being transparent. It's not your fault the system went down, but it's your responsibility now to do right by your customers."

Have a Disaster Recovery Plan

Mitchell A. Thornton, professor and director of the Cyber Security Institute at Southern Methodist University, advises:

> "Because it's impossible to predict every cyber disaster, a robust and well-tested disaster recovery plan is key to protecting an organization's assets and operations. It is essential that companies conduct periodic 'dry runs' to test the viability of their ... recovery plans, including testing their backup and restoration systems."

Back Up Data

Thornton also highlights the importance of thorough disaster recovery planning:

> "Some companies recommend storing backups in geographically distant locations; however, reliance on the internet to access backups can be a problem, so dedicated lines or other reliable means should be available for geographically distant backup storage.
>
> Many times, it is essential for disaster recovery to not only be comprehensive but quick to employ. The frequency of backups is another consideration—can a particular company afford to resume business with backup data that is one week/day/hour old?"

CHAPTER 27
Department of Defense

Crisis Exercises and Simulations

No one is born with the ability to communicate strategically, effectively, and efficiently about a crisis that strikes their company or organization.

But they can learn.

Indeed, executives could learn a thing or two about crisis communication in a disciplined, organized, and trained manner from the US military, which is known, after all, for the emphasis it places on discipline, organization, and training.

The armed forces have a lot of experience communicating about crisis situations. Examples include a Navy training jet that crashed into a residential neighborhood, the use of hazardous and toxic chemicals in firefighting foam at a Marine Corps base, and an active shooter on an Army installation.

A good way to take advantage of the Pentagon's experience and expertise is to use the crisis communication portion of its PAVILION website. The website is a portal to a searchable knowledge base of resources that are curated, developed, and pulled from training courses, fleet, field, and industry and crowd-sourced from the Department of Defense community.

The portal supplements the US military's in-person communication training for members of the armed services, select Department of Defense civilians, and international military personnel.

PAVILION is not a military secret and has been scrubbed clean of any sensitive or classified information. Not surprisingly, the website has its share of military abbreviations, buzzwords, and jargon. The good news is that anyone can profit from the advice and insights of this online learning resource, which is free to use and paid for by US taxpayers.

The Pentagon's Perspective

The crisis communication section of PAVILION provides a unique perspective and resources for corporate executives about important aspects of connecting with the public and stakeholders in emergency situations.

Business executives and their staff may find the following resources on the site particularly helpful in preparing and communicating about a crisis.

Crisis Communication Portal

The crisis communication section features dozens of checklists, exercises, tests, and simulations on topics that will be familiar to business leaders and crisis managers such as using social media, crisis response teams, communicating about accidents, news conferences, and preparing for a crisis.

The following descriptions are excerpted from the exercises that were on the PAVILION's website in 2024.

Three Crisis Communication Exercises

When a crisis occurs and your reputation is on the line, it is vital to be prepared to communicate effectively. These three exercises will help you manage a crisis and facilitate a more positive response from your audience.

Exercise: Prepare for Any Crisis

When the worst happens, it's natural to be overwhelmed in the moment, so it's important to rehearse your response in advance. Establishing a plan will help you and your team regain control as quickly as possible after the crisis occurs. Being prepared in case of an emergency is critical. When you plan ahead, you can do your part in the moment without panicking.

To be more confident during a crisis, practice and prepare by starting with these checklists, templates, and planning documents *before* a crisis occurs. They will provide you with structure and guidance, so you are ready before the pressure is applied during and after a crisis. Do your part and remember: you've got this.

Exercise: Keep Your Cool When Things Heat Up—Plane Crashes During Air Show

Your mission is to communicate vital information about the aircraft crash to the public and internal audiences while still protecting the privacy of victims during this crisis situation. Resources and other information regarding the mission will be provided to help you along the way.

Exercise: Using Social Media During a Crisis

In a crisis, you may look to social media to get information out quickly to your publics, but this is not always the right approach. Even if you have a well-established social media space, you cannot count on your [audiences] going there for information.

Practice, Practice, Practice

The more often your company practices and prepares for different crisis scenarios, the better.

It helps to make the training sessions as authentic as possible. Some business executives use computer simulations so their companies and organizations will be as prepared as possible for a variety of worst-case crisis scenarios.

From cyberattacks to mass casualty events, the simulations can provide the kinds of experiences, insights, and lessons that tabletop and other in-person exercises can't match.

Advice

- Online resources can supplement in-person crisis training and exercises.
- Business leaders and their staff can pick up important tips about managing and communicating about a crisis from how companies and organizations in different industries and professions prepare and train for crisis situations.
- The more often you practice and prepare for different crisis scenarios, the more likely it is you will be ready when a crisis hits.
- When practicing responses to different crisis scenarios it helps to make the training sessions as authentic as possible ... some business executives are using computer simulations so their companies and organizations will be as prepared as possible for a variety of worst-case crisis scenarios.

CHAPTER 28
Department of Homeland Security

Disinformation and Misinformation

False information can have real-world consequences. In worst-case scenarios, disinformation and misinformation can make bad situations worse, and even create new crises. One example in 2024 was their impact on efforts to recover from Hurricane Helene and Hurricane Milton.

Pausing Recovery Efforts

"Aid to several communities impacted by Hurricane Helene was temporarily paused in parts of North Carolina over the weekend due to reports of threats against Federal Emergency Management Agency responders, amid a backdrop of misinformation about responses to recent storms," *CNN* reported.

Protecting FEMA Workers

"Door-to-door outreaches resumed after about a day, a FEMA spokesperson said ... FEMA wanted to ensure it protected staff on the ground while the agency worked with local law enforcement officials to assess the threats and how serious they were, according to the spokesperson," reported the news outlet.

A Popular Post-Helene Rumor

"Some of the rumors floating around in Helene's wake seem designed to tap into people's preconceived political biases. A popular rumor, promoted by former President Donald Trump and X owner Elon Musk, suggests the federal government is confiscating or otherwise diverting aid meant for Helene relief efforts as part of a political ploy," *CNN* explained.

False Online Information

Homeland Security Secretary Alejandro Mayorkas thought that false information online about the hurricanes was "extremely pernicious" and warned that it's hampering efforts to assist victims of the crisis," *The Hill* reported.

Mayorkas said on *CBS' Face the Nation* that the false information is "deliberately spread to impact people's behavior and perceptions."

"It is extremely pernicious," he added. "We have individuals in need of assistance, who are entitled to assistance, who aren't seeking it because of the false information." Mayorkas called for officials to debunk the false claims because "we're not seeing enough of that ... I find that to be incredibly irresponsible and irresponsible to the people who are survivors of these extreme weather events."

Harassment and Death Threats

The New York Times reported that meteorologists have faced harassment and death threats because of disinformation about the hurricanes. "Weather experts say the spiraling falsehoods, especially claims that the government is creating or controlling storms, have gotten out of hand."

How Misinformation Thrives

"Misinformation thrives when people feel they're being kept in the dark, and our polarized political culture has only deepened mistrust, not just in government but between citizens themselves," observes Amanda Orr, a public relations expert at Orr Strategy Group.

Increased Urgency

Clifford Oliver is a retired former senior executive at FEMA and now the principal at Nanticoke Global Strategies, which provides emergency management, homeland security, and business continuity services. He said fighting disaster response disinformation took on added urgency when the response to both Hurricanes Helene and Milton became hyper-politicized and added new challenges for recovering from the weather-related crises:

"Previously, disaster response disinformation, while present, was more of an extreme dialogue mostly found on fringe social media and chat rooms that only had minimal operational impact on disaster response operations.

The recent 'mainstreaming' of disaster response disinformation has forced public affairs officials and representatives across all levels of government to divert attention from messaging important disaster response information to disaster survivors and coordinating the response to the disasters to addressing the disinformation."

Disinformation can add to the stress of hurricane survivors and the officials who are trying to help them. Oliver goes on:

"As a result of the extreme stress disaster survivors experience, they are a highly at-risk population that are vulnerable to disinformation; government officials have had to react to disaster response disinformation in as near to real-time as possible."

In addition to the added stress levels false information can make it harder to help hurricane victims:

"This has distracted from and disrupted disaster response planning and response, potentially delaying urgently needed information and resources from reaching disaster survivors."

Making Matters Worse

Oliver offers the following advice:

"It is important to note that those responding to the current disasters, emergency management officials, volunteers, and first responders are also under significant distress that the current disinformation only serves to make worse. As an almost 40-year member of the emergency management/first responder community, I find the situation disheartening. Those responding are heroes and deserve better."

Media Literacy Is Essential

Orr of Orr Strategy Group recommends the following:

"In the long term, a comprehensive federal media literacy program is essential for fighting the spread of misinformation ... The effort must be bipartisan, with equal funding from all political affiliations, to ensure it transcends partisan divides. Questioning government actions is a cornerstone of democracy and should be encouraged, but it's troubling when those questions are rooted in inflammatory rhetoric often fueled by extremist propaganda. A well-executed media literacy program would empower the public to critically evaluate information, paving the way for a more informed and productive dialogue."

Why Business Leaders Should Take Note

Oliver highlights the importance of business leaders engaging with misinformation:

"Business leaders should take note of the ability of disinformation players to quickly overwhelm 'official' communications concerning an unfolding crisis by generating what are often outrageous/bordering on sublime allegations of wrongdoing that are often tied to the current heightened distrust of government officials/leaders and the officers of large corporations."

Speed Matters

Oliver explains how corporate executives have even less time today than they did before to respond to disinformation and misinformation:

"In the often-perverse world of social media, the most outrageous allegations often draw the most hits. Another concern for business leaders to consider is the now near real-time speed with which the social media postings occur in response to an unfolding crisis which leaves business leaders with little if any time to 'get out ahead' in terms of communications.

Not long ago, businesses often had days to react to an unfolding crisis. Currently, businesses have hours, at best, to react and to push out 'their side of the story' through various communication channels."

The failure to control the story about a crisis can create its own crisis:

"No matter how well a business is prepared for and responds to a crisis, it is now nearly impossible to 'control the narrative' on social media, and businesses need to accept the fact that disinformation can create a crisis, in and of itself."

CHAPTER 29
Didi and Metro Bank

Rumors

The longer business leaders delay in responding to a damaging and unfounded rumor, the more likely it is the rumor will spread and grow, making it more difficult to set the record straight. Indeed, many people might assume that unless you *immediately* tell your side of the story, there could be some truth to the rumor.

That's why corporate executives should consider following the example set by an official of Didi, the Chinese app-based ride-hailing service, who acted quickly in response to an unfounded rumor about his company.

Fast Action by Didi Executive

The New York Times reported in 2021 that a Didi executive wrote on social platform Weibo "that he had seen rumors saying that because the company had gone public in New York, it had to turn over user data to the United States." The executive said that Didi stored all its Chinese data on servers in China, and that the company reserved the right to sue anyone who said otherwise.

"The message was reposted on Didi's official Weibo account 16 minutes later, with the comment: 'We hope everybody avoids spreading and believing rumors!'" according to the newspaper.

Business leaders usually have enough to worry about when dealing with the facts of a crisis. Their workload can increase, however—and a crisis made even worse—when rumors about the crisis start to circulate.

UK's Metro Bank Sets the Record Straight

Metro Bank, an independent bank in the UK, was forced in 2019 to respond to a false rumor in the middle of a crisis. *Reuters* reported at the time that the bank had been "battling to shore up confidence after a major accounting error in January wiped more than 1.5 billion pounds off its market value and forced it into a 350-million-pound ($455 million) fundraising."

"We're aware there were increased queries ... about safe deposit boxes following false rumors about Metro Bank on social media and messaging apps," a spokesperson stated.

According to the news organization, "Pictures on social media showed queues of customers at Metro Bank branches in West London, with Twitter users reporting that concerns about safety deposit boxes had been raised on community WhatsApp groups in the area."

"There is no truth to these rumors, and we want to reassure our customers that there is no reason to be concerned," the spokeswoman said as Metro Bank reiterated that it never takes ownership of customer items held in safe deposit boxes.

Government Role Models

Companies and organizations might learn how to respond to and control rumors from the US government. FEMA has a coronavirus rumor control page on its website, as does the US Defense Department; the Cybersecurity and Infrastructure Security Agency maintained a rumor control page about the 2020 elections.

Rumor control is nothing new for the federal government. According to Wikipedia:

> "The well-developed crisis control centers established during the Cold War were among the earlier examples of effective rumor control mechanisms. In the United States, during the civil rights movement, rumor control centers were set up and operated with the assistance of the Community Relations Service (CRS), a 'peacemaker' agency created by the Civil Rights Act of 1964.
>
> Rumor control centers have been established in the United States at different levels of governance, including municipal, regional, state-wide and national. Permanent rumor control centers serve a specific, local population, and have often been set up in response to specific incidents."

Advice

Monitor

- Have a staff member or consultant monitor all social media platforms for any mention of your company or organization.

Educate

- Educate employees and vendors about the potential damaging effect rumors could have on the organization, and why it is important they let officials know immediately when they hear or see any rumors about the company.

Respond

- As soon as you become aware of a rumor online, immediately respond with your side of the story.
- Depending on the nature and impact of the rumor, consider posting information about it on the company's website and social media platforms.
- If news organizations find out about the rumor, respond to their requests for information and provide your point of view and facts about the matter.

Update

- Update your crisis management plan to include policies and procedures for detecting and responding to rumors.

Practice

- The next time you conduct crisis management practice sessions involving various scenarios, include at least one scenario about responding to a false rumor.

CHAPTER 30
ExxonMobil

Setting the Record Straight

All publicity is not necessarily good publicity—especially when it may create a crisis for your organization by damaging its image or reputation. That's why it's important to immediately set the record straight when somebody conveys the wrong impression or says something harmful about your company or industry.

ExxonMobil's Tweet

A good example was when then-former President Donald Trump described during a rally in the midst of his re-election campaign in 2020 a fictitious telephone call between him and the CEO of Exxon. As reported by *CBS News*, in that hypothetical conversation, the CEO agrees to give the Republican presidential candidate $25 million in exchange for energy exploration permits from the government.

The company quickly sought to set the record straight, lest anyone think an actual bribe had occurred: "We are aware of the president's statement regarding a hypothetical call with our CEO ... and just so we're all clear, it never happened."

The Truth About Wind Turbines

Sometimes it's not just one corporation but an entire industry that may be maligned and required to set the record straight.

Trump has made false statements about wind turbines, including that the noise from the machines causes cancer and that "windmills kill all birds."

In response to these claims, the American Wind Energy Association posted this message on its website:

> "This weekend, the President made a series of inaccurate statements about wind energy while omitting the many benefits it brings to communities throughout the country, particularly in the Midwest. A number of media outlets have already fact-checked the President's remarks ..."

The message went on to include a series of reality checks about wind energy.

Fauci's Response to Trump Ad

Politicians can be quite adept in monitoring and immediately responding when rivals try to twist or distort their policy positions, voting record, or public statements. It's unusual, however, when a non-elected public official has to defend himself.

Dr. Anthony Fauci had to set the record straight on his own behalf when a Trump campaign ad in 2020 made it appear as if the nationally known and respected infectious disease expert was praising the President's response to the pandemic. Fauci told *CBS 60 Minutes*:

> "I do not and nor will I ever publicly endorse any political candidate. And here I am, they're sticking me right in the middle of a campaign ad. Which I thought was outrageous. I was referring to something entirely different. I was referring to the grueling work of the task force that, 'God, we were knocking ourselves out seven days a week. I don't think we could possibly have done any more than that.'"

If Not You, Who?

Whether you work for a company or organization or are a high-profile individual, setting the record straight should always be a top priority if you are attacked or maligned. As comforting as it would be for others to come to your aid, every minute that passes without a response can threaten to turn wrong information into accepted "facts" and conventional wisdom.

Some news organizations are quick to set the record straight without any prompting from the injured parties. This was particularly true in the 2020 election with several news outlets conducting and publishing the results of their own fact-checking about the claims, promises, and statements of presidential candidates.

But you may not have the allies you need to come to your defense or the luxury of time to wait until others do. If you fail to respond right away to damaging allegations about what you've said or done, who will step forward for you?

CHAPTER 31
Facebook

Attacking Critics and Changing Its Name

One of the challenges for companies that respond forcefully to allegations and charges that are made about their role in a crisis is that the comments can appear to be *too aggressive*. They run the risk of overshadowing the organization's arguments and creating sympathy or additional support for critics, providing more ammunition to opponents—and extending or worsening the crisis.

Facebook launched a series of counterattacks before, during, and after a 2021 Senate Commerce subcommittee hearing and the riveting and headline-making testimony of whistleblower Frances Haugen.

Facebook's Tactics

Business leaders should keep in mind the effects these and other tactics could have when they respond to crisis situations at their companies or organizations and whether that would help or hurt their efforts to address and resolve the crisis.

Question Credibility

ABC News reported that:

> "Minutes after her testimony, Facebook issued a statement attempting to discredit Haugen, stating that she worked for the company for less than two years, had no direct reports, never attended a decision-point meeting with C-level executives—and testified more than six times to not working on the subject matter in question."

Challenge Accuracy

The Washington Post said that Facebook sent out an early morning blog post defending itself, saying that "protecting our community is more important than maximizing our profits." Facebook also asserted, "It is not accurate that leaked internal research demonstrates Instagram is 'toxic' for teen girls."

Ridicule

In a memo to employees that was posted for the public on Facebook, CEO Mark Zuckerberg said:

> "Many of the claims don't make any sense. If we wanted to ignore research, why would we create an industry-leading research program to understand these important issues in the first place?
>
> If we didn't care about fighting harmful content, then why would we employ so many more people dedicated to this than any other company in our space—even ones larger than us?
>
> If we wanted to hide our results, why would we have established an industry-leading standard for transparency and reporting on what we're doing?
>
> And if social media were as responsible for polarizing society as some people claim, then why are we seeing polarization increase in the U.S. while it stays flat or declines in many countries with just as heavy use of social media around the world?"

Deny

In the same post, Zuckerberg went on to say:

> "At the heart of these accusations is this idea that we prioritize profit over safety and well-being. That's just not true.
>
> For example, one move that has been called into question is when we introduced the Meaningful Social Interactions change to News Feed.
>
> This change showed fewer viral videos and more content from friends and family—which we did knowing it would mean people spent less time on Facebook, but that research suggested it was the right thing for people's well-being. Is that something a company focused on profits over people would do?"

Challenge the Reasoning of Others

Again, from the same post, Zuckerberg claimed that:

> "The argument that we deliberately push content that makes people angry [so we can make money] is deeply illogical.

> We make money from ads, and advertisers consistently tell us they don't want their ads next to harmful or angry content. And I don't know any tech company that sets out to build products that make people angry or depressed. The moral, business and product incentives all point in the opposite direction."

Avoiding Responsibility

Ann Skeet, senior director of leadership ethics at the Markkula Center for Applied Ethics at Santa Clara University, comments:

> "Zuckerberg's response reads, in part, [as if it were sent] from someone on a high school debate team. He's hoping to 'win' an argument rather than accept responsibility for the harms inflicted by his company's products."

No New Thinking

Skeet goes on:

> "Unfortunately, dated regulation allows for this lack of accountability, and the governance choices the company has made along the way remove any checks and balances to Zuckerberg's opinion.

> [Zuckerberg] runs a company that provides service akin to those of utilities, without the counsel of a governing board, or the regulatory oversight of a public commission. Governance at its best generates new thinking about how to approach institutional challenges. Unfortunately, there is no evidence of new thinking in the company's response."

Comments Hurt Facebook

Julianna Sheridan, vice president of precision and crisis communications at Matter Communications, a digital marketing agency, observes:

"I believe Mark Zuckerberg's comments hurt Facebook. Two key elements of any crisis communications response are transparency and accountability.

In his latest employee message, [Zuckerberg] hides behind jumbled words and portrays Facebook as the victim of an unfair accusation. [His] own credibility has been called into question time and again, and recent events have also put the standing of Facebook on a precipice as well. These [latest] comments were drafted in a way [as] to distract from Facebook's major shortcomings and lack true accountability.

Businesses of all sizes need to ensure they are communicating a clear, consistent message when facing [a] crisis head-on."

Advice

- The approach, attitude, and tone of your responses about a crisis and your critics are as important as the words that are spoken or written.
- Before issuing a response to critics, ask for feedback to the statement from others whose opinions and guidance you trust. Do they think it is a good idea to respond? Why or why not?
- Put your remarks in perspective—what do you hope they will accomplish and how do they fit into your plans to address and resolve the crisis?

Name Change

Weeks after attacking whistleblower Frances Haugen—and the negative headlines Facebook received for criticizing her—Zuckerberg announced that the company had changed its name to Meta—Greek for "beyond." The move was an example of a tactic that has been used to divert attention from an organization that has received negative publicity and is confronting a crisis situation.

It was doubtful, however, that the name change would do anything to help alleviate any of the crises or controversies now confronting the company. Indeed, the product known as Facebook is still called Facebook. Mark Bayer, president of Bayer Strategic Consulting, notes that:

"A name change now—when Facebook is under intense scrutiny—reinforces the perception the company is trying to elude responsibility for its lengthening list of misdeeds. Even if disconnected from the current crisis, the name change will be seen as a clumsy PR move. It's a gift for comedy writers everywhere."

Zuckerberg said the name change was made to:

"... reflect who we are and what we hope to build ... Building our social media apps will always be an important focus for us. But right now, our brand is so tightly linked to one product that it can't possibly represent everything that we're doing today, let alone in the future.

Over time, I hope that we are seen as a metaverse company. I want to anchor our work and our identity on what we're building towards."

Michael Grimm, vice president of national strategic communications firm Reputation Partners, told *Forbes.com* that:

"Introducing a new name that can act as a parent company overseeing sub-sidiary groups like Instagram, WhatsApp, Oculus, and, of course, Facebook can help divert negative publicity to each business unit while trying to keep the overarching new brand name clean from blame and negative reputation.

We've seen other companies like Google do this with the creation of Alphabet. It will be up to 'Meta' and Mark Zuckerberg to prove that this switch wasn't an obvious crisis communication strategy to divert from the crises plaguing Facebook and that it backs up its rebranding explanations for the switch with real value for consumers and shareholders."

Business consultant Jeff Pedowitz makes the following observation:

"I think the timing feels strange given the recent scrutiny the company is under. Name change aside, the company has a lot of work to do to rebuild trust and confidence in consumers and demonstrate that it can really protect privacy while maintaining balanced and fair standards that are applied to everyone, not just select individuals.

They need to take tangible steps to reaffirm the brand promise. Demonstrate real transparency and accountability. Right now, they are papering over the issues, and everyone sees right through it. They should consider replacing some of their key executives and invest in outside agencies to review and provide oversight of their changes. That would go a long way to demonstrating they are serious about improving their image and what they really stand for."

No Impact on Brand

In an article on *Forbes.com*, Terry M. Isner, owner and CEO of Jaffe PR, advises that:

"A name change or a logo change does not change a brand. It can't hide or erase the past with a face lift. If the perception is that they are using it to remove themselves from past issues, they are actually giving more life to that thought process by making this change [as] opposed to deflecting it because they hope everybody will be distracted by a new shiny name and logo."

"Shining a Light on Their Problems"

However, Isner goes on to say:

"They are shining a spotlight on their problems while also creating more doubt around the brand. The name 'Facebook' associated the tool with people and humanity and a need to collaborate, share and connect. 'Meta' actually fits as a name, as it appears they are moving towards a data-driven platform and not connecting people."

CHAPTER 32
Dr. Anthony Fauci

Responding to Critics

Business leaders should be ready to respond to people who publicly criticize or question their handling of a crisis. Otherwise, their allegations could make a bad situation worse—and damage careers and reputations.

Dr. Anthony Fauci has more experience dealing with criticism over the course of a decades-long career than most corporate executives. His appearance in 2024 before a House committee was an example of how he handles critics.

Fauci was unequivocal in his response to the latest round of criticism. The former government scientist who is "both celebrated and despised for his work on [COVID-19], on Monday forcefully denied Republican allegations that he had helped fund research that sparked the pandemic or had covered up the possibility it originated in a laboratory, calling the accusations 'absolutely false and simply preposterous,'" *The New York Times* reported.

Criticism can lead to the resignation of executives who don't do or say enough in response to their critics. Harvard University president Claudine Gay resigned after weeks of calls for her to step down over her response to antisemitism on campus—and her testimony on the topic at a fiery House hearing. In response to questions by a Republican committee member, Gay said that calling for genocide of Jews may or may not have violated university rules on bullying and harassment "depending on the context." Though Gay later apologized, these comments sparked sharp criticism from Congress, the Harvard community, and the public, and fueled calls for her resignation.

Best Practices

Executives who come under fire for their management of a crisis should remember the following best practices:

- **Respond quickly:** The sooner you respond to criticism, the better. Otherwise, unanswered allegations or aspersions could lead people to assume that the charges are true. Monitor social media and news organizations for how they are covering your response to the crisis and what critics are saying about your management of the situation.
- **Set the record straight:** Cite facts, figures, and other relevant information that effectively counters the charges others make.
- **Be consistent:** Ensure that what you say and how you say it are consistent with the messaging and information that were originally shared about the crisis. Creating an element of doubt or giving new reasons for others to question your management of the crisis could deepen or extend it.
- **Seek allies:** Ask others who have the appropriate and relevant expertise to speak up on your behalf. Their voices could help bolster your credibility, put critics on the defensive, and help make the criticism a non-issue.
- **Keep it short:** Don't say anything more than necessary to refute the allegations. Brevity is critical and can ensure that others—including news organizations—will quote or repeat your response.
- **Admit mistakes:** If criticism for how a crisis was managed is justified, immediately own up to the mistake and explain the steps that will be taken to ensure it is not repeated.
- **Practice:** When testing crisis management plans, include scenarios in which the decisions, actions, and judgment of those who managed the crisis are publicly called into question.
- **Be proactive:** When a crisis strikes, consider how others will react to your management of the situation. Then prepare a list of the worst accusations that could be made for how the matter was handled—and how your organization would respond to those charges.

CHAPTER 33
Federal Emergency Management Agency

Prepare, Prepare, Prepare

Business leaders who want to prepare for a crisis or update their crisis management plans could learn a lot from the Federal Emergency Management Agency (FEMA). The agency has worked on thousands of declared disasters and emergencies according to Clifford Oliver, a retired former senior executive at FEMA and now the principal at Nanticoke Global Strategies.

In the Trenches

Oliver knows what it's like to be in the trenches of crisis management. He worked in the field in various technical staff and management positions, including serving as the deputy federal coordinating officer, which is the President's official representative.

In Washington, he filled a broad range of roles and coordinated field activities that provided temporary housing assistance to victims of Hurricane Katrina, conducted field investigations into the safety of buildings after disasters, and ensured the continuation of essential services in communities after a crisis.

Advice
Be Flexible

Delays can be deadly in a crisis. Every moment spent jumping through hoops before a decision can be made or action taken in an emergency simply prolongs the crisis and can make things worse.

Oliver says how FEMA "... tends to issue guiding principles and as few regulations and rules as possible ... then relies on experienced and empowered leaders to manage crisis situations with the established framework." Although FEMA has crisis planning templates, "... they often act as 'frameworks' [because] each disaster is unique."

Oliver notes that after Hurricane Katrina the agency reviewed and revised its national response plan and turned it into a national response framework: "That framework now serves as the comprehensive guide on how the US responds to all types of disasters and emergencies."

The framework itself is based on a national incident management system that Oliver claims "guides all levels of government, nongovernmental organizations, and the private sector to work together to prevent, protect against, mitigate, respond to, and recover from disasters and other disruptive incidents."

Be Agile

It is important in any crisis to move quickly, learn from your mistakes, and modify your activities, policies, and procedures accordingly.

"As we often hear, most government agencies are known for being highly rule-bound and inflexible. No two crises are the same, [which means] the responses must be adjusted based on what is happening on the ground," Oliver observes.

He says FEMA regularly adjusts its operations and policies based on the lessons it learns from crisis situations: "The buzz word today for this approach is 'agility' and FEMA excel[s] at it, especially for a federal government entity."

Put a Priority on People

Organizations can get so wrapped up in a crisis that they may forget about the importance of the human factor in addressing and recovering from the situation.

FEMA hires staff and managers who work well under pressure in challenging and ever-changing situations, are good communicators, and are team-oriented, Oliver explains. Indeed, "... no matter what was going on operationally, FEMA leadership has kept stressing 'people first' [and] has been able to manage its ever-changing portfolio of work while keep[ing] their staff safe."

To ensure the agency can respond to a crisis at a moment's notice, FEMA maintains a corps of standby workers. These "on-call reservists" are organized into 23 groups or cadres, and become the main FEMA workforce during emergencies and disasters. They must be available to travel on 24–48 hours' notice and willing to be deployed for 30 or more days.

The number of reservists fluctuates, according to Oliver. "As with any large 'on demand' surge workforce, there is always churn, with people leaving and people being removed for not accepting assignments." He notes that there was widespread agreement among other federal agencies and Congress that a larger reservist workforce is needed, which FEMA sought to expand.

Practice

Testing your crisis management plan on a regular basis helps guarantee it will work when needed and that all members of your crisis response team can work well together.

Oliver reports that FEMA conducts tabletop and field exercises throughout the year to ensure it is ready for all crisis situations. Every two years, it holds a national exercise in which all levels of government and the private sector can participate. Each simulation has a different crisis scenario.

Recommended Skills and Relationships

Oliver points out that the most important skills for corporate crisis managers are the same ones that help the government agency do its job: agility, communication, trust, and empathetic leadership. He recommends that business leaders support and empower their crisis managers so they can do their jobs in good times and bad. He suggests that company crisis managers should also develop strong professional networks by joining trade groups such as the Association of Continuity Professionals and building relationships with their local and state emergency management officials.

In 2024, FEMA announced the launch of its National Disaster & Emergency Management University. The university—which is open to the business community—will "help train emergency managers to keep pace with the rapidly changing threat environment," according to the agency.

Then-FEMA administrator Deanne Criswell issued the following statement:

> "Emergency managers are our nation's chief problem solvers ... The new university provides an opportunity for emergency managers to further their professional development and prepare to solve an expanding set of challenges in an ever-changing threat landscape. This is a groundbreaking moment that will be transformational for the field of emergency management."

Courses Are Available to the Private Sector

The announcement was good news for business leaders and their staff who need all the help they can get to prepare for disasters and emergencies—and to keep pace with constantly evolving risks and threats including climate change and cyberattacks.

The online and in-person courses are available to private sector and non-governmental organizations. Independent study courses are available at no cost.

CHAPTER 34
Federal Reserve Bank

Investigating a Crisis

A logical and necessary step after any crisis is to determine the cause and what can be done to prevent it from happening again. Two federal agencies did just that in the aftermath of the collapse of Silicon Valley Bank in March 2023. The Federal Reserve blamed itself for failing to "take forceful enough action" to address the risks the bank took that led to the headline-making collapse of the financial institution.

Critical Review

"A sweeping—and highly critical—review conducted by Michael S. Barr, the Fed's vice chair for supervision, identified lax oversight of the bank and said its collapse demonstrated "weaknesses in regulation and supervision that must be addressed," *The New York Times* reported.

"Regulatory standards for SVB were too low, the supervision of SVB did not work with sufficient force and urgency, and contagion from the firm's failure posed systemic consequences not contemplated by the Federal Reserve's tailoring framework," Barr wrote in a letter accompanying the report.

There were other major contributing factors to the bank's demise.

The Federal Deposit Insurance Corporation's "report confirms that SVB, with its $209 billion in assets, failed mainly because it focused too heavily on tech startups and venture firms along with bond investments sensitive to interest rate hikes. So as the Federal Reserve rapidly raised rates in the past year, it left the company overexposed and, ultimately, drained of capital," according to *Forbes*.

"The bank was growing much too fast, and its demise occurred when word of its struggles spread and customers began pulling out deposits in droves, the report says. The next day, regulators were forced to shut the company down," *Forbes* reported.

Raising Questions

The General Accountability Office chimed in as well, noting in a report that the SVB's failure "raised questions about bank management, federal supervision, and the events leading to regulators' decisions to use emergency authorities."

The House and Senate held hearings into the crisis as well. According to *CNBC*:

> "Members of the Republican majority [in the] House challenged many of the decisions made by regulators in the hours and days after SVB collapsed and Signature Bank followed 48 hours later. Chief among these was what regulators did, or didn't do, in the three days from the time they each learned of SVB's looming collapse, on Thursday to Sunday, when they decided that the failures of SVB and Signature Bank posed a systemic risk to the financial system."

Rep. Ann Wagner, R–Mo., said:

> "Despite U.S. regulators having clear knowledge of insufficient risk management, it seems the examiners and your supervisors were asleep at the wheel while signs that Silicon Valley Bank was heading towards a collapse were staring them right in the face for many, many months."

It made sense, of course, that the FDIC [Federal Deposit Insurance Corporation], General Accountability Office, and Congress would quickly look into the collapse of a government-regulated organization. In other parts of the corporate world, however, decisions about who should investigate a crisis may not be as obvious, clear-cut, or easy to determine.

Optics Matter

A lot can be at stake. If not properly handled, a post-crisis investigation can trigger another crisis by raising questions or doubts about the credibility, objectivity, and validity of the inquiry.

When to Hire Experts

A fundamental question corporate leaders will face is whether an investigation should be conducted by those in the organization or outsourced to independent counsel, experts, or others.

The answer can help determine how the inquiry will be perceived, how the findings will be received, and the steps that are taken to ensure the crisis is not repeated. By having an external investigation—instead of one that is conducted in-house—the conclusions and recommendations will often be considered more credible and objective.

That's why companies and organizations might decide to hire outside firms—such as attorneys, accountants, other experts, or prominent individuals—to conduct thorough and speedy investigations. Their jobs are to find out what happened, why it happened, and what can be done to ensure it does not happen again.

For example, the United States Soccer Federation hired former US Attorney General Sally Yates to investigate allegations of sexual abuse of players. Her report about the scandal made headlines around the world.

Reality Check

Depending on the nature of the crisis—such as fraud, embezzlement, sexual abuse, or other illegal activity—companies might not have a say in the investigation because law enforcement agencies would naturally investigate these allegations.

Business leaders can face their own set of challenges when the time comes to investigate the cause of a crisis that strikes their company or organization.

Lynn Neils is a former in-house lawyer at Johnson & Johnson. She is a partner at the Elliott Kwok Levine Jaroslaw law firm, where she represents businesses and executives in criminal prosecutions, regulatory investigations, and other high-stakes disputes. Neils comments: "How the company responds to and investigates the causes of the crisis can have far-ranging implications for the company and the perception of the investigation's independence."

When to Hire Outside Experts

Neils offers the following advice:

"Corporations or other entities should in most instances hire outside experts—particularly outside counsel—to lead the investigation of a corporate crisis ... Not every allegation of wrongdoing at a company needs to be investigated using outside resources, but one that amounts to a 'corporate crisis' suggests conduct that could seriously impact the reputation, and even the viability, of the company.

If the investigation is conducted by outside counsel that is independent of the company, that helps increase confidence that the findings are accurate and helps bolster the perception that the company is doing what it can to uncover any wrongdoing and remediate the issues. Using outside counsel also helps to ensure that the investigation, and its findings, are subject to the attorney-client privilege and work-product protections."

Three Benefits of Using Internal Resources

Neils suggests using in-house resources to conduct crisis-related investigations as they will:

- Be less expensive for the company—the cost of outside counsel and forensic services, for example, can be very high.
- Likely be faster—in-house resources understand the business and do not need to get up to speed on people and issues.
- Often be less intrusive—they are people that company employees already know and will be more sensitive to the business interruptions; but using only in-house resources can lead to allegations of bias or a cover-up.

CHAPTER 35
Firefly Aerospace

Misconduct

Corporate executives who are supposed to help prevent a crisis can be the same people responsible for causing a crisis.

If details about that misconduct go public, what company officials are alleged to have done behind closed doors—and how organizations responded to those allegations—can play out in front of a national or international audience. Some forms of misconduct are more obvious and public than others and can make national headlines.

That was the case with rocket maker Firefly Aerospace in 2024 when it announced that Bill Weber would no longer serve as CEO of the company. "The move follows reports the company was investigating allegations of an inappropriate relationship between Weber and a female employee," according to *Yahoo Finance*.

Proactive Approach

Rather than wait until executives get themselves or their company into hot water, some businesses are being proactive in protecting their bottom lines.

As reported by the *Wall Street Journal*, "Companies are withholding more of their top officers' pay for longer, hoping to avoid the hassle of recouping money when—or if—executives are later found responsible for misconduct." Examples cited in the story include Bristol-Myers Squibb Co. and drugstore chains CVS Health and Walgreens Boots Alliance. CVS was also holding back some pay even after an executive leaves the company.

A CEO's actions and words have the potential to inflict serious harm on organizations. Depending on the nature of the misconduct, a company's image, reputation, bottom line, and relations with stakeholders can be at risk.

Protecting Their Brand

The sooner an organization responds to allegations of a CEO's misconduct, the sooner it will be able to defend its brand.

Stacy Rosenberg, an associate teaching professor at Carnegie Mellon University's Heinz College of Information Systems and Public Policy, recalls:

> "In July 2018, CBS chairperson and CEO Leslie Moonves was accused of sexual assault. The board launched an independent investigation, issued a clear statement, replaced Moonves, and withheld $120 million in exit payout funds.
>
> These swift decisions separated the actions of the CEO from the media network—which helped protect their brand and demonstrated that sexual misconduct will not be tolerated at any level of the organization."

Boards that do not move quickly when they see a CEO doing something wrong or questionable do so at their peril and can risk facing legal and other issues.

Reality Check

Companies should not allow employment agreements to excuse the misconduct of their leaders.

Mitchell S. Muncy, executive vice president of the Ethics and Public Policy Center at Prospera, a crisis and executive management firm, told *Forbes.com*:

> "Though contractual protections are important, there is no substitute for realism on the part of board members. No hiring process or employment contract can substitute for a willingness to recognize bad behavior for what it is and to act promptly.
>
> In my experience, board members delude themselves about what they've seen or heard about a CEO's behavior far more often than they're simply ignorant of it. A board almost always has sufficient time to act before the crisis is upon them.
>
> One of the rules I give board members is 'Things are exactly as they appear.' If they identify something in a CEO's past or current behavior that strikes them as a problem, the chance that their instincts are wrong is negligible. On the contrary, bad CEO behavior is like icebergs and cockroaches: You ought to presume that what you see is a tenth of what there is."

Signs of a Larger Problem

The misdeeds and misbehavior of high-level company officials may be a sign of deeper problems and issues at an organization.

CHAPTER 36
Fisher-Price and Peloton

Delayed Product Recalls

Although product recalls are nothing new, why and when they are recalled can create a crisis for companies and organizations, especially if they delay in issuing a recall for products that have been shown to be unsafe—or even deadly.

Every day that a business postpones recalling a product can create negative publicity that damages its image, reputation, and standing in the eyes of the public.

Peloton's Delayed Recall

There have been several headline-making product recalls, including Peloton, which recalled two million exercise bikes due to fall and injury hazards.

In 2021, Peloton recalled its Tread+ and Tread treadmills several weeks after fighting against an "urgent warning" from the Consumer Product Safety Commission (CPSC). On May 5, 2021, the federal agency said:

> "To date, CPSC is aware of 39 incidents including one death. CPSC staff believes the Peloton Tread+ poses serious risks to children for abrasions, fractures, and death. In light of multiple reports of children becoming entrapped, pinned, and pulled under the rear roller of the product, CPSC urges consumers with children at home to stop using the product immediately."

On that same day, *Reuters* reported Peloton had announced a recall of its products "reversing course just weeks after saying there was 'no reason' to stop using the exercise machines despite reports of multiple injuries and the death of a child in an accident."

In a statement posted on the company's website, Peloton CEO John Foley said: "I want to be clear: Peloton made a mistake in our initial response to the Consumer Product Safety Commission's request that we recall the Tread+. We should have engaged more productively with them from the outset. For that, I apologize."

News that a product has been recalled is a sign, of course, that something associated with the product can make it dangerous or hazardous to consumers or the public. The crisis can be made even worse, however, if the company refuses to recall the product in question.

Robert Bird, professor of business law at the University of Connecticut's School of Business, explains:

> "Peloton's problems are tied to market demand, but they are also tied to values. Any company, no matter how popular or how rapidly it grows, must not lose touch with its core ethical values. Such values cannot be generated overnight but must permeate through the organization via a culture of integrity. That way, when a crisis appears suddenly, a company like Peloton can respond organically and with authenticity.
>
> Peloton didn't do that when the Consumer Product Safety Commission reported a number of serious accidents with its treadmill. Its first instinct was to dispute the information and respond defensively. That does not reassure consumers or investors. Instead of resisting public accusations, it should have offered to make amends immediately. Peloton didn't have the culture of integrity to do that, and now it is paying a heavy price."

A Legal Obligation

The Consumer Product Safety Commission explains that businesses have a legal obligation to immediately report the following types of information to the federal agency:

- A defective product that could create a substantial risk of injury to consumers.
- A product that creates an unreasonable risk of serious injury or death.
- A product that fails to comply with an applicable consumer product safety rule or with any other rule, regulation, standard, or ban under the Consumer Product Safety Act (CPSA) or any other statute enforced by the CPSC.

Failure to fully and immediately report this information may lead to substantial civil or criminal penalties. CPSC staff's advice is "when in doubt, report."

Factors to Consider

How frequently the defect occurs, how many units it affects, the cost of repair, and the consequences for consumers if the issue isn't addressed all matter here. It's also important to consider the consequences of inaction from a financial, moral, and legal perspective.

Fisher-Price

Fisher-Price's recall in 2021 of its 4-in-1 Rock 'n Glide Soother for infants—a year after the reported deaths of four infants—underscored why business leaders need to ensure their companies' actions are always in sync with corporate values. According to the Consumer Product Safety Commission:

> "There have been reports of four infant deaths in the 4-in-1 Rock 'n Glide Soother. The infants were reportedly placed on their backs unrestrained in the product and later found on their stomachs.

> These incidents occurred between April 2019 and February 2020. The fatalities were a 4-month-old from Missouri, a 2-month-old from Nevada, a 2-month-old from Michigan, and an 11-week-old from Colorado. There have been no fatalities in the 2-in-1 Soothe 'n Play Gliders."

The commission warned that "Infants who are placed unrestrained in the product and later found on their stomach are at risk of suffocation."

Statement from Fisher-Price

A statement from a Fisher-Price spokesperson said:

> "The 4-in-1 Rock 'n Glide Soother is a safe product when used in accordance with its safety warnings and instructions. Given the reports of four fatalities in which infants were placed in the 4-in-1 Rock 'n Glide Soother without safety restraints and left unsupervised and contrary to the safety warnings and instructions, we believe that the voluntary recall of the product is the right course of action to reduce the risk of additional occurrences."

Speed Matters

When problems or issues arise, the sooner they are addressed, the better. The failure to act quickly usually makes matters worse and can prolong or exacerbate a crisis.

According to the Fisher-Price website, "Since our founding, safety has been our highest priority. For more than ninety years, we have maintained an unrelenting focus on product safety, quality, and compliance."

But actions speak louder than words.

In apparent adherence to that priority, Fisher-Price issued a recall for its 4-in-1 Rock 'n Glide Soother following the deaths of the four infants. However, the recall occurred more than a year after those deaths.

CHAPTER 37
Goldman Sachs

Departing Employees Who Criticize Their Company

Although headline-making crisis situations often fade from the public's memory, they can quickly resurface in connection with current news or events.

A case in point was reported by *The New York Times* about the departure of Jake Siewert, the global head of corporate communications at Goldman Sachs. "For nearly a decade," the paper noted, "... Siewert led Goldman Sachs's post-crisis efforts to shed its image as one of Wall Street's most mysterious, and maligned, money machines."

According to *The Times*, Siewert did not have an easy job: The day after his hiring was announced in 2012, "... a former Goldman banker published a now-famous Op-Ed, 'Why I Am Leaving Goldman Sachs,' accusing the firm of fostering a 'toxic and destructive' environment."

It can be instructive for business leaders to get Siewert's take on what happened, how Goldman responded to the allegations, and his advice for corporate executives on how to deal with similar situations.

Quick Response

Siewert recalls that:

> "We put [out] a statement right away, posted on social media, and put out another statement after the review of the allegations. We also did a series of TV appearances around [the op-ed author's] book tour (he appeared on *60 Minutes* and participated in numerous stories around the firm's culture."

Goldman Takes Issue

As *The Times* reported at the time:

> "Goldman Sachs took issue with the opinion piece, defending the investment bank's practices and its treatment of clients. 'We disagree with the views

expressed, which we don't think reflect the way we run our business,' said a spokesperson for Goldman Sachs. 'In our view, we will only be successful if our clients are successful. This fundamental truth lies at the heart of how we conduct ourselves.'

Within hours, the public resignation letter had sparked a storm of comment on the Web and Twitter, with some calling it a 'must read' and others a 'public relations disaster.'"

Thorough Review

Siewert says that Goldman:

"... took the somewhat vague allegations he made very seriously, undertook a thorough review, and found no real substance behind them. Like many notes of the type, his writing reflected his own dissatisfaction with how his career had unfolded [rather] than the reality of the firm he left."

More Transparency Needed

Siewert observes:

"As a brand-new employee at the firm, the press reporting at the time underscored the importance of creating more transparency at the firm.

There was a big mismatch between how highly clients and my colleagues at the firm felt about Goldman and how the public saw it. The data showed then and still does that clients highly valued working with the firm and employees loved working there. We needed to give the public a closer look at the people of the firm, the work they did with clients, and why the clients found it so helpful."

Steps Taken

Siewert explains how Goldman Sachs took several steps to address the issues that were raised in the op-ed.

"We've made it much easier to see the firm and its people. Nine years ago, it was extremely difficult to get a sense of Goldman if you didn't work with the firm closely. And that was necessarily a very small group of people.

We've made it much easier to see the firm and its people.

Now you can listen to a Goldman podcast (*Exchanges*) with experts from around the firm sharing the insights we give clients. *Exchanges* is published twice a week and has been around longer than *The Daily*.

You can watch a 'Talks at GS' where CEOs, entrepreneurs, professors, leading thinkers, and even journalists answer a wide range of questions from people at Goldman.

Our people appear weekly on *CNBC*, *Bloomberg*, Cheddar, Yahoo Finance, and other networks to discuss issues our clients are facing."

Results

Siewert goes on:

> "... the research shows across the board that there's been a dramatic improvement in the firm's reputation as more people see the reality and not the cliched Goldman that the press sometimes portray."

Advice for Others

Siewert's advice for business leaders facing a similar situation is "to reflect on what it says about the firm and how you can use the occasion to strengthen your culture even if you don't agree with the messages conveyed."

CHAPTER 38
Google

Emotional Arguments in the Workplace

The heat and smoke that are often generated about hot-button issues can be matched by employees in the workplace who argue about the pros and cons of those issues.

The spillover from civil discussions that escalate into emotional arguments, confrontations, and protests can create a crisis for companies by damaging morale, productivity, and the retention of employees.

Why Google Fired Employees

In today's polarized political environment, it's not unheard of for workers to protest their company's business activities. That was the case in 2024 when Google fired 28 employees for staging a protest against the company's contract with Israel that it shares with Amazon.

"Physically impeding other employees' work and preventing them from accessing our facilities is a clear violation of our policies and completely unacceptable behavior," the company noted in a statement.

"Google said it had concluded individual investigations, resulting in the termination of 28 employees, and would continue to investigate and take action as needed," *Reuters* reported.

What Employees Think About Political Discussions

According to the results of a 2024 survey of 1,000 US workers by Resume Help, a platform for resume and career advice and services:

- 45 percent regretted having political discussions at work.
- 51 percent believed workplace political discussions hurt the work environment.
- 57 percent of women felt there was a negative impact from talking about politics at work compared to 44 percent of men.

"These findings suggest that political discussions at work can have a negative impact on employees' experience in their workplace," Maria Correa, a career expert at Resume Help, says in a story posted on the company's website.

"It's No Surprise"

According to Kraig Kleeman, founder and CEO of CEO Branding Worldwide:

> "With the political thermometer hitting new highs each election cycle, it's no surprise that our workplaces are buzzing with more than just the usual coffee machine chatter. These days, it feels like every cubicle and conference room has turned into a mini political arena."

Ways to Keep the Peace

"A Bit of Structure"

"A bit of structure never hurt anyone. Setting up some ground rules for political banter can help keep the peace. It's not about silencing voices; it's about making sure everyone gets heard without turning the office into a free-for-all," Kleeman counsels.

Provide Space

Tracy Pearson, J.D., Ed.D., an investigation and implicit bias expert, offers the following advice:

> "The mistake that employers make is not providing space and opportunity for discussions. Politics is in everything we do and the choices we make. Politics align with values and beliefs. By clamping down on these conversations, it creates tension, and the tension finds its way out in other ways."

Heated political discussions in the workplace "can lead to others feeling very uncomfortable and changing how they engage with their co-workers," says Luke Blaney, CEO of recruitment firm Chief Negotiations. "I've seen firsthand how it can ruin a company's culture."

Establish Guidelines

Justin Goldsberry, CEO and founder of Goldsberry Management Group, highlights the need for companies to be proactive:

"During a presidential election year, people are more inclined to discuss politics, and these conversations may not always be avoidable.

Consequently, it's important for companies to proactively incorporate guidelines into their professional development programs and handbooks, detailing empathetic approaches to avoid political discussions. This includes offering advice on how to tactfully and respectfully withdraw from them if they do occur."

CHAPTER 39
Kamala Harris

Choosing a Second in Command

Democratic presidential nominee Kamala Harris's selection of Minnesota Governor Tim Walz as her running mate in 2024 was a reminder for CEOs about the importance of the criteria they use when choosing a second in command.

Who leaders choose and why can be especially important when a crisis strikes their companies.

Be careful, though, if a possible second in command appears to be *too* eager to please and agrees with everything the leader says or does. That's because in crisis situations, it's always a *good* idea to have people who are not afraid to *speak up*, raise questions, and express their doubts or concerns—before it's too late.

In the corporate world, choosing the right person can send an important message about a leader's judgment and priorities. But naming the wrong individual can raise doubts and concerns about a leader—and the future of the organization.

Harris, of course, had her own reasons for picking Walz to be her vice president: "Tim is a battle-tested leader who has an incredible track record of getting things done for Minnesota families. I know that he will bring that same principled leadership to our campaign, and to the office of the vice president," she wrote in a fundraising message, according to *USA Today*.

Walz's political appeal was also a consideration, according to news reports. His credentials "as a veteran and gun owner who previously represented a Republican-leaning, rural part of Minnesota in Congress could help Harris appeal to working-class White voters who have turned away from Democrats and helped fuel Donald Trump's political rise," *The Washington Post* reported.

Additional Factors

What business leaders look for in a second in command can depend on personal and professional preferences, chemistry, and their experience in the company's industry or profession. However, there are other factors that executives could include in the selection equation.

Alignment

Malika Begin, a business owner and an adjunct professor at Pepperdine University and business consultant, suggests:

"First and foremost, ensure the candidate aligns with the organization's mission and values. This alignment is crucial as it sets the tone for consistent decision-making and helps maintain a cohesive culture. When your number two shares the core values and vision of the organization, it not only strengthens the internal team dynamic but also reinforces the organization's identity externally."

The right alignment can pay off in other beneficial ways:

"This shared commitment to the mission makes it possible to navigate challenges, manage resilience during change, and drive the organization toward long-term goals, instead of getting distracted by all the 'shiny objects' one may chase when not completely focused on shared goals."

"A Blend"

Emily Walton, a certified executive coach and founder of Alo Coaching, cautions:

"You need to observe a blend of trustworthiness, credibility, adaptability, and grit. You want to be able to trust them and their ability to stand, speak, and act on your behalf when you aren't present. If something were to happen to you today, they would be the ones who could step in tomorrow."

Track Record

When choosing a number two, evaluating their past performance can yield important clues about how well they might perform in the future. Walton goes on:

"A consistent track record goes a long way in determining who your second in command should be. Do they follow through? Do they get the big picture? Do they have their priorities right? When you see someone who reminds you of you, but better, pour into them. They are your second in command in the making."

"Look for someone with a history of delivering results and demonstrating leadership potential. Their past performance can be a reliable indicator of their ability to handle increased responsibilities," says Smita Das Jain, a personal empowerment life coach and executive coach from India.

"Mitigating Weaknesses"

A second in command doesn't necessarily need to be an exact copy of the CEO. "Leaders should choose a second in command who complements their strengths and mitigates their weaknesses. This ensures a balanced leadership team capable of handling diverse challenges effectively," Jain points out.

Having someone who is too eager to please and agrees with everything a CEO says or does may not be the best choice. Steve Taplin, CEO of Sonatafy Technology, observes:

> "Look for a strategic thinker who can challenge you constructively and drive the organization forward. Integrity, loyalty, and the ability to inspire and lead teams are non-negotiable qualities. Ultimately, your second in command should be someone who can seamlessly step into your role if needed, ensuring continuity and stability."

CHAPTER 40
Hershey

Advertising During a Crisis

Depending on the nature of a crisis, companies and organizations could wrestle with the decision of how or whether to continue running ads for their products and services. A lot can be riding on the decision, including the image, reputation, and credibility of the organization—not to mention its financial success.

Hershey faced that difficult decision during a supply chain crisis in 2021.

Behind the Hershey Company's Decision

Melissa A. Poole is vice president of investor relations for The Hershey Company. In a call with analysts, she said their decision to reduce advertising during the supply chain crisis:

> "... was driven by the fact that we have such elevated demand and given that the supply chain challenges just wouldn't enable us to be able to meet further demand that we would create through our very impactful advertising.

> It just didn't make sense. It put more pressure on the supply chain and also, we probably wouldn't get a good ROI because we wouldn't be able to fulfill that incremental demand ... we're seeing a lot of people manage advertising to supply as a challenge and will continue to focus on optimizing it. [We] will invest as much as we can, as much as we think we can sell. Certainly, we're investing in capacity going forward and we are very agile in how we're handling support behind our brands."

Protect Brand Value

Bridget Arik, chief operating officer at Redmill Solutions, observes that:

> "During a crisis there will be a temptation for advertisers and marketers to cut costs to protect their revenue in the short-term.

However, it is actually essential that they continue advertising to protect brand value in the short-term and accelerate growth in the long-term. [In 2020], supply chain disruptions became a reality for many companies during the pandemic and those that continued with their advertising investment were able to keep communicating their brand's value with the consumers, and as a bonus, they were not dragged into tough conversations to get out of media commitments that had been made previously.

Research shows that consumers don't want advertisers to stop advertising altogether during times of crisis. Although the messaging in the advertising might need to change, the potential for brand value still remains high; we've seen that brands that adopt this strategy are able to enjoy higher sales and market share."

Advice

Kristen Gall, president of Rakuten Rewards, advises in a story for *Forbes.com* that:

"... retailers can certainly get creative and smart with how they're spending so that they are driving the most value.

For example, retailers can shift their [budget] to focus on offloading existing inventory so that they can push out products that they already have in-hand while they work out the supply chain issues on the back end."

CHAPTER 41
Jeep

Threats to Brands

Jeep temporarily distanced itself from Bruce Springsteen when it learned he was arrested in November 2020 on DUI charges. Jeep announced it had "paused" the airing of a commercial featuring the rock legend that debuted during the Super Bowl.

"It would be inappropriate for us to comment on the details of a matter we have only read about, and we cannot substantiate," a Jeep brand spokesperson told *ABC News* in a statement. "But it's also right that we pause our Big Game commercial until the actual facts can be established. Its message of community and unity is as relevant as ever. As is the message that drinking and driving can never be condoned."

"According to documents related to Springsteen's arrest, an officer approached the rock star on November 14 after observing him 'consume a shot of Patron tequila and then get on his motorcycle and start the engine.'" The report states that "Springsteen claimed that he had two shots" within a 20-minute time span and that the musician "smelt strongly of alcohol coming off his person and had glassy eyes," *The Washington Post* reported.

Refused Breath Test

"The musician, who refused a preliminary breath test according to the document, was asked to complete several field sobriety tests. The officer statement recalls Springsteen 'visibly swaying back and forth' when the officer observed his eyes and taking '45 total steps instead of the instructed 18' during what's known as a walk and turn test," according to *The Washington Post*.

News of Springsteen's arrest did not surface until February 10, 2021. Jeep reinstated the ad when charges against the singer were dropped, *Variety* said.

Whether caused by external events or their own actions, companies that fail to pay close attention to potential threats to their brands run the risk of losing their competitive edge, customers, market share, and tarnishing their reputation.

One-way companies can help prevent their brands from having a crisis is to follow the news to ensure that nothing is said or done in connection with the brand that would be seen as questionable or in poor taste.

Advice

When corporate brands are facing a crisis:

- Get all the information you can, as soon as you can.
- When you know the facts, share them with the public immediately.
- Use all available and appropriate communications channels and methods to share the information and updates.
- If you are to blame, admit it.
- When appropriate, express remorse, sympathy, and empathy for those who were affected by the crisis.
- Use all available communication channels to tell your side of the story.
- Explain what steps you will take to ensure the crisis is not repeated.

CHAPTER 42
Jeopardy!

The Right Public Face

It's hard to imagine that a well-known brand or company would have a parade of different people serve as its "public face" over a short period. Such a merry-go-round of spokespersons would raise questions about and send the wrong message concerning the organization's image, stability, or direction.

Then there's *Jeopardy!*.

After the death of long-time host Alex Trebek in 2020, the game show held a series of public auditions for a new host, a process that encountered a few bumps along the way—and generated less than favorable publicity for the show.

Mehmet Oz

In March 2021, interim host Mehmet Oz created a crisis for the show because of controversial comments he made about pseudoscience and bogus health claims. According to *Variety*:

> "Notable instances mentioned in past coverage of Oz include his claiming, on his show, that arsenic is present in apple juice and that green coffee beans are an effective weight-loss supplement ... Elsewhere, he promoted hydroxychloroquine, the baseless and ineffective COVID-19 treatment. He has also provided a megaphone to vaccine denialists and to antigay conversion therapy."

Mike Richards

Mike Richards was named the new host of *Jeopardy!* a month later. But Richards quit the high-profile position "days after a report by *The Ringer* revealed offensive and sexist comments he had made on a podcast several years ago," *The New York Times* reported. It was "the latest in a series of scandals that tarred his brief tenure."

Richards said in a statement:

"I was deeply honored to be asked to host the syndicated show and was thrilled by the opportunity to expand my role. However, over the last several days, it has become clear that moving forward as host would be too much of a distraction for our fans and not the right move for the show."

An End to Rotating Hosts

Ken Jennings and Mayim Bialik were eventually named to host the show on a rotating basis in 2022. But Bialik took a break from her hosting role to show solidarity with striking Hollywood writers. The game of musical chairs came to an end in December 2023 when Bialik was dropped from the line-up, and Jennings was named the sole permanent host of the show.

Maintaining Continuity

The show announced it "made the decision to have one host of the syndicated show next season to maintain continuity for our viewers, and Ken Jennings will be the sole host for syndicated *Jeopardy!" Newsweek* reported.

The statement added that the show executives "are truly grateful for all of Mayim's contributions to *Jeopardy!* and we hope to continue to work with her on primetime specials."

"I am incredibly honored to have been nominated for a primetime Emmy for hosting this year, and I am deeply grateful for the opportunity to have been a part of the *Jeopardy!* family," Bialik explained in her own statement. "For all of you who have supported me through this incredible journey and to the fans, contestants, writers, staff, and crew of America's Favorite Quiz Show, thank you."

Look Before You Leap

Before jumping on an opportunity to be associated with another brand, companies should make a reality check to ensure that the arrangement makes sense and would be a good fit. That includes asking the tough questions about the proposed partnership, including:

- What does each side bring to the table?
- What are their respective strengths and weaknesses?

- Will they be co-equal partners, or will one oversee the other?
- What are the strengths and weaknesses of each brand?
- Who are their target audience?
- How long will it take for the arrangement to work?
- How will success be measured?

A Different Kind of Crisis

Long delays in filling top leadership positions in organizations can result in a crisis for companies by creating doubt or confusion about their long-term future. This is especially true for publicly held companies whose value and credibility can decrease the longer they go without a full-time and permanent leader.

That's why all companies need to have up-to-date succession plans in place and a deep bench of prospective leaders who are prepared and ready to fill unexpected vacancies in organization charts.

CHAPTER 43
Kellogg

Weigh Your Words Carefully

Companies and their executives should always weigh their words carefully and consider how others will hear and interpret what they say and how and when they say it. Otherwise, those words could be perceived as callous and unsympathetic—or worse, create a controversy or a full-blown crisis.

This critical crisis management lesson came through loud and clear in 2024 after news reports that Kellogg's CEO Gary Pilnick told *CNBC*:

> "The cereal category has always been quite affordable, and it tends to be a great destination when consumers are under pressure. If you think about the cost of cereal for a family versus what they might otherwise do, that's going to be much more affordable."

In the interview with the news organization, Pilnick also said:

> "The company was advertising cereal for dinner to consumers looking for more affordable options. 'Give chicken the night off', the ad's cheery tagline reads."

WK Kellogg owns cereals such as Frosted Flakes, Froot Loops, Corn Flakes, Raisin Bran, and others.

Blowback

The CEO's comments did not go down well with some consumers and were the focus of critical stories by news organizations. "'Let them eat Corn Flakes' appears to be Kellogg's CEO Gary Pilnick's advice to cash-strapped shoppers who are spending the highest portion of their income on food than at any point in the last 30 years," *CNN* reported.

Social Media

Clips of the interview started popping up on social media, including on a subreddit called *NotTheOnion* where people share real news that sounds like it could have come from the satirical website the Onion, according to *The Washington Post:*

> "On Reddit, some people complained about the cost of cereal, corporate profits and 'shrinkflation'—where the amount of food in a package is reduced, but the price stays the same—while others noted that the sugary breakfast food isn't actually a good substitute for a nutritious meal."

"Tone Deaf" Comments?

"Some consumers have called the comments tone deaf from an executive who made more than $4 million [in 2023]. They note that boxes of popular cereals now cost more than $7 and cereal is not an adequate substitution for a full dinner," *CNN* said.

"A Serious Issue"

"The plight of families dealing with high inflation and exorbitant prices at the grocery store is nothing to capitalize on," John Goodman, CEO of John Goodman PR, comments:

> "It's a serious issue for families and a huge mistake by Kellogg's CEO Gary Pilnick to even suggest this idea. And if the goal was to get some quick media coverage by floating the idea of cereal for dinner, it backfired. The price of that media coverage was a terrible hit for Kellogg's image, and it received the negative backlash it so deserved."

Pilnick Received a Second Chance

Corporate executives who quickly learn about the negative reaction to their words should carefully consider taking advantage of opportunities to retract or apologize for them.

Jennifer Donahoe, group account director for public relations and social media at Planit, an advertising, branding, and marketing firm, observes in a story for *Forbes.com:*

"After his comments on *CNBC*, Pilnick was then asked if cereal for dinner has the 'potential to land the wrong way' with consumers and he responded confidently saying 'We don't think so,' immediately citing data on consumers who eat cereal outside of breakfast time.

This only reinforced the perception that Pilnick is not only out-of-touch but does not care about the struggle of the average American or the importance of being able to provide your family nutritious food.

This negative perception isn't just that of Pilnick, but as a representative of the company who is also running a major ad campaign promoting cereal for dinner, the negative perception extends to the company as well."

Courtney Haywood, the head of Haywood Agency Partners, a strategic communications firm, highlights the importance of a sensitive approach:

"Business leaders should always approach sensitive topics like financial hardship with empathy and sensitivity, recognizing the real-life struggles that many individuals and families face—even now more than ever with companies having a surge of layoffs.

By demonstrating a genuine understanding and compassion, leaders can foster trust and uphold a positive reputation within their companies. It's vital for leaders to intimately know their audience [and understand] their diverse experiences and challenges. ...

Making statements that lack awareness or come across as insensitive can alienate consumers, employees, and tarnish the company's reputation. Therefore, leaders should prioritize staying connected with their customer base, employees, and being mindful of their perspectives."

CHAPTER 44
KFC

Tone Deaf

KFC's apology for a message it sent to German consumers provides business executives with several lessons about best practices for preventing, managing, and communicating about a crisis. The fried chicken company sent a promotional message to customers in Germany in 2022, noting that "It's memorial day for Kristallnacht! Treat yourself with more tender cheese on your crispy chicken. Now at KFCheese!" Kristallnacht is widely seen as the beginning of the Holocaust.

The United States Holocaust Memorial Museum's website explains:

> "The Nazi-led series of attacks in the country in 1938 left more than 90 people dead and destroyed Jewish-owned businesses and places of worship ... The Nazis came to call the event *Kristallnacht* ("Crystal Night," or "The Night of Broken Glass"), referring to the thousands of shattered windows that littered the streets [afterward], but the euphemism does not convey the full brutality of the event."

KFC said that it "sincerely" apologized for the "unplanned, insensitive and unacceptable message," the *BBC* reported. Reaction to KFC's "mistake" came swiftly, according to news reports.

Daniel Sugarman, director of public affairs for the Board of Deputies of British Jews, tweeted that the promotion was "absolutely hideous." Arsen Ostrovsky, head of the pro-Israel legal group International Legal Forum, said he was "utterly speechless and repulsed."

Crisis Management Best Practices

How and when KFC responded to the distribution of its promotional message provides several lessons for business leaders.

Act Quickly

About an hour after sending the first message, the company sent an apology, which blamed the mistakenly sent communication on "a fault in our system," according to *The Guardian*.

The company announced that its app communications had been suspended while an examination of the communications took place, the *BBC* reported.

Explain What Happened

"On November 9, an automated push notification was accidentally issued to KFC app users in Germany ..." a KFC spokesperson said in a statement that was picked up by several news organizations. "We use a semi-automated content creation process linked to calendars that include national observances. In this instance, our internal review process was not properly followed, resulting in a non-approved notification being shared," the spokesperson explained.

Ensure the Crisis Is Not Repeated

"We are very sorry," KFC said, noting that, "we will check our internal processes immediately so that this does not happen again. Please excuse this error," *The Guardian* reported.

"We have suspended app communications while we examine our current process to ensure such an issue does not occur again," according to the company's statement.

Be Sincere

"We understand and respect the gravity and history of this day and remain committed to equity, inclusion, and belonging for all," KFC said.

"There is much to be said about the value of a sincere, heartfelt apology, but KFC's response was not an example [of] that," comments Irina Tsukerman, president of Scarab Rising, a reputation management and crisis communications strategic advisory company.

An Effort to Avoid Accountability

On the contrary, Tsukerman continues:

"It was a self-evident effort to avoid accountability by blaming the tone deaf and borderline offensive messaging on an unspecified 'error in their system', which nevertheless clearly required human input due to the specificity of the occasion.

It is unlikely that KFC globally will suffer serious consequences, such as boycotts, over such an incident. But even if the problematic communication is unintentional, it leaves (excuse the pun) a bad taste in one's mouth and points to a lackadaisical approach to communications in [general], which reflects poorly on the corporate culture overall."

Care About Your Communications and Audience

Tsukerman advises the business management at KFC to review their practice:

"What the business management in KFC and elsewhere should carry away from this incident as the best way to avoid even accidentally offensive messaging is to care about communications overall and about your audience.

When you think deeply about what your target market cares about, you will be inspired to put out well-thought-out and clear messages that connect and work without having to worry about putting your foot in your mouth by jumping opportunistically at any occasion to push your product or service.

At the end of the day, genuine mistakes can be forgiven, but opportunist callousness will sooner or later become a pattern and damage one's business reputation."

Don't Misuse History

Diane Saltzman, director of Survivor Affairs at the US Holocaust Memorial Museum, said in a statement to *The Washington Post* that recent incidents misusing Holocaust history have been increasing in frequency and intensity:

"Holocaust survivors, and everyone—especially in Germany—concerned about historical truth, should never have to see such a blatant attempt to minimize and capitalize on their pain. We hope people remember, learn from and study this history, and refrain from its misuse."

CHAPTER 45
King Charles III

Sending the Right Message

Words matter in a crisis. And so do the timing, tone, pace, and purpose of the person who delivers them. Missteps can have damaging consequences by prolonging a crisis or making matters worse.

In the aftermath of the death of Queen Elizabeth II in 2022 there were concerns and speculation about the future and role of the British monarchy, how the new King Charles III would conduct himself, and what his priorities would be.

"Hitting All the Right Buttons"

The king's recorded television speech—his first public remarks since the passing of his mother, Queen Elizabeth II—appeared to hit all the right buttons for all the right reasons.

At the start of the speech, the king said:

> "Queen Elizabeth's was a life well lived; a promise with destiny kept, and she is mourned most deeply in her passing. That promise of lifelong service I renew to you all today."

He then went on to say that:

> "As the queen herself did with such unswerving devotion, I too now solemnly pledge myself, throughout the remaining time God grants me, to uphold the Constitutional principles at the heart of our nation. And wherever you may live in the United Kingdom, or in the realms and territories across the world, and whatever may be your background or beliefs, I shall endeavor to serve you with loyalty, respect, and love, as I have throughout my life."

What the king said and how he said it provides essential lessons for corporate leaders about communicating during a crisis. Katie Waldron, public relations consultant, observes in a story for *Forbes.com*:

"Executives can use King Charles III's thoughtful language choices and his paced and confident delivery as a guide for crafting their own crisis communications statements.

Today's leaders can apply his transparency to their messaging [just] as he did regarding title changes within the monarchy and how his charities will function as he takes on his new role as king.

Showing respect for Queen Elizabeth's lifelong work while reassuring the public that he'll carry out his duties as king in a similar manner are also key examples of ways leaders can honor predecessors and give stakeholders insight into future leadership plans.

His speech is a sterling example for executives to replicate because people need to feel stability and continuity during times of transition."

"True to the Brand"

Shannon Peel, branding expert, writes in an article for *Forbes.com*:

"King Charles III was true to the brand of [the] monarchy as defined by his mother, Queen Elizabeth II.

By telling the story of the Queen's promise to her subjects and continuing the promise by dedicating his reign to the service of the people in the UK and Commonwealth, he ensured we feel there will be no change with his taking over.

By staying on brand, keeping the tone similar to that of the Queen, and communicating the pared-down monarchy, he affirmed his role and what we can expect from King Charles III—a pared-down executive, a business-as-usual approach, and affirmed his role to serve the people of the UK and Commonwealth."

Achieving Important Objectives

Amy Levy, president of Amy Levy Public Relations, said in a statement:

"As a crisis communications professional, I feel that he showed an appropriate sense of authority, calm, warmth and empathy for his constituents in the UK and around the world who are mourning the loss of his mother.

In a crisis or massive change in a company or government, the public wants to be reassured by those in a position of power. He was eloquent and appropriate as he spoke kindly of his wife and children.

King Charles III acknowledged that the responsibilities of his new title would likely cause him to step back from some of his charitable efforts and concentrate on areas where he is most needed."

Sending the Right Messages

"King Charles checked off all the boxes in an effective crisis communication public address," Kirk Hazlett, an adjunct professor of communication at the University of Tampa, believes:

"First and foremost, he immediately went out into the public to see and be seen. He made it clear that he is not going to be an aloof monarch. Finally, not only did he pay a beautiful tribute to his mother, he also made it clear that his own children remain an important part of his life.

In all crisis situations, those affected want to know [what's next], and King Charles made it clear that he is 100 percent committed to continuing his mother's legacy. He also made sure that the countless individuals and organizations receiving some sort of support from one of his many charitable endeavors will continue to do so ... he's not simply dropping the ball and moving on."

CHAPTER 46
Lyft and Uber

Working Together in a Crisis

Depending on the nature of the crisis, some companies have put their rivalries aside and worked together to address a crisis situation. That was the case when Uber and Lyft announced in 2021 that they had joined forces to help ban drivers who were accused of sexual assault from working for the two ride-hailing companies, *NBC News* reported.

"We want to share this information with each other and hopefully in the near future with other companies so that our peers in this space can be informed and make decisions for their own platforms to keep those platforms safe," said Jennifer Brandenburger, head of policy development at Lyft.

Scott Berkowitz, president and founder of the nonprofit Rape, Abuse & Incest National Network, commends the companies for working together. "Uber and Lyft have demonstrated thoughtful leadership with the Industry Sharing Safety Program," he notes on the company's website. "By putting aside competition, they are placing users first and building a safer rideshare community for all."

Meeting Larger Challenges

COVID-19

The larger the crisis—such as COVID-19—the more likely it is that larger companies and entire industries will work together to help those who are affected by the crisis.

"Key examples include retailers sharing information about stock levels, pharmaceutical organizations working together to develop a vaccine, technological giants collaborating for the greater good, and charities forming alliances for a joint cause," according to a report by the National Institutes of Health's National Library of Medicine.

Cybersecurity

One example of an industry working together is the Cybersecurity Tech Accord, which was signed by more than 150 companies. According to a press release about the accord:

> "The Cybersecurity Tech Accord, the private sector as a whole, global human rights organizations and the UN's High Commissioner for Human Rights are today united in expressing grave concerns on the current draft Convention on law enforcement cooperation against cybercrime.

> Originally intended to deliver a targeted instrument to counter the growing threat of cybercrime, the negotiations are in danger of producing a broad UN surveillance treaty that would undermine both privacy and security in the digital environment."

Nick Ashton-Hart, head of the Cybersecurity Tech Accord delegation to the negotiations, said in a press release:

> "As presently drafted, the Convention presents grave risks to human rights and legitimate commerce. It risks undermining global cybersecurity, making it easier, not harder, for criminals to engage in cybercrime."

Advantages and Benefits

There can be advantages and benefits for companies that collaborate to address a crisis.

- Pooling or sharing expertise and resources can help ensure that a crisis is addressed as effectively, efficiently, and strategically as possible.
- Coordination can ensure the companies are not sending the public mixed messages or wrong information about the crisis.
- Businesses that work together can strengthen their brands and reputations by showing that they can put their rivalry aside and work together for the good of the public.

The Importance of Communication

Make sure that those who are affected or would be interested in the partnership are kept informed and updated as needed.

Don't Wait

Competitors should not wait until there is a crisis to figure out how to work together when the crisis strikes. Cheryl Fenelle Dixon, a marketing and communication executive and adjunct professor in the M.S. strategic communications program at Columbia University, offers the following advice:

> "Like any good crisis communication response, competitor outreach should be planned well in advance. A pre-established communication network, company agreement or industry association can be a vehicle for information sharing and brainstorming.
>
> Companies should alert competitors when there is a threat to the industry as a whole or shared challenge such as a tainted ingredient or issue with a manufacturer that serves multiple companies in an industry."

CHAPTER 47
Maersk and Target

Supply Chain Bottlenecks

The fragility of the world's supply chains has often been underscored by crisis situations, such as the collapse of the Francis Scott Key Bridge in Baltimore, tensions in the Red Sea, and when a container ship blocked the Suez Canal.

Shipping companies, for their part, would avoid and reroute cargo ships away from these trouble spots. For example, when the Key Bridge collapsed in 2024, Danish shipping company Maersk said on its website:

> "For cargo already on water, we will omit [the port of Baltimore] and will discharge cargo set for Baltimore in nearby ports. From these ports, it will be possible to utilize land-side transportation to reach [its] final destination instead."

Target took matters into its own hands in 2021 when it chartered its own container ship in an effort to help keep shelves stocked for customers. The company noted on its website:

> "It takes a village, and as the second largest U.S. importer, we'll continue to partner with our vendors to tackle supply chain challenges together this season and beyond to ensure we can deliver for our guests.

> We also chartered our own container ship to regularly bring Target merchandise from overseas ports to the U.S. As co-managers of the ship, we can avoid delays from additional stops and steer clear of particularly backed-up ports. Once products arrive stateside, we're partnering closely with our vendors and transportation partners to move them quickly to our stores, keeping our shelves well-stocked and ready for guests."

Blinders?

Corporate leaders who delay in ensuring they can get the materials and supplies their organizations need when there is a disruption to supply chains can be putting their companies at risk. And denying that they will ever face such a crisis could be the equivalent of wearing blinders, which is never a good look for business executives.

Brian Alster, CEO of Altrata, a global wealth intelligence company, and former general manager of Dun & Bradstreet's North American finance and risk business, makes the following observations:

> "The disaster of the moment becomes a global phenomenon because it is yet another reminder of the interconnectedness that comes with globalization and our reliance on each other as contributors to the global supply chain. Companies have developed a higher level of dependency on suppliers and third parties from other countries, and that dependency is highlighted when a link in the supply chain is impacted.
>
> In today's ever-changing world, it is not enough to simply onboard vendors and complete annual health and due diligence assessments on them. Companies must develop a data-driven risk-based assessment process to identify and continuously monitor a variety of risks that could impact the productivity of their supply chain—creating a more flexible and agile network that can quickly pivot in any circumstance or during any unexpected event.
>
> By working to create a more modern supplier operation today, companies will be in a better position to manage the unprecedented events of the future, enabling an agile supply chain that can withstand any challenges."

Alster recommends that corporate executives adhere to the following short and long-term best practices.

Short-Term

- Develop a risk-based assessment process that helps identify and continuously monitor a variety of risks that could impact the productivity of your supply chain. Risk conditions can include a range of incidents, from natural disasters such as hurricanes, to trade wars and worker shortages due to a pandemic.
- Complete an assessment of all tiers of suppliers to ensure your suppliers' suppliers are not going to negatively impact your business.
- Monitor your supply chain and make sure that you are monitoring the risks associated with all tiers of suppliers to ensure your company has a complete view of your global supply chain.
- Identify alternative suppliers in non-impacted regions of the world to diversify the supply chain and limit dependencies on any one supplier of a geographic region.

Long-Term

- Focus on digital transformation. Supply chain leaders must act now to digitally transform their supply chain operations using data-driven insights that offer real-time transparency into the financial and operational health of every supplier across all tiers.
- Build policies and contingency plans for your supply chain. Identify geographically diverse suppliers to onboard in the event of future emergencies. A company should also consider dual sourcing for critical components within your supply chain.

CHAPTER 48
Maui

Ignoring Warnings

The wildfire crisis on the island of Maui in Hawaii in 2023 was a reminder for business leaders that all the planning and safeguards in the world are useless for preventing or warning about an emergency or disaster if those plans and safeguards fail or are ignored. A lot can be riding on the success or failure of those preparations, plans, and warning systems, including reputations, careers, credibility—and lives.

Expertise

When appointing someone to oversee the preparation for and management of a crisis, make sure they are properly and fully qualified and are the best person for the job.

"Herman Andaya was not an expert in emergency management when he was hired to lead the Maui Emergency Management Agency in 2017," according to the Honolulu *Civil Beat*:

> "Trained in political science and the law, he has no formal education in disaster preparedness or response. And prior to his current role, he never held a full-time job dedicated to emergency management.
>
> Instead, his main qualification was being chief of staff to then-mayor Alan Arakawa. But in that role, he told *Civil Beat* that he assisted during emergency operations. And he said he participated in online FEMA trainings and workshops throughout the years."

Fire Protection Plan

In 2014, government officials in Hawaii approved a Western Maui Community Wildlife Protection Plan. But, as *NPR* reported, the state has struggled to implement the report's recommendations.

Clifford Oliver, a retired former senior executive at FEMA and now the principal at Nanticoke Global Strategies, says:

> "As with all government budget processes, there is never enough money to go around, so elected officials, usually with community input, set priorities, and the money runs out before you get to the lower-priority items."

100+ Recommendations

Oliver notes that:

"There are over 100 community-provided recommendations [in the plan], many of which cost money to implement. To make these mitigation actions a higher priority would mean lowering the priority of others, what many might consider more urgent needs, such as schools, police protection, etc. Getting state and local elected officials to make this difficult decision requires true leadership and a political commitment."

Emergency Notification

No Warning

According to *The New York Times*:

> "None of the 80 warning sirens placed around Maui were activated by the island or the state's emergency management agencies in response to the devastating Lahaina fire, a spokesman confirmed on Saturday.
>
> "Residents who survived the fire have wondered aloud why no one activated the sirens, which emit noises at a higher decibel level than a loud rock concert and can be heard from more than half a mile away."

CNN noted that although the emergency response was still being reviewed, authorities believed the sirens were 'essentially immobilized' by the extreme heat, according to Gov. Josh Green. He explained that some of the sirens were broken, and that was part of an ongoing investigation.

He asked the state's attorney general "to do a full review of everything: decisions, policies, policies on water, and then, of course, the sirens."

"I do not" regret not sounding the sirens, Maui Emergency Management Agency administrator Herman Andaya told *CBS News* at a news conference in his first public comments about the wildfires.

The Accidental Warning

This was not the first time that there were issues with the state's emergency notification system.

In January 2018, an alert was accidently issued warning citizens to take shelter because of an incoming ballistic missile. "It took nearly 40 minutes for officials to issue a correction. But after the shock wore off, many were left with frustration and anger," *Hawaii News Now* said.

Water Pressure

Making a bad situation even worse were water pressure-related issues.

"Hoping to control the blaze as it took root among homes along the hillside nearly a mile above the center of town, fire crews encountered water pressure that was increasingly feeble, with the wind turning the streams into mist," *The New York Times* reported. "Then, as the inferno stoked by hurricane-force gusts grew, roaring further toward the historic center of town on the island of Maui, the hydrants sputtered and became largely useless."

Warning by 2021 Commission

"Prompted by the increase in wildfires, a Maui County government commission in July 2021 examined the local prevention and response system and warned county and state officials of the growing fire threat," the *Wall Street Journal* said.

"The investigation found that the number of incidents from a combination of wild/brush/forest fires appears to be increasing, and that this increase poses an increased threat to citizens, properties, and sacred sites," the commission's report concluded.

"The report said not enough was being done to address the concerns. It recommended a number of solutions, including better management of vegetation around power lines and creating fuel buffers around the lines," according to the news organization.

Concerns Voiced in 2022

In 2022, Hawaiian Electric warned that the risk of its utility system "causing a wildfire ignition is significant." The company said it needed the funding to ensure its facilities were not "the origin or a contributing source of ignition for a wildfire," *NBC News* reported.

Advice

Remember What's at Stake

- Remember what's at stake for your company or organization if you do not have a crisis management plan in place—or have not updated it to reflect the dangers your business could face.

Assume Nothing

- When it comes to preparing for a crisis, don't assume that your crisis management plan will work when needed.
- Make sure that the crisis early warning systems you have in place for your company are functioning. This includes monitoring and being notified immediately about critical comments about your business on social media platforms that could be an early warning of a pending crisis.
- Take steps to practice the plan on a regular basis and ensure that you have the resources necessary to implement the plan.

CHAPTER 49
Former House Speaker Kevin McCarthy

Trust

The unprecedented ouster in 2023 of House Speaker Kevin McCarthy by hard-right fellow Republicans—and the turmoil it created—provides several crisis-related lessons for business leaders. It is a cautionary tale of placing too much trust in others and giving potential adversaries too much control over your future.

McCarthy's removal from the top leadership position of the House of Representatives was promoted by Rep. Matt Gaetz (R-Fla.) who had threatened for months to force a vote to fire him. Gaetz angered many fellow Republicans who charged that his actions and threats were self-serving and took attention away from conducting legislative business.

Consequences of Unethical Behavior

"The turmoil in the House of Representatives should remind leaders of what can happen when people behaving unethically are allowed to continue in their roles without sanction," Ann Skeet, senior director of leadership ethics at Santa Clara University's Markkula Center for Applied Ethics, points out. "There is always the potential for their behavior to have spillover effects and disrupt the focus of an organization."

Impact of Broken Relationships

Stacy Rosenberg, an associate teaching professor at Carnegie Mellon University's Heinz College of Information Systems and Public Policy, says:

> "When we think of a senior executive being ousted from a corporation, often a scandal—such as misconduct—comes to mind ... However, much like in former Speaker Kevin McCarthy's case, the reason can be attributed to broken relationships and weak performance in the leadership role."

Examples in the corporate world parallel the events leading up to the vote that removed McCarthy from his leadership position.

A lot of leaders and CEOs stepped down in 2023, "many because of pressure they were receiving by the people they oversaw," observes Amani Wells-Onyioh, a Democratic political strategist and partner and operations director of Sole Strategies.

Time to Think Outside the Box?

The Speaker does not have to be a member of Congress. The House can consider appointing an outsider with appropriate leadership and crisis management experience to be its leader.

In the business world, there are a number of current and former CEOs who could be a good fit for this critical and demanding role.

Expect the Unexpected

McCarthy's ouster "highlights the unpredictability of leadership roles when faced with unforeseen challenges and the importance of maintaining stakeholders' trust," Lakesha Cole, founder and principal publicist at she PR, comments. Like their counterparts in the corporate world, members of Congress did not expect the events to unfold the way they did in the House chamber.

Fortunately, House rules require that the Speaker designate someone to replace them should the unexpected happen. Immediately after the Speakership was declared vacant, Rep. Patrick McHenry (R-North Carolina) became interim Speaker until McCarthy's successor was approved.

This is another lesson business executives can learn from the historic chaos in the House: No matter how remote a worst-case scenario may seem today, it can become a nightmare reality tomorrow.

Plan accordingly.

CHAPTER 50
McDonald's

Perspective is important in a crisis. Without it, business leaders may not be able to tell the difference between an issue that could quickly disappear, a slowly simmering controversy that can take its toll over time, or a rapidly growing problem that will create an avalanche of negative publicity. Knowing the difference could help determine how or if a company's credibility, image, and reputation will be affected and the steps that are necessary to address the situation.

McDonald's is a case in point. According to the *Wall Street Journal* in 2021, McDonald's franchisees had been upset for some time about company-supplied ice-cream machines that kept breaking down.

An Old Complaint

The *Wall Street Journal* reported that:

> "Owners of McDonald's outlets have long complained the devices are overly complicated and their breakdowns hard to fix. The machines require a nightly automated heat-cleaning cycle that can last up to four hours to destroy bacteria. The cleaning cycle can fail, making the machines unusable until a repair technician can get them going again, owners say."

Adding fuel to the fire were reports that the Federal Trade Commission was investigating the matter; some franchisees said they have been contacted about the issue. The Federal Trade Commission told me they had no comment about an investigation, adding, "For context, the FTC does not comment on or confirm the existence of investigations."

Statement from McDonald's

In response, according to *USA Today*, McDonald's USA issued this statement:

"Intrinsic to the interest in our soft serve machines is our fans' love of McDonald's iconic McFlurry desserts and shakes. Nothing is more important to us than delivering on our high standards for food quality and safety, which is why we work with fully vetted partners that can reliably provide safe solutions at scale."

The Right Approach?

At first glance, it appeared the fast-food company reacted appropriately to the situation.

Alice M. Walton is president of Walton Strategies, a boutique strategic communications firm. She notes in a story for *Forbes.com* that, "The company is doing two important things here. One, they are acknowledging the problem and two, they are educating consumers on what is needed to solve it. This could ultimately strengthen confidence in the brand."

Stacy Rosenberg, associate teaching professor at Carnegie Mellon University's Heinz College, observes, "While McDonald's might be trending in the news today, it is unlikely the reports of an FTC investigation into malfunctioning ice-cream machines will have a long-term, negative influence on the corporation's valuation [or] on their brand."

Staying Focused

Rosenberg goes on:

> "Given the relatively innocuous nature of the equipment failure, McDonald's should focus on resolving the issue to satisfy the FTC as well as its dessert-loving customers. Other business leaders would be wise to similarly distinguish between bad news ... and very bad news. In this case, McDonald's brief statement focused on the quality of their food ..."

She advises that was all that was necessary, "as customers will return despite broken ice-cream makers. After all, sundaes and shakes are not their core product."

CHAPTER 51
Microsoft, Rolls-Royce, and Walmart

Bribery

The federal indictment of New York mayor Eric Adams on bribery-related charges in 2024 triggered reminders about allegations of bribery that have been made against business leaders and organizations in the corporate world. Adams denied any wrongdoing, according to *Reuters*, and pleaded not guilty at his arraignment, *CBS News* reported.

The headline-making indictment of the first term mayor may have raised concerns and questions for executives about how to respond if their organizations are ever confronted with bribery charges—whether against employees or the entire company—and the steps to take to help prevent bribery-related behavior.

Corporate Examples

Colin Ram, a civil litigation attorney with Colin Ram Law, points out:

> "Bribery is a particularly dangerous charge, as the underlying facts may not only trigger criminal and civil liability, but for companies engaged in business overseas, the Foreign Corrupt Practices Act may come into play if bribes were paid to even low-level foreign government officials."

Microsoft

In 2019, a wholly-owned subsidiary of Microsoft Corporation based in Hungary agreed to pay a criminal penalty of more than $8.7 million to resolve the government's investigation into violations of the Foreign Corrupt Practices Act (FCPA) arising out of a bid-rigging and bribery scheme in connection with the sale of Microsoft software licenses to Hungarian government agencies, the Justice Department announced on its website.

Walmart

Also in 2019, Walmart "agreed to pay $282 million to settle a seven-year bribery investigation by the US government concerning certain payments that were made to foreign officials in places like Mexico and China," *Forbes.com* wrote at the time.

Rolls-Royce

In 2017, Rolls-Royce plc, the United Kingdom-based manufacturer and distributor of power systems for the aerospace, defense, marine, and energy sectors, "agreed to pay the US nearly $170 million as part of an $800 million global resolution to investigations by the department, U.K. and Brazilian authorities into a long-running scheme to bribe government officials in exchange for government contracts," according to a press release that was posted on the Justice Department's website.

How to Respond to Bribery Allegations

There are several steps companies can take when they become aware of allegations of bribery about their organizations or executives.

Move Quickly

Adrienne Uthe, founder and strategic advisor at Kronus Communications, a public relations firm, told *Forbes.com*:

> "When allegations of bribery arise, transparency and swift action are essential. Companies should immediately acknowledge the issue, initiate an independent investigation, and keep stakeholders informed throughout the process. Handling it [in] this way limits speculation, protects the company's reputation, and demonstrates a commitment to integrity."

The initial period after allegations become known to corporate officials is important. Ram, the civil ligation attorney, recommends:

> "The first few hours and days after the bribery allegations come to light are critical—companies want to avoid making haphazard comments to the public because what they say in the early days may not only prove to be inaccurate but can be used against them later. Company employees should be cautioned

against feeding the rumor mill at work. An off-the-cuff remark about the bribery charges made in a private text message can create headaches for the sender down the line."

Investigate

Investigating the allegations is critical—and so is who conducts the investigation. Amanda Orr, a public relations expert at Orr Strategy Group, advises:

"As soon as an allegation surfaces, companies must launch an independent, thorough investigation led by a neutral third party to demonstrate a commitment to accountability and allow leadership to assess the scope of the issue before making public statements."

Disclose

David Greiner, a corporate law and governance attorney, says in an article for *Forbes.com* that it is best to "disclose issues transparently while the investigation is ongoing. Express commitment to compliance and ethical conduct. Outline corrective actions, like placing executives on leave. This reassures stakeholders the company takes governance seriously."

Act Based on Findings

Greiner also suggests taking "definitive action based on findings. If executives are cleared, reinstate them. If found guilty, terminate them immediately and cooperate fully with authorities. The company must show illegal behavior is not tolerated."

Communicate

Amanda Orr observes:

"In the court of public opinion, silence can be the right move, but in allegations of bribery, it can be perceived as guilt. Companies should communicate with stakeholders promptly, acknowledging the allegation and outlining the steps they are taking to address it. The key is to express responsibility without prematurely admitting fault."

Repair Damage

Greiner emphasizes the importance of taking action to rebuild trust:

> "Work to repair reputation damage. Issue a sincere public apology acknowledging mistakes. Highlight strengthened controls and ethical policies to rebuild trust. It takes time, but companies can recover by demonstrating real change."

Prevention

There are several actions businesses can initiate now to discourage executives from taking or offering bribes. Orr advises, "Demonstrating that the company is taking steps to prevent future issues is essential. This could include enhancing compliance programs, retraining staff, and working with regulators to rebuild trust."

Some companies have strict bribery-related policies which other organizations could consider emulating.

Microsoft

"We prohibit corrupt payments of all kinds, including facilitating payments. We expect our representatives to share our commitment to integrity, and if we see signs that a representative is unethical or could be engaging in corrupt conduct, we prohibit doing business with them," Microsoft says in a statement on its website.

Rolls-Royce

"Following bribery allegations, Rolls-Royce implemented extensive internal changes, including stronger anti-corruption policies, which helped restore its credibility," Orr recalls.

On its website, Rolls-Royce says that its policy is to:

- Not give or receive bribes, and will report to the Ethics and Compliance team if we are asked for, or offered, bribes or facilitation payments;
- Only offer, or accept, gifts or hospitality allowed within policy; and

- Consult our Ethics and Compliance team about any business partners that we engage with to make sure that we are conducting the appropriate due diligence on the partner.

Walmart

According to the retail giant Walmart's website: "We compete fairly and honestly everywhere we do business around the world. We never attempt to gain a business advantage through bribery, and we do not tolerate bribery or corruption in any form."

Similarities and Differences

The bribery allegations against Microsoft, Rolls-Royce, and Walmart share important connections with and differences from those that New York Mayor Eric Adams faced.

Federal and Foreign Focus

All of the allegations were the result of federal investigations into suspected wrongdoing by the businesses and mayor. The charges had something to do with seeking favors from or trying to influence the decisions of foreign governments.

Fines and Settlements

Each of the three companies agreed to pay fines to settle the cases and put the matters behind them.

Adams, however, pleaded not guilty to the bribery and other charges. He vowed "to fight the case, even as a growing number of New York politicians call for his resignation and as Gov. Kathy Hochul, a fellow Democrat, weighs whether to force him from office," according to *CNBC*.

Resources and Priorities

Compared to elected officials, corporations have much deeper pockets and more extensive resources for fighting bribery charges. Businesses may be more inclined to settle and pay hefty fines in the hopes that memories of the allegations will fade from the public's memory. Politicians, on the other hand, might decide to dig in, deny the charges, and fight as long as they can in the hope of clearing their name.

Of course, having anti-bribery policies is no guarantee that corporate executives will not offer or accept bribes. But enacting and enforcing those policies would be good first steps in the right direction.

CHAPTER 52
MSNBC and *NBC*

Blowback to Controversial Hires

Hiring individuals for high-profile positions who may not be the best fit for organizations can be a recipe for creating crisis situations and can include blowback from employees who go public with their concerns and criticisms.

NBC News found that out in 2024 when it hired Ronna McDaniel, the ousted chair of the Republican National Committee, to be a commentator on all its platforms.

A Reversed Decision

In the wake of the unprecedented on-air opposition to her hiring by hosts on *MSNBC*, *NBC* announced that she would no longer be joining the network, *The Washington Post* reported.

"No organization, particularly a newsroom, can succeed unless it is cohesive and aligned," Cesar Conde, *NBCUniversal's* News Group chairperson, wrote in a memo. "Over the last few days, it has become clear that this appointment undermines that goal," according to the *Wall Street Journal*.

Going Public

The fact that several *NBC* employees publicly expressed their concerns and objections about McDaniel during a nationally broadcast television program served only to compound the situation—and generated headlines across the country.

A panel of journalists on *Meet the Press* criticized *NBC News* executives "for their decision to hire someone who had long attacked the network," according to *The Washington Post*.

"We Weren't Asked Our Opinion"

"The on-air criticism continued ... on *NBC's* cable cousin *MSNBC,* where *Morning Joe* host Joe Scarborough said that he and his co-hosts 'strongly objected' to the hire," according to the newspaper.

"We weren't asked our opinion of the hiring, but if we were, we would have strongly objected to it for several reasons," Scarborough noted, "including but not limited to, as lawyers might say, Ms. McDaniel's role in Donald Trump's fake elector scheme and her pressuring election officials to not certify election results while Donald Trump was on the phone," the *Wall Street Journal* reported.

Calls to Reverse Decision

If there's one thing worse than hiring the wrong person for a high-profile job, it's waiting too long to reverse course and allowing a crisis to drag on unnecessarily.

"We hope *NBC* will reconsider its decision" to hire McDaniel, said Mika Brzezinski, co-host of *MSNBC's* four-hour morning show with her husband, former GOP congressman Joe Scarborough," the *Associated Press* reported.

On her *MSNBC* show, Rachel Maddow said she hoped *NBC News* would "reverse their decision" to hire McDaniel. "If you care what I think about this, the fact that McDaniel is on the payroll at *NBC News*, to me that is inexplicable."

What Was at Stake

Christine M. Haas, CEO and founder of Christine Haas Media, observes:

> "Given the landscape of employee activism, social media scrutiny, and increasing societal expectations for corporate accountability, the stakes involved in executive recruitment are higher than ever ... A misstep in hiring decisions could lead to repercussions and damage an organization's reputation."

Best Practices

Thoroughly vetting a potentially controversial hire is one of the best HR practices to help guard against a possible crisis. So is giving others in the organization an opportunity to meet and question the candidate and provide feedback before they are offered a contract.

Another option is to give the job candidate an assignment or retain them on a probationary basis to see how they perform and ensure they are a good fit for the organization.

Chuck Todd, a former moderator of *Meet the Press*, said on the show:

> "[I]f you told me we were hiring [McDaniel] as a technical advisor to the Republican Convention, I think that would be certainly defensible.
>
> If you told me, 'We're talking to her, but let's see how she does in some interviews and maybe vet her with actual journalists inside the network, [let's] see if it's a two-way, what she can bring [to] the network.'
>
> Unfortunately, this interview is always going to be looked at through the prism of, who is she speaking for? I don't think it's going to bring the network what they think it wants to bring to the network. I understand the motivation, but this execution, I think, was poor."

CHAPTER 53
Elon Musk

Ego

While Elon Musk's ego may not explain all of his decisions since buying Twitter in 2022, it was likely part of the equation that helped create its worsening crisis.

"Twitter is dying before our eyes, and not of natural causes. Its present owner, Elon Musk, is killing it. Ego, impulsiveness, and lack of self-discipline are the proximate causes of its decline," David Frum wrote in *The Atlantic*. He also noted, "The company is alienating advertisers, shedding valuable users, and attracting the anonymous trolls that Musk supposedly wanted to discourage."

A business executive's ego can help provide him or her with the confidence they might need to buy, start, or lead a company. However, that same ego, left unchecked, can lead them to create or extend a crisis that threatens the organization's future, according to leadership, mental health, and other experts and observers.

"Egos Can Create Huge Blind Spots"

"Egos can create huge blind spots for leaders, making them unaware of their impact on the business and on those around them," according to Moshe Cohen, founder of The Negotiating Table which provides negotiating, consulting, strategic advice, and negotiation training services, and a senior lecturer at Boston University's Questrom School of Business.

Trail of Destruction

Cohen goes on:

> "Whether leaders lay off employees on mass Zoom calls, announce major changes to their companies with a tweet, berate employees publicly, or make impulsive or contradictory decisions, they are often surprised by the trail of destruction to their organizations, people, and reputation in their wake.

Egos can also limit the ability of leaders to hear feedback and incorporate information from others into their decision-making, whether they are launching products, deciding to go to war, or determining their country's response to a pandemic. As a result, they sometimes make disastrous and entirely preventable decisions."

Bloated Egos

Victoria Clark, a licensed mental health counselor and executive coach, explains:

"A leader's ego by nature is likely to be a little bloated. The mentality of someone with not only the ability to lead the masses but the knowledge that they hold the power to do so can overtake some people.

A true leader is able to harness that ability and knowledge and actively work to ensure that these strengths are used positively. The benefit of a leader's ego or mentality is that they can lead. This sounds easy enough, but in reality, it's multifaceted and not everyone is capable of doing so. Leading well requires the ability to take oneself out of the picture and put the company and in turn its people first. While at the same time identifying others who can grow with a company and those that are not meant for it."

"The Quickest Route to Self-Destruction"

Lakesha Cole, founder and principal publicist at she PR, offers the following advice:

"The bull-in-a-china-shop approach, or always needing to be the smartest person in the room, is the quickest route to self-destruction, irreparable relationships, and loss of revenue, as we've seen with Kanye West and his relationship with Adidas.

The common denominator in all of your business endeavors is you. Understanding your internal self at your core is paramount. Get this right, and you'll know the areas in which you are strong and those which need some work—better positioning you and the company for improvement and growth."

Impact of Unchecked Egos

Clark warns:

> "If a leader's ego goes unchecked this can significantly harm a company and its employees, easily resulting in a crisis. One example of this could be a leader who takes over a company that does not help its employees grow due to the need for the leader to be in the spotlight. This can lead to the loss of valuable staff that are the backbone of a company. This type of crisis may occur behind closed doors, but it will not stay there. As others see the ship going down, they will likely jump ship to save themselves."

Be Self-Aware

The more executives are aware of their words and actions, the more likely it is that they could curtail or stop them.

The Best Approach

"When disasters do occur, the best approach is humility and communication, acknowledging that errors have been made and focusing the organization, its people, and the public on looking forward," Boston University's Cohen concludes.

CHAPTER 54
National Football League

Improving Safety

Not all crises are easily or quickly resolved, and new actions and decisions can be required to address the latest developments.

That happened when the NFL and NFL Players Association announced they had agreed to change the league's concussion protocol. The move came "following a joint investigation into the procedures after Miami Dolphins quarterback Tua Tagovailoa suffered what was described as a back injury against the Buffalo Bills ..." *CNBC* reported.

Crisis Communication and Management Lessons

Business executives can learn several lessons about managing and communicating about their corporate crisis from the NFL's actions to address the decades-long concussion controversy.

Regularly Review Protocols

Don't assume that the policies and procedures for addressing a crisis last year are still appropriate today.

Nesochi Okeke-Igbokwe, a health expert and CEO of the Dr. Nesochi LLC internal medicine practice, says:

> "Football is a contact sport in which there is a risk of traumatic brain injury. Nonetheless, concussion protocol must always be reviewed and updated by medical experts in the field to ensure that the health of current and future generations of players [is] well protected.

> One important lesson for any organization is that leadership plays a crucial function in establishing, solidifying, enforcing, and reinforcing a clearly defined safety protocol that cultivates a culture of health and safety for all members of the organization.

This safety framework and guidance should be routinely evaluated and amended as needed."

Explain Why New Policies or Procedures Are Needed

Don't change your company's approach to a crisis without explaining why the change is needed.

The league and players' union said in a joint statement that:

> "While the investigation determined that the team medical staff and unaffiliated medical professionals followed the steps of the Protocol as written, the NFL and NFLPA agree that the outcome, in this case, is not what was intended when the Protocols were drafted.
>
> As such, as has been done in previous cases, based on the advice of the parties' respective medical experts, the Protocol will be modified to enhance the safety of the players."

Under the new protocols, players will be unable to compete if they are experiencing ataxia, which describes a lack of coordination caused by poor muscle control, according to *CNN*.

Put Things in Perspective

Responding to a question at a fan forum in London, NFL Commissioner Roger Goodell outlined the league's "intensive focus" on the issue over the past 15 years and said its medical protocols have served as templates for other sports. "Our job really is to continue to modify those as medical experts or other experiences tell you this is something you can do differently," he explained.

Discuss What's Next

When policies or procedures change, it's a crisis communication best practice to explain how they will change the organization's approach to the crisis. Dr. Allen Sills, the NFL's chief medical officer, noted during a news conference about the new concussion protocols that the league "will take a 'conservative' approach to ruling players out.

"He acknowledged [that] players who might not have suffered a brain injury might still be ruled out anyway if ataxia [impaired coordination] is present," *CNN* reported.

Sills said, "... let's just go ahead and assume it is coming from the brain, and we will hold someone out. Because if we are going to be wrong, we would rather hold someone out who doesn't have a brain injury, but we are being cautious, than to put someone out who might have a brain injury, and we weren't able to diagnose it."

CHAPTER 55
National Women's Soccer League

Allegations of Abuse

Learning from the crises of others is one thing. But applying those lessons and avoiding similar situations is another. A case in point is the report released in 2022 about the alleged abuses in the National Women's Soccer League.

The report, prepared by former Acting US Attorney General Sally Yates, was published "a year after players outraged by what they saw as a culture of abuse in their sport demanded changes by refusing to take the field." It found that leaders of the NWSL and the United States Soccer Federation—the governing body of the sport in America—as well as owners, executives and coaches at all levels failed to act on years of voluminous and persistent reports of abuse by coaches," *The New York Times* reported.

Peter Loge, director and associate professor in the School of Media and Public Affairs at George Washington University, comments:

> "The best organizations are honest about their shortcomings and hold themselves accountable. The Yates report demonstrates that soccer needs to hold itself to the same standards off the field as it does on the field.
>
> The NWSL needs to treat the Yates report as it would a player who persistently fouls opponents and puts others in danger in the game. Dangerous behavior on the pitch gets punished by coaches and referees. Dangerous behavior off the pitch should be punished as well. The game sets the standard [and] everyone in the game needs to be held to that standard."

Statement from US Soccer Federation

US Soccer Federation president Cindy Parlow Cone says that the findings of the investigation are just a "first step" in changing an environment that allowed the abuse of professional women players to take place unchecked for many years. *ESPN* reported:

> "The misconduct and abuse [are] entirely inexcusable and have no place in soccer on or off the field … I think this report makes it clear that we need to make systemic changes at every level of our game.

This report is just the first step in taking a hard look at the entire soccer ecosystem in this country and what we need to do."

History Repeating Itself

Marc Lewis, an attorney specializing in sexual abuse cases, comments in a story on *Forbes.com*:

"It is tragic that we are seeing history repeat itself. Like USA Swimming, USA Gymnastics, and so many other national organizations, it seems like the culture of abuse is nowhere near ending.

On the positive side, [the League] should be commended for retaining Sally Yates and captaining what appears to be a full-scale investigation of the abusive culture. But issuing a report is just the beginning. [The League] will now need to clean house and be sure to actually take positive steps to combat the abusive culture.

At a minimum, the NWSL will need to change the culture—stop ignoring red flags, stop dismissing complaints, and encourage an environment where abuse victims feel safe and empowered to speak up. And no more 'passing the trash', moving abusers from one place to another rather than tackling the problem head on."

Accountability

"Take Appropriate Steps"

"In light of this crisis, a business leader should learn to take the appropriate steps to ensure safety in the place of business," Collen Clark, an attorney with law firm Schmidt and Clark, advises in an article for *Forbes.com*:

"People will feel safe in an environment where business leaders prioritize their workers' well-being. If there are serious misconduct allegations, they need to respond appropriately and immediately. They also need to take a deeper look at the culture they have imposed on their business. Does it employ physical, emotional, and overall psychological safety?

It should also be clear to business leaders that when abuse stems from a culture that encourages it, victims are forced to stay silent."

CHAPTER 56
Dolly Parton

Do What You Can, When You Can

When your company or organization deals with a crisis, "who will be your Dolly Parton?"

That was the question posed by Lance Kinney, an associate professor of advertising and public relations at the University of Alabama's College of Communication and Information Sciences in an online presentation for members of the Public Relations Society of America. To be sure, Parton—an award-winning actress, entertainer, song-writer, and director—is an unlikely example for business leaders on how to communicate during and recover from a crisis.

But she's had plenty of hands-on experience doing both.

In 2024 she announced a $1 million donation to the Mountain Ways Foundation, a non-profit that helped victims of the Hurricane Helene flood. That was on top of an other $1 million she donated in 2020 to help Moderna develop a vaccine for COVID-19.

Parton's Brand Equity

Parton's "rags-to-riches story is well known" and her Dollywood theme park and other tourist holdings are closely associated with the area, Kinney explains:

> "It's as if she spent the last 60 years prepping for this leadership opportunity ...
> In marketing communication terms, we might say that she possesses strong
> brand equity. Her multi-media career is built upon her down home, Appalachian
> persona as a practical, straight-talking woman directly from the Tennessee
> mountains."

Monitoring the Crisis

In 2016, wildfires ravaged areas of Parton's home state of Tennessee. Like any corporate crisis manager, she monitored the situation. As reported by *USA Today*, as the fire raged, she said in a statement:

"Today I have been watching the terrible fires in the Great Smoky Mountains and I am heartbroken. I am praying for all the families affected by the fire and the firefighters who are working so hard to keep everyone safe. It is a blessing that my Dollywood theme park, the DreamMore Resort and so many businesses in Pigeon Forge have been spared."

Taking Action

A basic rule of crisis management is that you should respond strategically, effectively, and efficiently to a crisis. Although Parton's business properties were unscathed, she sought ways to help those who had not been as fortunate. She put her brand equity to good use when she stepped up and used her high public profile to help those impacted by the crisis.

According to Kinney, Parton:

- **Obtained needed resources:** Called other music and media colleagues to help those impacted in her home area (Gatlinburg/Sevierville/Pigeon Forge).
- **Communicated with the public:** Immediately released video statements stressing the resiliency of the people in the area, the magnitude of the crisis, and her efforts to bring as much relief as possible to the region.
- **Created and repeated key messages:** Encouraged anyone who had planned a trip to the area to move forward with those plans—despite the fire. Her response to the question, "What's the best thing we can do to help?" was always "Visit."
- **Focused on what was important:** Consistently focused on the future. She never dwelt upon the crisis, nor did she ever seek help with appeals to pity or other base emotions. She concentrated on the "discourse of renewal," a concept in crisis communication which embodies the best values of an organization, centers on future opportunity and growth (rather than assigning blame), stands upon a reservoir of previously developed goodwill, and builds morale both inside and outside the organization.

Parton's efforts and messages paid off.

The year following the fires, tourism in the region broke all records, generating an estimated $1.3 billion in revenue—up 3 percent from the previous year.

Parton continued to help people recover from the wildfires. She:

- Staged a telethon that helped raise nearly $9 million for fire victims.
- Donated $1,000 a month for six months to families where the fire occurred.
- Pledged $3 million to help victims of the crisis.
- Donated an additional $5,000 to more than 900 families who were affected by the tragedy.
- Funded ongoing support programs.

Advice

Based on what Parton did during and after the crisis and how she did it, Kinney said business executives should remember the importance of:

- Being prepared for a crisis.
- Corporate citizenship.
- Looking forward (rather than stonewalling or dwelling upon cause/blame).
- Being able to step in front of the media and embody their company's best values.
- Knowing who, in their time of need, will be their Dolly Parton.

Helping in Another Crisis

In 1995, Parton jumped in to help out on a different types of crisis—early childhood literacy—and launched the Imagination Library, a book giveaway program that has donated more than 150 million books to schoolchildren around the world.

She recalled on the project's website that "When I was growing up in the hills of East Tennessee, I knew my dreams would come true. I know there are children in your community with their own dreams. They dream of becoming a doctor or an inventor or a minister. Who knows, maybe there is a little girl whose dream is to be a writer and singer. The seeds of these dreams are often found in books, and the seeds you help plant in your community can grow across the world."

Given everything Parton had done for the people of her state, it's hardly surprising that a Tennessee lawmaker introduced legislation to erect a statue in her honor on the grounds of the Capitol.

But it was an honor that the singer did not want. "Given all that is going on in the world, I don't think putting me on a pedestal is appropriate at this time," Parton said in the statement, which was posted on Twitter and Instagram.

In her statement, Parton, 75, left the option open for a statue to be erected in the future, writing, "I hope, though, that somewhere down the road several years from now or perhaps after I'm gone if you still feel I deserve it, then I'm certain I will stand proud in our great State Capitol as a grateful Tennessean."

CHAPTER 57
PGA Tour

Controversial Mergers

The headline-making announcement in 2023 that the PGA Tour, the organizer of professional golf tours in the United States, planned to merge with LIV Golf, a new professional golf league established by the Kingdom of Saudi Arabia, reverberated throughout the sports world. The unexpected move posed major challenges for the tour that threatened to permanently damage its brand, image, and reputation.

Money appeared to have been a factor behind the PGA Tour's decision to agree to a merger.

"We cannot compete with a foreign government with unlimited money," PGA commissioner Jay Monahan said in a speech to employees according to the *Wall Street Journal*. "This was the time. ... We waited to be in the strongest possible position to get this deal in place."

Tattered Reputation

An organization's controversial or unpopular actions or decisions can have unintended consequences. This pending merger was one example.

Bouncing Back

A crisis does not have to be a death blow for an organization. The Crisis Management Hall of Fame is rich with examples of how companies recovered from a variety of scandals, disasters, and other emergencies.

But comebacks are not automatic and require carefully planned strategies and tactics to help ensure success.

The Tour's "brand, built on a rich history and tradition, could face dilution or misalignment if the merger isn't managed with the utmost care," Casey Jones, the founder and head of marketing and finance at digital marketing agency CJ&CO, told *Forbes.com*.

Priorities

Before attempting to bounce back from a crisis, companies must map out and prioritize what should be done, when, how, and in what order. Jones advises:

> "To recover from any potential damage to its brand and reputation, the [PGA Tour] must prioritize transparency and clear communication. It's essential to articulate the benefits of the merger to all stakeholders, including players, sponsors, and fans, while also addressing any concerns head-on. This proactive approach can help maintain trust and credibility during the transition."

Reinforce Commitments

An important part of the crisis recovery process is to remind the public and stakeholders about the organization's core values and commitments.

"To recover from any damage, the PGA Tour can amplify its commitment to the core values of integrity and sportsmanship, underlining that these remain at the heart of its operations," Lakesha Cole, the founder and principal publicist of she PR, recommends.

Communications

How an organization communicates during and after a crisis can help ensure that those concerned about or affected by the situation are fully informed about efforts to address the situation.

Statement from PGA Tour

"We are confident that once all stakeholders learn more about how the PGA Tour will lead this new venture, they will understand how it benefits our players, fans, and sport while protecting the American institution of golf," the Tour said in a statement to *CNN*.

CHAPTER 58
Presidential Candidates

The Importance of Branding When a Crisis Strikes

A respected and trusted brand can help companies and organizations weather a crisis by helping to ensure that the public will trust the brand when worst-case crisis scenarios become a reality. Political candidates, who need to survive a variety of crisis situations, can offer valuable insights for executives about branding.

The strategies, tactics, and techniques that presidential candidates use to whip up and then sustain energy, enthusiasm, and support among voters can be employed by business leaders to successfully brand themselves and their companies.

Corporate executives can learn several lessons about effective branding by paying close attention to what the men and women who run for the White House say—and how and why they say it.

Clear Messaging

Unless people can understand what you are saying and why, nothing else matters.

Greta Maiocchi, the head of marketing and recruitment at the Open Institute of Technology, says in an email interview:

> "One significant lesson is the importance of a clear message. Barack Obama's 2008 campaign with its crisp slogan 'Yes, we can!' is a powerful example. It encapsulates his mission and passion, much like companies need to crisply communicate their mission, vision, and values to resonate with their target audience."

Jo Caruana, founder and CEO of Finesse group, a communications and public relations agency, observes:

> "Clarity is the ultimate example of things CEOs and brands can learn from presidential candidates that follow that rule. Who remembers Donald Trump's slogan from 2016? Yup, you know the one—and it's still being used by his campaign

today. What about Hillary [Clinton's] from back then? No idea. I am sure she had plenty of important things to say, but it wasn't clear enough for any of us to remember."

Simplicity

Make it as easy as possible for consumers to remember your messaging.

"The right marketing will be so simple that your clients can repeat it back to you—rather than you having to constantly repeat it to them. Kamala Harris's message in 2024 was 'We're not going back'—clear, easy to remember/repeat, and exactly what her target voter wants to hear," Caruana points out.

Authenticity

Coming across as fake and insincere can sink any branding campaign.

"Authenticity matters. Voters can see through manufactured personalities and disingenuous promises. Companies should build transparent brands that match their true values and mission," branding expert Haiko de Poel notes.

Relevancy

To ensure success, branding efforts need to stay current and in sync with those they are trying to reach.

According to Maiocchi:

> "Politicians' methods of staying relevant to their voters parallel how brands must constantly evolve to stay relevant to their consumers. Politicians often adapt their strategies based on audience feedback and show agility and responsiveness, reinforcing the importance of being attuned to customers' evolving needs—a lesson every brand should adopt.

> As an example, take Elizabeth Warren's [a Democratic Senator from Massachusetts] 2020 campaign, which did [extensive testing] of slogans and messages to see what resonated with voters. This reflects an approach commonly used by brands and marketers to refine their messaging."

Storytelling

Telling stories will help to hold the attention of consumers and avoid the risk of boring them.

"Politicians are masters of storytelling. They share powerful stories and testimonials to create an emotional connection with voters. Companies should do the same by highlighting customer success stories and sharing authentic experiences," de Poel suggests.

Understand Audiences

The more you know about your audience, the more likely it is that your messages will resonate with them.

"Deeply understanding your target audience is the cornerstone of branding. Trump has a laid-back, informal campaigning style, which resonates with his voters," Emily Williams, a content strategist and CEO of Web Copy Collective, points out. By contrast, Vice President Kamala Harris had "a disciplined, structured approach to campaigning, which connects more to her demographic. Policies aside, each does a great job of staying on brand and using that on their campaign."

Create a Movement

Lakesha Cole, founder and principal publicist at she PR, recalls:

> "The most successful campaigns don't just broadcast a marketing message— they create a movement that people feel compelled to join. For example, the Harris campaign has inspired voters to build their own diverse coalitions, like Win With Black Men, Beyhive for Kamala, Military Families for Kamala, Swifties for Harris, Republicans for Harris, and even White Dudes for Harris.
>
> These grassroots groups bring together people from different backgrounds, united by their shared belief in the candidate's vision and values. From a marketing perspective, these voter-led coalitions show the power of community-driven marketing."

Turn Customers into Advocates

Build an identity that "resonates so deeply with various audiences that they become advocates and feel personally invested in the brand's success," Cole advises:

> "It's about turning customers into fans who will spread your message because they believe it represents them. The Harris campaign has shown that by embracing the unique identities and passions of these groups, you not only strengthen your core base but also expand your reach and impact. That's a powerful lesson for any CEO looking to build a brand that truly connects."

Data

The ability to quantify the impact and success of your branding campaigns is critical.

"Data-driven decisions are key. Politicians constantly analyze polls and metrics to optimize their messaging. Companies must analyze metrics like customer satisfaction, retention, and lifetime value to make strategic branding choices," de Poel recommends.

Reinforcement

Sarah Mitchell, marketing director for Relyir, a manufacturer of artificial grass, offers the following advice:

> "An essential lesson comes from Barack Obama's campaign of 'Hope and Change.' He reinforced this message at every opportunity, silently affirming it through his demeanor, speeches, and the cultural zeitgeist he embodied. Corporations can learn the importance of consistency—every touchpoint a customer has with your brand should uphold the key messaging and brand ethos."

Alignment

Make sure that your branding efforts are in sync with what people know about the products or services you are marketing to them.

According to Mitchell:

> "Politicians embody their branding—every action and every statement aligns with their brand image. You can't dispute the fact that Donald Trump's 'Make

America Great Again' and his bold, direct approach fed seamlessly into each other. Corporate leaders should similarly live their brand, fostering an authentic connection with consumers."

Consistency

Don't zig and zag.

Nikkia Adolphe, founding partner and head of media strategy at Tenet Consultancy, advises in an email interview:

"Candidates who succeed do so by consistently communicating their values and vision across every platform, whether it's social media, TV, or live events. This is exactly what strong brands do—they maintain a clear, unified message that resonates with their audience.

[One example] is how President Biden's campaign consistently used the themes of 'restoration' and 'unity' to differentiate him from opponents, which created a strong emotional connection with voters."

CHAPTER 59
Jen Psaki

Dealing with the Media

The ability to communicate effectively, strategically, and efficiently is a critical skill when dealing with news organizations, especially during a crisis.

Jen Psaki served as President Joe Biden's first press secretary. The White House briefings she conducted provided important lessons about communicating in a crisis. Her televised meetings with reporters immediately became a continuing education class for business leaders on how to communicate clearly and effectively with the media and the public during a crisis—or any other time.

Patience and Grace

Mike McCurry, a former White House press secretary (1993–98), said Psaki "handled the chores of daily briefings superbly and that was important since the daily press briefing was an endangered species. Being accountable, taking tough questions, even the ridiculous ones, requires some patience and grace ... And she did that and probably passed some ethic of respect for the press to her capable successor ..."

Overcoming a Bad Precedent

Cheryl Fenelle Dixon is a marketing and communication executive and adjunct professor in the M.S. strategic communications program at Columbia University. She notes that Psaki "took over a tenuous and adversarial relationship between the White House and the press where insults, lack of objectivity, and personal agendas were the norm."

The situation she inherited made her job even more difficult. Dixon goes on:

> "Overcoming this kind of precedent is not an easy task for any communicator. She started her job with a distrusting and browbeaten audience and needed to earn credibility while setting a new tone for how they would work and communicate together. Jen was inclusive and called on reporters with an adversarial history—not dodging the questions that were likely to be challenging."

The ability to project confidence in the face of adversity was a contributing factor to Psaki's success as a communicator. Dixon believes she was:

"consistently calm and professional in her tone and delivery. Even when she pushed back against a reporter or delivered an edgy rebuttal, she did so with an even tone that prevented an exchange from escalating. She displayed humor and warmth when appropriate but stayed on course."

Consistency

Stacy Rosenberg is an associate teaching professor at Carnegie Mellon University's Heinz College of Information Systems and Public Policy. She says:

"One of Psaki's greatest strengths was consistency. Unlike the previous administration that set the record for the longest time without an official White House press briefing, Psaki maintained visibility through regular briefings. This created a sense of transparency. Business leaders who are accessible either directly or via their media relations team can similarly show a commitment to open communication."

Professionalism

Rosenberg points out that:

"... Psaki is also credited with professionalism. She treated every journalist, regardless of political affiliation, with respect. She was not thrown by a challenging question. Crisis communicators can model Psaki's command of the room by pivoting from a heated question to a key talking point to remain on message."

Respect

Zach Friend is a national public policy, political campaign, and communications expert. He says Psaki:

"... found a way to successfully navigate a political world that awards silos and fierce partisanship with a calm, measured, factual approach.

One of her greatest successes has been in making the role of White House press secretary respected again—even among media outlets that have audiences not supportive of the President's policies. She has successfully toned down the rhetoric from the podium, ably and sincerely represented the President even against a backdrop of constant national and international crises, all with a command of facts and approach."

Messaging

Peter Schwartz is an international business consultant with 30 years of experience in marketing, business development, recruiting, and crisis communications. He comments on *Forbes.com*:

"As part of the first-ever all-female communications team for the Biden White House, she made sure to structure her answers in a way that would appeal to progressive supporters as well as [the] middle of the road voters. Some have criticized her lack of effort attracting the support of conservative voters, although there was very little chance of that, to begin with.

There are lessons to learn since, in some ways, Psaki represented a return to the more traditional role of a press secretary. And she showed it could be effective. Psaki's answers were usually long and more detailed than other recent spokespersons.

She made a point of not ignoring antagonistic media outlets like Fox. And she conducted herself in a matter-of-fact, restrained manner. All of these characteristics can be real assets in crisis communications."

CHAPTER 60
Publix

Consumer Protests

It was not the first boycott of a company or organization, nor will it be the last. But a protest against Publix Super Markets—a multi-billion-dollar grocery chain with 1,200 stores in southeastern USA—had an interesting plot twist that created international headlines and provides important lessons about crisis communication for all business executives.

The protest in 2021 was unusual because it was not sparked by anything the corporation said or did, but by the actions of a member of the family that owns the company. As reported by *The Guardian*, "Families are boycotting Publix after a member of the founding family donated $300,000 to the Trump rally that preceded January's deadly Capitol attack."

In responding to the crisis situation, Publix appeared to do the right things, the right ways, and for the right reasons.

Setting the Record Straight

Publix sought to distance itself from the actions of Julie Jenkins Fancelli, one of the daughters of the man who founded the company in the 1930s.

According to the *Miami Herald*:

> "Publix's communications director Maria Brous released the supermarket chain's response to the *Miami Herald*: "Mrs. Fancelli is not an employee of Publix Super Markets, and is neither involved in our business operations, nor does she represent the company in any way. We cannot comment on Mrs. Fancelli's actions."

Publix's statement continued:

> "The violence at the Capitol on Jan. 6 was a national tragedy. The deplorable actions that occurred that day do not represent the values, work or opinions of Publix Super Markets."

Publix posted a similar message on Twitter.

Advice for Business Executives

Corporate officials should take several factors into account before responding to any protests that are launched against their companies or organizations. Depending on the nature of the protests and your business, there may be no clear-cut answers on how—or whether—to respond.

Reality Check

Nick Kalm is the founder and CEO of Reputation Partners, a national strategic communications firm. He says:

> "While studies have shown that boycotts don't dramatically affect an organization's sales, they can and often do have a significant impact on reputation.
>
> Deciding on whether and how an organization should respond needs to be a very careful calculation. Understanding how the offending action relates to an organization's line of business, core values, and brand proposition, as well as if it was deliberate and who or what caused it, are all critical factors when considering a response.
>
> In most cases, it makes sense for an organization to respond. Otherwise, those who are leading the boycott can further fuel their campaign by saying the organization clearly doesn't care or value the perspective of those who have been offended."

Choose Your Words Carefully

Kalm offers the following advice:

> "Sometimes the comment can be a simple one-time apology and a pledge to do better. Or it can be a comment that clarifies the organization's position—or lack of relationship with the person or action generating the controversy. If the boycott involves a more systemic issue inside the company, more than just one comment will be required.
>
> But, if the boycott is triggered due to an overtly political issue, the organization would be wise to choose its words very carefully or risk alienating approximately half the country in its response."

CHAPTER 61
Queen Elizabeth II

Succession

The death of Queen Elizabeth II in 2022 and the immediate succession of her son Charles provides lessons from the British monarchy about leadership transition for companies, organizations, and corporate leaders. The Queen's death at age 96 was another reminder for business executives to have succession plans in place and ensure those plans are updated on a regular basis as needed.

Leadership transitions—whether they are planned or unexpected—can create a crisis for any organization if they are not handled strategically, effectively, and efficiently.

"A Watershed Moment"

"The death of Queen Elizabeth II, which Buckingham Palace announced, is a watershed moment for Britain, at once incomparable and incalculable," *The New York Times* reported.

"It marks both the loss of a revered monarch—the only one most Britons have ever known—and the end of a figure who served as a living link to the glories of World War II Britain, presided over its fitful adjustment to a post-colonial, post-imperial era and saw it through its bitter divorce from the European Union," the paper observed.

"King Charles has been planning his entire life to take the throne. He has planned and replanned again and again," retired US Navy Captain Barbara Bell comments. She is an adjunct professor of leadership and ethics at the United States Naval Academy, and author of *Flight Lessons: Navigating Through Life's Turbulence and Learning to Fly High*. She was one of the first women to graduate from the US Naval Academy and the US Naval Test Pilot School. She goes on:

> "There is a lesson in that. A succession plan must be a living, breathing entity. We must observe, prepare, and refresh our plans for the next leader to take over. And as CEO, we must be a willing and active participant in our own succession planning. Where is the company now, where is it going or should be going, and what type of leader is needed for the future?

"In the Navy, it was always that way for me. While in command, I led and planned for the next commander to take over after me."

David Braun, founder and CEO of Capstone Strategic, a mergers and acquisitions strategic consulting firm, explained in a statement how the monarchy's succession plan:

"... is codified in efficiency and dictated by centuries of history and traditions. While companies need not have a minute-by-minute plan, they can learn the power of having 'the next in line' ready to go, followed by precision in their announcements and actions. Detailed plans that can be implemented quickly make a big difference in how companies are perceived and how they keep their business moving forward."

Provide for Smooth Leadership Transitions

CNN reported:

"Charles had already been taking on some of the Queen's engagements this year as her health had become enough of a concern for her to cancel some of her commitments, including the State Opening of Parliament.

Both Charles and Prince William had been prioritizing the Queen's diary over theirs. Both of them had been activated as Counsellors of State, where the Queen delegates her sovereign power for specific purposes, and they were obligated to be even more available for those duties."

"This is the greatest lesson for business—be ready and develop a strong bench so that you can act quickly and safeguard a smooth transition," Amy Clark, chief human resources officer of the Better Business Bureau National Programs and founder of the Growth Minded Leadership group, told *Forbes.com*.

She points to two examples in the corporate world:

"As part of a long-planned leadership transition, WD-40 groomed Steve Brass to succeed Garry Ridge, who retired as their chief executive officer this week [September 2022]. This is a terrific example of a well-controlled, communicated, and deliberate plan to take the WD-40 into the future.

Compare this with the emergency replacement plan that JPMorgan Chase had in place and effectively activated in response to Jamie Dimon recovering from a health scare in 2020.

Two senior JPMorgan executives were prepared and ready to effectively manage the company with confidence until Dimon was ready to return as CEO."

Carefully Groom Your Future Leaders

Position potential successors as true leaders, not figureheads.

Charles "was never positioned as a person who was a leader," Catherine Rymsha, visiting management lecturer at the University of Massachusetts Lowell, says:

> "The monarchy could have strategically managed his leadership brand preparing for this moment over time yet failed to position him well in terms of strength or confidence. While he may have the skills and support needed to lead, even the headlines and hearsay over the years saying that the crown may skip him and go to Prince William showed there may be something lacking in his preparedness.
>
> While this may not be [the] case due to related succession laws set forth by the monarchy, it does show how Prince William is seen as a leader more so than his now reigning father."

The monarchy no doubt had its plan for how this day would proceed for years. The plan was written, the successor was in place, and now "management" was ready to execute it.

Depending on the size, nature, and age of a company, businesses may have already groomed second-tier leaders, such as vice presidents or division heads, to assume the leadership mantle.

Only 12 percent of companies reported confidence in the strength of their bench, according to Development Dimensions International's 2023 "Global Leadership Forecast Report." That was hardly an improvement over 2021, which showed only 11 percent had confidence in their bench of leaders.

If a board of directors has not already taken steps to groom or identify their future leaders, then the chaos in the House of Representatives was an important reminder of why they should.

Crisis Management Planning

Companies and organizations should not leave succession planning to chance. But they should account for sudden vacuums in leadership in their crisis management and crisis communication plans.

Family Businesses

Succession was the popular HBO series that followed the power struggles and efforts to control Waystar Royco, a fictional dysfunctional family-owned conglomerate. The series mirrored the challenges and issues that face many real family-controlled businesses.

One of the many parallels in *Succession* with real companies was the failure of Waystar Royco to have a succession plan. The inability to have and implement a plan can create a crisis situation that simmers for years, then explodes without warning into a full-blown disaster, scandal, or other corporate emergency.

More Similarities

There are other important similarities worth pointing out and for owners of family-owned companies to keep in mind. The parallels focus on efforts to keep a company's leadership and ownership within the family—and being able to discuss the topic with family members in the first place.

This is especially important, considering that 85 percent of surveyed family-owned businesses said it was very or extremely important that their business remains in the family for at least another generation.

Succession Issues

According to the results of the inaugural Private Business Owner Survey of 400 family-owned businesses by Brown Brothers Harriman's Center for Family Business:

- 43 percent said it was a challenge to choose a successor, knowing it will cause conflict within the family.
- 84 percent of respondents said that a business decision or discussion has led to severe disagreements or resentment within their family.
- 75 percent of these business owners say the family members' roles are either not well defined or not fully communicated.

CHAPTER 62
Rosendin Electric

Responding to Back-to-Back Crises

The COVID-19 pandemic created a ripple effect of other crisis situations that made a bad situation worse for millions of companies and organizations. Like other business leaders, the executives at Rosendin Electric faced and overcame back-to-back challenges and emergencies that tested the strength, determination, resilience, and resources of their companies.

Their experience provides important crisis management lessons for all business executives.

Underestimating COVID-19

In January 2020, about a month after Mike Greenawalt became CEO of Rosendin Electric—the US's largest private electrical contractor with 7,000 workers, 16 offices, and $2 billion in annual revenues—he and his colleagues started to pay serious attention to COVID-19.

Their early focus was on the company's supply chain and how the coronavirus—then confined to China—could impact the company's projects in the US. Rosendin's executive committee and regional managers started to discuss how different "what-if" scenarios could impact the organization. "It is clear now that we underestimated the gravity of the situation until the week of February 24," Greenawalt said.

Starting in early March, the company canceled all non-essential travel, conferences, and large group meetings; established daily executive committee conference calls to discuss what was going on around the country; developed action plans; and told office employees to work from home. It also sent a series of video updates to workers about what Rosendin officials knew at the time, the company's action plans, and thanks to workers for trusting in the procedures and protocols that were being put into place.

Just the Beginning

But that was only the beginning. In the months that followed, Greenawalt said the company had to contend with:

- The impact of government lockdowns and stay-at-home orders around the country. The degree of difficulty depended on the location of projects; in several markets construction work was not deemed essential.
- A continuing and growing labor shortage of qualified workers.
- The large number of construction workers who chose to stay home.
- The risk of losing veteran key employees who had to homeschool their children after brick-and-mortar schools shut down.
- Challenges in processing payrolls for 5,000 field workers.
- Dealing with issues related to social injustice and ensuring all employees felt welcome and safe coming to work.
- Spreading wildfires in the western US that were a continual threat to operations and employees. In many cases, Rosendin had to pull its workforce from projects until air quality improved.

Prepared for the Resurgence

Although the pandemic had raged on and worsened across the country, Greenawalt recalled that Rosendin was:

> "... better equipped to handle [the resurgence] because of the first round. We developed procedures and policies and a response plan. Round one of COVID-19 was devastating because we were scrambling to respond.

> But because we have remained diligent and our employees remain vigilant, we aren't feeling the impact nearly as much. Yes, the numbers [of COVID-19 cases] are higher, but they seem to be less severe. Had we seen case numbers like this in the first round, the impact would have been much more significant. But we're actually doing all right—our response plan is working."

Advice

Based on his experience, Greenawalt says there are several steps business executives can take to respond to, manage, and recover from back-to-back crisis situations:

- Don't hesitate: time is not your friend.
- Utilize all the resources available at the time and promptly develop an action plan for each crisis as it occurs.
- Listen to the leaders you have surrounded yourself with before the crisis, as they are looking to you for support as well.
- The term "we will get through this together" should resonate regardless of which crisis you are dealing with.
- Communicate your plans frequently and with certainty to those you lead.

CHAPTER 63
Secret Service

Security Failures

A series of security failures by Secret Services tarnished its image, reputation, and credibility, and led to improvements and reforms to help ensure those lapses were never repeated.

In 2024, a sniper wounded former President Donald Trump at an outdoor rally in Pennsylvania. The attempted assassination led to the resignation of the director of the Secret Service and a congressional hearing about the headline-making incident.

Ronald Rowe Jr., the agency's acting director, told lawmakers that "he considered it indefensible that the roof used by the gunman in the attempted assassination of former President Donald Trump was unsecured and said it was regrettable that local law enforcement had not alerted his agency before the shooting that an armed subject had been spotted on a nearby roof," the *Associated Press* reported.

"What I saw [when he visited the roof later] made me ashamed. As a career law enforcement officer and a 25-year Secret Service veteran, I cannot defend why that roof was not better secured," he admitted.

The US Secret Service has had to deal with other embarrassing crises over the years, which were often followed by investigations, calls for reforms, and commitments that the situations would never be repeated.

In 2022, one crisis led to the agency immediately suspending four of its agents, *Reuters* wrote.

According to *CNN*, two men "... allegedly provided 'rent-free apartments' estimated to cost more than $40,000 annually each to a [Department of Homeland Security] employee and members of the US Secret Service, all while impersonating federal agents," an affidavit said. The document "details substantial gifts the two defendants allegedly gave federal agents."

Infiltrating the Secret Service

The Washington Post reported that: "Federal law enforcement officials did not say what motivated the men or what they wanted in return as they, according to prosecutors, "ingratiated themselves with and infiltrated" Secret Service agents and DHS personnel who lived in their D.C. apartment building.

"'We have not verified the accuracy of his claims, but [one of the men] made claims to witnesses he had ties to ISI, which is the Pakistani intelligence service," US Attorney Joshua Rothstein commented.

Statement from the Secret Service

In a statement posted on its website, the Secret Service explained it:

"... has worked, and continues to work, with its law enforcement partners on this ongoing investigation. All personnel involved in this matter are on administrative leave and are restricted from accessing Secret Service facilities, equipment and systems.

The Secret Service adheres to the highest levels of professional standards and conduct and will remain in active coordination with the Departments of Justice and Homeland Security."

According to *Homeland Security Today*:

"The Secret Service experienced several protection-related security incidents on the White House complex from 2012 through 2017. These incidents included attempts to gain access to the White House complex by foot, car, and air."

It also included an incident in September 2014 when "an intruder jumped a fence, passed several layers of security, evaded US Secret Service personnel, and entered the White House before being detained."

In 2012, *ABC News* said that:

"Secret Service agents hired prostitutes while traveling in El Salvador, Panama, China and Romania years before the scandal involving President Obama's trip to Colombia that April, according to a Homeland Security investigation ...

The probe, by the department's inspector general, contradicts Secret Service Director Mark Sullivan's May testimony to Congress that 'this just is not part of our culture.'"

Criticisms

In a story on *CBS' Sunday Morning*, correspondent Jim Axelrod reported on the publication of *Zero Fail: The Rise and Fall of the Secret Service*. The book by Pulitzer Prize-winning *Washington Post* reporter Carol Leonnig was critical of the agency and how it has responded to its crises.

Among those interviewed in the *CBS* story was former agent Jonathan Wackrow, who was with the Secret Service for 14 years, where he served on the details protecting President and Mrs. Obama. Wackrow's experience "... gives him insight into another problem plaguing the Secret Service that more money can't address: a culture lacking transparency and accountability."

The agency also provided a link to a report by the inspector general of the US Department of Homeland Security with the title: The Secret Service Has Taken Action to Address the Recommendations of the Protective Mission Panel.

Implementing Recommendations

The Government Accountability Office (GAO) issued a report that found the agency was working to address a series of reform-related recommendations. According to the report:

> "In Dec. 2014, an independent panel of experts made 19 recommendations for improvements to the Secret Service. For example, the panel cited a 'catastrophic failure of training' and recommended certain divisions train 25% of the time.
>
> We found that the agency is working to address these recommendations. For example, in 2021, the Secret Service mandated that agents who protect the President and Vice President train for at least 12% of their work hours by FY 2025."

Homeland Security Today reported that the GAO concluded that the Secret Service had "... taken actions to address 13 of the 19 recommendations, including two since GAO's last assessment in 2019." For example, the agency revised its budget processes to incorporate principles of mission-based budgeting in its budget formulation process.

"The Secret Service is in the process of implementing the remaining six recommendations," according to the article.

Corporate and other executives can learn from the agency's failures by not assuming that their organizations are completely safe and secure from risks and threats, testing regularly to ensure that the protections they have in place are working, and adding new protections when new or evolving threats are identified.

CHAPTER 64
Silicon Valley Bank

The Law of Unintended Consequences

When, how, and why companies communicate about a crisis can make a crisis even worse. Blame it on the law of unintended consequences. Take Silicon Valley Bank, for example.

Silicon Valley Bank dominated the tech industry, according to *The Washington Post*:

> "The bank's pleasant blue-and-white logo was omnipresent at tech conferences. It loaned money to both the venture capitalists investing in start-ups and the start-ups they were investing in. When a founder who might not have a real salary but was running a promising start-up needed a mortgage, they went to SVB. It even built up a business banking for Napa Valley wine producers, giving its tech clients access to California's best wine and exclusive vineyard parties."

On March 8, 2023, the bank issued a press release that it was seeking to raise cash. But the announcement had the opposite effect when the bank's stock collapsed and there was a run on the bank. *The Washington Post* reported:

> "The bank lost scores of customers, many of whom frantically pulled their money out over a chaotic few days last year in a bank run that shocked the tech industry and triggered a government rescue. Hundreds of employees were laid off, while others left voluntarily, taking their customers to competing banks. Since then, the bankers that remain have been trying to rebuild trust and get out the message that they're still around."

Control of Silicon Valley Bank was taken over by the FDIC [Federal Deposit Insurance Corporation] and soon shut down. That, in turn, created a ripple effect that led President Joe Biden to assure Americans that the banking system was safe, created jitters on Wall Street, and spurred investigations by the Justice Department and SEC.

"An act meant to shore up its balance sheet did the exact opposite—because the bank failed to explain its actions to customers, who were already wary from the closure of Silvergate Bank just days before," *Axios* observed.

A year after its collapse—the third largest bank failure in US history—the bank was trying to make a comeback. But its future was uncertain.

Why Silence Is Not Golden

Staying quiet about a crisis is not a recommended option. The longer business leaders refrain from sharing information about a crisis, the more likely it is that they will be accused of trying to cover up the situation or avoid discussing an embarrassing situation.

And that can be a costly mistake.

In 2017, the failure of credit score monitoring company Equifax to disclose a data breach for six weeks sparked headlines and investigations.

According to the *Wall Street Journal* in October of that year:

> "Attorneys General in at least five states are looking into why credit-reporting firm Equifax Inc. didn't tell the public for nearly six weeks about the massive data breach that potentially compromised the personal information of 145.5 million Americans.

> As the broader investigation into the Equifax breach continues, some state officials want to know why Equifax didn't say something sooner. The inquiries are aimed at determining whether Equifax might have violated state laws requiring companies to notify consumers promptly when cyber-thieves steal personal data."

The crisis was the subject of a detailed report by the US Government Accountability Office and an in-depth analysis by *Bloomberg Businessweek*.

Key Questions

There are steps to help avoid repeating Silicon Valley Bank's communication crisis—or creating a worse situation for your company or organization.

Before saying anything about a crisis, executives and their staff should ask themselves the following key questions. The answers can help ensure that communications and decisions about the crisis will be strategic, effective, and efficient.

What

- What do we know about the situation?
- What is the source of information about the crisis, and how trustworthy is that source? Is it accurate, credible, and current?
- What don't we know about the situation, and when will we know?
- What will be the impact when we tell people what we know about the crisis? Could it make matters better or worse, or have no effect?
- What questions could we be asked about the crisis, and do we have answers to those queries? If not, why not?
- What steps will we take to address the crisis, and what will we tell people about those actions?
- What resources do we have—or have access to—in order to respond to the crisis?
- What's the worst that could happen if we stay quiet about it, and are we prepared for the possible consequences?

When

- When will we announce what we know about the situation?

Who

- Who are the most important audiences that we should tell about the crisis?
- Who will be our spokesperson for the crisis, and why?
- Who should we give a heads-up that we will make the announcement?
- Who can we get to be surrogates to help tell our side of the story about the situation?

Where

- Where will we make the announcement?

Why

- Why will we share the information about the crisis?

How

- How will we share that information?

Remember that a crisis can be very fluid, and what you think you know about it now could change. So be ready to update your answers to the questions as needed.

CHAPTER 65
Will Smith

Apologizing for Creating a Crisis

Actor Will Smith apologized to Chris Rock a day after he slapped the comedian in response to a joke about Smith's wife at the 94th Academy Awards ceremony in 2022. (See a related story in Chapter 1.)

As angry as Smith was with Rock, he could have handled the situation—and the apology that followed—better. While he was entitled to be angry or upset about what Rock said about his wife, marching up onto the stage and slapping the host crossed the line. When faced with the need to apologize, company executives can learn the following lessons from Smith's apology that he posted on Instagram:

- **Don't wait:** Although Smith apologized to the Academy and his fellow nominees when he accepted the Best Actor award the same night he slapped Rock, he made no mention of Rock.
- **Be direct:** He called his own behavior "unacceptable and inexcusable."
- **Make it personal when appropriate:** Smith said later that "I would like to publicly apologize to you, Chris."
- **Explain what prompted your actions:** In his statement, Smith admitted that "... a joke about Jada's medical condition was too much to bear, and I reacted emotionally."
- **Be clear:** Make it clear why you were wrong. Smith wrote that "I was out of line, and I was wrong."
- **Express embarrassment/remorse/regret:** He pointed out, "I am embarrassed, and my actions were not indicative of the man I want to be." Smith wrote that "I deeply regret that my behavior has stained what has been an otherwise gorgeous journey for all of us."
- **Put things in proper perspective:** The actor said that "There is no place for violence in a world of love and kindness." He admitted that "I am a work in progress."
- **Don't leave anyone out:** He ended his apology by saying, "I would also like to apologize to the Academy, the producers of the show, all the attendees, and everyone watching around the world. I would like to apologize to the Williams Family and my *King Richard* family."

Criticisms

While some on social media said they could understand why Smith got angry at Rock, few condoned his violent response.

On Twitter, actor Rob Reiner wrote "Will Smith owes Chris Rock a huge apology. There is no excuse for what he did. He's lucky Chris is not filing assault charges. The excuses he made tonight were [BS]."

"Let me tell you something, it's a very bad practice to walk up on stage and physically assault a comedian," comedian Kathy Griffin wrote on Twitter. "Now we all have to worry about who wants to be the next Will Smith in comedy clubs and theaters," according to *ABC News*.

People magazine reported: "Noting that she thought Will's outburst was a result of 'a lot of stuff built up,' including a joke that Rock, 57, made at Jada's expense at the 2016 Oscars, Whoopi Goldberg added, 'I think he overreacted.'"

"Will Smith's carefully managed engagement with his fanbase, strategic choice of roles, and embrace of both digital and real-world platforms for interaction offer a blueprint for business leaders and public figures looking to rebuild their brand," says Tenyse Williams, an adjunct digital marketing instructor at Columbia University, George Washington University, and University of Central Florida. "These actions, characterized by a blend of authenticity, strategic planning, and personal touch, illustrate how challenges can be transformed into opportunities for deeper connection and brand evolution."

Best Practice

Corporate executives can learn several lessons from the situation and follow these crisis management best practices:

- **Don't act compulsively**: Carefully consider your actions and words before you do or say anything. You can never unring the bell.
- **Ask others**: Weigh the potential consequences or impact of what you are thinking of doing or saying. Time and circumstances permitting, consult with trusted advisors, colleagues, and friends for their feedback and guidance.
- **Don't wait**: The sooner you can end a crisis and begin the recovery process, the better. Sometimes that means doing what has to be done to take yourself, your company, or your organization out of the headlines as quickly as possible.

- **Keep ego in check:** Don't let ego, pride, or arrogance get in the way of doing the right thing.
- **Be proactive:** It can be better to be proactive and penalize yourself than to drag out a crisis endlessly and wind up being punished or sanctioned by others.
- **Express remorse:** When resigning, express the appropriate level of regret and remorse and apologize for your actions.
- **Avoid the blame game:** Do not blame others for the crisis, damage, or harm that you caused.

CHAPTER 66
Southwest Airlines

Modernization

Southwest Airlines, which struggled to recover from its weather-related meltdown in December 2022 through the following January, provides several crisis management and crisis communication lessons for corporate executives.

Failing to keep up with technology and update your software could eventually create a crisis for your company.

A System Prone to Trouble

Wendy L. Patrick, a lecturer at San Diego State University's Fowler College of Business, observes in an article for *Forbes.com*:

> "The biggest lesson other business leaders can take from the Southwest implosion is the importance of modernization.
>
> Southwest's failures admittedly arose from its outdated business practices. This includes the use of decades-old scheduling software, which failed to adjust to weather disruptions, to an old point-to-point baggage model that ships luggage from one city to another, instead of the modern hub-and-spoke model where routes are connected to a major hub."

Southwest Airlines used a point-to-point system that allows it "to pick up different crews daily. When travel conditions are normal, this allows it to fly more routes in a 24-hour span than other airlines," according to the *Dallas Morning News*. "But when there's a delay or a busy period, this can prove to be troublesome. And having crews scattered all over the country compounded the airline's problems over the last week when it needed to reschedule lots of flights," the newspaper noted.

It's hard to spend too much money on the right IT infrastructure. Indeed, the best policies and procedures in the world are useless without the right and updated technology to implement them.

Don't Avoid Responsibility

Moshe Cohen, founder of The Negotiating Table and a senior lecturer at Boston University's Questrom School of Business, explains:

> "Instead of taking responsibility, Southwest's management ... responded by blaming the weather, the FAA, and its own employees for the crisis.
>
> While the airline's executives have kept largely out of sight, refusing to provide interviews, passenger horror stories, unfavorable comparisons with other airlines, and employee complaints have instead painted a picture of chaos and helplessness at Southwest.
>
> Repeated apologies from the company's management have done little to reduce people's frustration and have provided little confidence in the airline's ability to restore its service or take care of its passengers."

A C+ Effort

Gigi Marino, a communications consultant, recalls in an article on *Forbes.com* how Southwest Airlines CEO Bob Jordan:

> "... made a decent effort in his December 27 apology. Were I still in the classroom, I would grade it a C+.
>
> Let's begin with what he did right. First, he apologized. He spoke with empathy. He promised that customers will receive refunds and reimbursements. And he acknowledged Transportation Secretary Pete Buttigieg's concerns—although it would have been a grave error to ignore the person who characterized the situation as a 'meltdown,' a term the media immediately glommed onto, which essentially branded the crisis."

Falling Short

Marino goes on:

> "That said, Mr. Jordan fell short in a few areas. His apology should have been the first thing he said, not the second. And it should have reflected what the thousands of travelers are experiencing and feeling right now. Rather than plunging

into an explanation of why the delays are snowballing, he simply should have said, 'We should have done better, and we will.'"

Speaking to the Wrong Audience

Jordan also addressed Southwest employees, "which [was] a positive, but saying that he is 'apologizing to them daily,' again is something that should be communicated separately to employees—not to bone-weary travelers," Marino comments.

Don't Wait to Say Something

Shane Allen, a public relations consultant, recommends in a story on *Forbes.com*:

"Don't let other parties get ahead of your story ... The Southwest flight attendants' and pilots' unions got in front of journalists days before Southwest did, allowing someone else to control the narrative in the media by planting words like 'meltdown' early on. It's okay if you don't have all the information, as long as you're transparent in saying that. But don't wait.

Practice crisis communications responses. I'm not saying Southwest doesn't do this, but stress testing your crisis communications response at least once a year will allow your response to be much smoother when something happens in real life. Across all industries in today's world, you're not planning for if you need to use it—but when."

Pivot Before You Have an Emergency

Lindsey Walker, owner of the Walker+Associates Media Group, offers the following advice in an article that was published on *Forbes.com*:

"As leaders in business, we must always stay on the cutting edge of our operations management and customer service. What worked in one season will not always work in the next.

Southwest's crisis was a warning for leaders in businesses of any industry [that] the demands and increase of your product or service will always require an increase in the tools, technology, and resources."

Act Quickly on Feedback from Employees

Walker also points out that:

> "Southwest pilots have had complaints regarding the scheduling issues ... and executive leadership was well aware, but they did not move on it in enough time to solve the problem ... As a leader, you have to be willing to implement when employees and staff are giving consistent feedback regarding the resources and tools necessary for them to do their jobs."

CHAPTER 67
Starbucks

Corporate Turnarounds

Starbucks' decision in 2024 to hire Brian Niccol, the chair and CEO of Chipotle Mexican Grill, as its fourth CEO in two years underscores the challenges boards of directors can face when searching for the right people to help turn around their struggling companies.

Depending on the problems that they are seeking to address, companies may consider a range of characteristics, credentials, and qualities when hiring a new CEO to help rebound from a crisis.

Starbucks' Challenges

In Starbucks' case, its sales "have fallen for two straight quarters. Customers have expressed frustration with high prices, slow pickup orders on Starbucks' app and lackluster food options. The company, historically considered a progressive employer, has also seen a wave of union organizing at stores stemming from frustration with working conditions, pay and benefits, and that will also be a challenge for Niccol to tackle on his first day on the job," *CNN* reported.

Starbucks' board of directors apparently thought that Niccol was the right person for the right reasons and at the right time.

"Brian is a culture carrier who brings a wealth of experience and a proven track record of driving innovation and growth," Mellody Hobson, Starbucks' board chair and new lead independent director, said in a statement on Starbucks' website. "Our board believes he will be a transformative leader for our company, our people, and everyone we serve around the world."

Leadership Bench Strength

A board that thinks it could easily find someone who is already on the company payroll as the new leader of the organization should think again.

A study in 2023 by Development Dimensions International found that only 12 percent of surveyed companies had confidence in the strength of their leadership bench. The percentage had hardly improved over the years. In 2021, only 11 percent of surveyed organizations reported they had a "strong" or "very strong" leadership bench, the lowest it had been rated in the previous 10 years.

The leadership bench problem can be traced to a failure by companies to provide leadership development and transition training for newly hired and current executives, according to DDI, which conducts the surveys. The highest global average rating for bench strength was 18 percent in 2011.

Hiring Priorities

Although there are several key CEO competencies companies should keep in mind when considering candidates, some can be more important when trying to rebound from a crisis.

Dawn Cone, a management consultant and executive coach at DSC Consulting Solutions, offers the following advice in a *Forbes.com* article:

> "They must be a strategic thinker who can focus on short and long-term issues simultaneously; they must be able to make tough, often unpopular, decisions—often a series of them—in order to cut further losses, stop the bleeding and move in a different, more profitable direction; and they must be a skilled communicator [who] can share the vision, inspire enthusiasm for that vision in the midst of tough times, and enlist buy-in for the necessary change."

Beyond the Basics

Depending on the nature of the crisis, companies may look for someone with more than a pedigree education and track record of success.

Nancy Newman, founder and CEO of Extract Talent, observes:

> "A company in severe crisis needs a transformative leader. These individuals are rare. A transformative leader is committed to creating a new future for the company that's visionary, inspiring, and one that boldly steps away from the past. Clear to this leader is that in order to fulfill the mission and goals of the organization, everyone must own the new future as if it were their own creation."

Data-Driven

Cameron Gawley, co-founder and chief growth officer at Arrival, a social commerce app, comments:

> "A key attribute is the ability to make unemotional, data-driven decisions to right the ship. An effective turnaround CEO will have a keen understanding of financial and operational levers to pull in order to stop the bleeding and set the business back on a path to growth. They should also have expertise in strategic planning to identify new opportunities, partnerships, and revenue streams to diversify risk."

Striking the Right Balance

Lucas Botzen, CEO and HR expert at Rivermate, a global HR and employment platform, suggests that:

> "They must be innovative and agile enough to make the hard decisions required for restructuring, cost-cutting, or even strategic pivoting. Otherwise, the new CEO has to engender confidence in the workforce and investors, foster a work culture of accountability, and deliver results.
>
> The board of directors has, therefore, to zero in on a leader who will be in a position to strike a balance between recovery in the short term and the long-term growth strategies to ensure that the company not only survives the crisis but also thrives in the years to come."

Potential Red Flags

It's important for a board to conduct their due diligence and do a thorough vetting of potential CEOs to help ensure that there are no issues that could cause an internal or external crisis later on.

The list includes:

- Inflated or inaccurate resumes.
- Taking credit for the work that was done by others.
- Being a "yes-man" or "yes-woman" who cannot make tough decisions.
- A lack of emotional intelligence, and an inability to read the room.
- Allegations of sexual abuse, harassment, or other wrongdoing.

Some companies and organizations have learned the hard way about the importance of digging deep into a candidate's background. Examples include the following.

Yahoo

Yahoo CEO Scott Thompson was out of his job in 2012 four months after he had been hired when it was discovered he had padded his resume with an embellished college degree, according to *CNN*.

Southern Baptist Convention

Willie McLaurin, the acting president of the Southern Baptist Convention's Executive Committee, resigned in 2023 after he admitted he had falsified his resume, *The New York Times* reported:

> "'McLaurin's education credentials that he presented in his résumé are false,' the committee's chair, Philip Robertson, said in a statement. In his resignation letter, Mr. McLaurin wrote that a recent résumé submitted to the committee 'included schools that I did not attend or complete the course of study,' according to the statement from Mr. Robertson."

CHAPTER 68
Supreme Court

Codes of Ethics

Business leaders can't prevent their companies and organizations from having a crisis that is caused by employees. But they can take steps to lessen the chances by establishing, promoting, and enforcing standards for the conduct and ethics of their workers. The documents can also be useful in addressing crisis situations.

An analysis by ethics experts of the US Supreme Court's first code of ethics in 2023 provides key insights for corporate boards of directors and other business leaders to consider when preparing or reviewing their own organization's code of ethics.

Best Practices

A code of ethics "is a reflection of the priorities, risks and values of leadership," says Patricia Harned, CEO of Ethics & Compliance Initiative.

She notes that a good code:

- Is a clear communication of an organization's overall commitment to doing what is right in all its operations.
- Outlines things that all members of the organization should not do.
- Helps employees understand what right conduct looks like (or what they should do).
- Contains clear information about how to report suspected wrongdoing.
- Is compiled by taking into account the values, risks, standards, and intended impact of an organization.

Falling Short

The Supreme Court's new code appeared to fall short in important ways, according to ethics and leadership experts and observers.

"A Dismissive Attitude"

Nicholas Creel, an associate professor of business law at Georgia College and State University, makes the following observations:

"In essence, the court opens [its statement about the code of ethics] by making the claim that the recent spate of scandals which have made the public question the integrity of the court were not actually scandals at all. If that is the case, then the court must necessarily believe they were already operating within the parameters of what the following code would allow, making it superfluous in their eyes.

Beginning the code with such a dismissive attitude no way makes it seem like the code itself will actually change the way they operate."

"No Real Consequences"

Creel goes on:

"Overall, this document is best described as vague and modestly proscriptive, with seemingly no real consequences for noncompliance. As such, it is hard to imagine how this code would actually make the court any more ethical."

Redundant

The Court's new code is "a muddle of law, compliance, and ethics. To say that 'a justice should respect and comply with the law' is redundant, imprecise, and belittling. It's not unethical to break the law, it's illegal," Rabbi Yonason Goldson, author of *Grappling With Gray: An Ethical Handbook for Personal Success and Business Prosperity*, comments.

No Oversight

Ben Michael, an attorney with Michael & Associates, says in a story for *Forbes.com*:

"The Supreme Court, while being the highest court in the land, has virtually no oversight itself. The code of ethics is an attempt to govern the Court. However, it's still being left up to the judges on the panel to enforce the code, so it leads one to wonder how effective it will be."

Going Forward

"My hope is that when ethics issues arise, the Court will consider those issues as an institution in light of the Code (instead of leaving recusal decisions entirely to individual justices, as has largely been the practice in the past). If the Court does so, then I think the Code will be an effective tool," Cassandra Burke Robertson, a law professor and director of the Center for Professional Ethics at Case Western Reserve University's School of Law, predicts.

Advice

Business leaders can't prevent their companies and organizations from having a crisis that is caused by an employee or vendor. But they can take steps to lessen the chances by establishing, promoting, and enforcing standards for the conduct and ethics their workers, members, and suppliers should follow. The documents can also be useful in addressing crisis situations.

There can—and should—be consequences for failing to adhere to codes of ethics and conduct. Otherwise, the documents are nothing more than empty and meaningless gestures that do nothing to enhance an organization's reputation or help prevent, mitigate, or address a crisis.

"Codes of conduct/ethics give everyone in an organization a road map to point to whether in [a] crisis or day-to-day dealings," notes Michael Elkins, a partner and founder of MLE Law, a labor and employment/business law firm. "Without a road map, an organization can easily get lost when a crisis arrives."

Catalyst

Kia Roberts, founder and principal of Triangle Investigations, explains:

> "Rapidly changing sensibilities about what is inappropriate behavior should be a catalyst for organizations to brush up [on] their code of conduct, if need be, or to create a code of conduct where there is none.

> Countless CEOs have resigned over the last few years due to embarrassing and damaging press reports about sexual harassment and discrimination within their organizations.

Codes of conduct are essential for employees to understand what is and isn't acceptable behavior within the workplace. Once these codes of conduct are created and implemented, organizations must then do the work of ensuring that their work matches the words—that there is appropriate corrective action taken for employees who do not follow the code of conduct."

CHAPTER 69
T-Mobile

Data Breach

The T-Mobile data breach that impacted 40 million people in 2021 highlighted—again—the need for companies and organizations to adopt and follow best practices for preparing and responding to crisis situations.

Not the First Time

According to the website Ars Technica in August 2021:

> "By some counts, T-Mobile has experienced as many as six separate data breaches in recent years. They include a hack in 2018 that gave unauthorized access to customer names, billing ZIP codes, phone numbers, email addresses, and account numbers. In a breach from last year, hackers absconded with data including customer names and addresses, phone numbers, account numbers, rate plans and features, and billing information."

Best Practices

Don't Wait for Others to Disclose Your Crisis

An important crisis management best practice is to immediately disclose information about a crisis, and not leave it for others to discover it themselves. If others—such as news organizations—find and report details of the crisis before you do, it can raise questions about your failure to announce the crisis.

News of the cyberattack on T-Mobile was first reported by digital media and broadcasting company *Vice*, not T-Mobile. The attack was confirmed a day later by the telecommunication company, which did not provide additional details about the incident at the time.

Joseph Nwankpa is an assistant professor of information systems and analytics at the Farmer School of Business at Miami University. He notes in a story on *Forbes.com* that:

"In this era of ubiquitous cyberthreats, T-Mobile's delayed reaction in discovering and disclosing the breach calls to question the effectiveness of its responsible disclosure program.

These responsible disclosure programs are designed to be a digital equivalent of 'if you see something, say something,' like with the goal of providing clear reporting guidelines to the public or anyone who stumbles on potential data breaches or security vulnerabilities."

Keep People Posted

T-Mobile issued a news release that was also posted on its website with the latest information about the data breach.

The company noted in the release that:

"We take our customers' protection very seriously and we will continue to work around the clock on this forensic investigation to ensure we are taking care of our customers in light of this malicious attack. While our investigation is ongoing, we wanted to share these initial findings even as we may learn additional facts through our investigation that cause the details above to change or evolve."

Help Those Impacted by the Crisis

CNN reported that:

"The company is recommending that all T-Mobile postpaid customers preemptively change the PINs protecting their accounts, though it said it has no evidence those PINs have been compromised. Account PINs belonging to the 850,000 prepaid customers were compromised, however, and T-Mobile said it has unilaterally reset those PINs as a security precaution."

T-Mobile announced it would offer two years of free credit monitoring to affected customers.

Advice

A Challenge to Stay Secure

Bruce Dahlgren, CEO of risk management and compliance software company MetricStream, observes in article for *Forbes.com* that:

> "As hackers become more sophisticated, it's a challenge for companies to stay secure. It's not a matter of if a breach is going to happen, but when. Because of this, it is critical for organizations to have an incident response team comprised of legal, corporate communications, and IT staff, as well as to have contingency plans in place.

> Additionally, management should conduct regular risk assessments in order to identify potential gaps and areas where cybersecurity and response plans can be improved.

> Lastly, response teams need to be aware of data protection and disclosure regulations that may impact response processes and disclosure details. Having these in place now will pay dividends down the road, dramatically improving corporate transparency, market credibility and customer loyalty."

Notify Immediately

Kevin Breen, director of cyber threat research at cybersecurity training company Immersive Labs, says in an article for *Forbes.com*:

> "When it comes to mitigating the risk of a mega-breach like this, it's important to place applications that hold large volumes of data under additional scrutiny in terms of their security monitoring, patching policies, and audit logging. This is even more vital for public-facing applications. The speed and efficiency with which an organization identifies and responds to a vulnerability could be the factor that halts a breach in its footsteps.

> Sadly, there's nothing new about this attack—and I have no doubt that we'll see more of its kind.

> "While no financial information has been compromised, significant amounts of personal data could now be in the hands of those who would use it for malicious intent. This particular incident might fade into the noise of the current news cycle, but there are people who will suffer at the hands of the fraudsters that now hold their personal information."

Pitfall to Avoid

Miami University's Nwankpa comments:

"Companies need to avoid the pitfall of attempting to find all the answers to a potential data breach by surveying the damage, identifying the attackers, limiting the damage prior to going public, and notifying the affected parties. Part of the damage limitation process during the initial response to a breach involves notifying affected parties.

Yet often, we see firms losing public goodwill by delaying the notification in an attempt to get all the answers before going public."

CHAPTER 70
Taylor Swift

When You See Something, Do Something

After a fan at a Taylor Swift concert in Rio de Janeiro apparently died as a result of sweltering temperatures in 2024, the music superstar did something that was an important crisis management lesson for corporate executives.

Swift postponed a scheduled performance because of the heat. The lesson: When you see something, do something.

In a post to her Instagram account, Swift wrote, "I'm writing this from my dressing room in the stadium. The decision has been made to postpone tonight's show due to the extreme temperatures in Rio. The safety and well-being of my fans, fellow performers, and crew have to and always will come first," *USA Today* reported.

This was not the first time Swift said or did something because of a crisis-related situation.

Tell Your Side of the Story

When Ticketmaster canceled its planned public sale of tickets to Swift's Eras tours in November 2022, fans went crazy, according to *The New York Times*. The company cited "extraordinarily high demands on ticketing systems and insufficient remaining ticket inventory to meet that demand."

For her part, Swift took steps to tell her side of the story about the crisis that had upset so many of her fans.

> "It's really difficult for me to trust an outside entity with these relationships and loyalties and excruciating for me to just watch mistakes happen with no recourse.

> "There are a multitude of reasons why people had such a hard time trying to get tickets, and I'm trying to figure out how this situation can be improved moving forward. I'm not going to make excuses for anyone because we asked them multiple times if they could handle this kind of demand, and we were assured they could."

Ticketmaster said in a statement:

> "We strive to make ticket buying as easy as possible for fans, but that hasn't been the case for many people trying to buy tickets for Taylor Swift's 'The Eras' Tour. First, we want to apologize to Taylor and all of her fans—especially those who had a terrible experience trying to purchase tickets."

Speed Matters

While Taylor Swift's statement was being praised online, one public relations expert thought that it came too late.

Swift "had ample opportunity at every major change in the pre-sale and general admission process to acknowledge frustrations and note any steps she was taking with Ticketmaster to alleviate the problem," Christy Reiss, a crisis communication professional, points out.

Danielle Grossman, a senior media consultant at Sevans PR, says:

> "While her statement acknowledges that she is 'extremely devoted to fans', she waits until she is called upon for a statement to give one—and rather than showing action, places blame. While Ticketmaster did release a lengthy explanation as to why the entire situation happened, it's one of those 'it's a little too late' for an explanation or apology situations.

> Ticketmaster did admit that they did not anticipate demand, which is something quite inexcusable for a company that has one purpose: to sell tickets for large-scale events and tours like Taylor's.

> It is also unfortunate that the company's internal team [apparently] did not follow what has been trending, what is popular, and anticipate the demand for this show. In its entirety, they did not handle this situation well and should have been prepared before the tickets even went on sale."

CHAPTER 71
Tesla, United Airlines, and Zillow

Silence Is Not Golden

A traditional best practice for companies when confronted with a crisis is to immediately tell their side of the story about the situation.

Tesla apparently decided to go in a different direction.

The Washington Post reported in November 2021 that a Tesla employee had "filed a rare lawsuit against the electric vehicle maker, alleging Tesla fostered a climate of sexual harassment at its Fremont, Calif., factory, where she says she was subjected to catcalling and aggressive physical touching."

Missing from the article, however, were any comments or reactions from Tesla about the allegations. But it was not for lack of trying by the news organization. According to the *Post* story, "Tesla did not respond to multiple requests for comment. The company, which has not had an active public relations department since 2020, does not typically respond to press inquiries."

Sending the Wrong Message

A company that does not immediately acknowledge and address a crisis runs the risk of damaging its image, reputation, and credibility and making the crisis worse. Saying "no comment"—or nothing at all—can send the wrong message to the public about the organization's actions, concerns, or culpability about the crisis.

United Airlines' Delayed Response

A passenger was dragged off a United Airlines flight in April of 2017, and videos taken of the event were widely shared on social media, which led to threats of boycotts and demands for answers from the company about what had happened, and why.

But it was not until the following day that United Airlines said anything about the headline-making incident. The company apologized for overlooking the matter.

Later that same day, the company released a statement from CEO Oscar Munoz "that was unsatisfactory to many. United Airlines finally acknowledged responsibility two full days after the incident," according to Cheryl Fenelle Dixon, a marketing and communication executive and adjunct professor in the M.S. strategic communications program at Columbia University.

A Bad Idea

Executives should avoid the temptation to stay quiet when a crisis hits, hoping that the matter will blow over.

That's often a bad idea and can make matters worse.

Dixon advises that:

> "If the company isn't talking, others will certainly fill in the blanks through speculation or with their own version of the story. When a crisis hits, people will try multiple channels to get answers—employees, partners, holding companies, and brand ambassadors.
>
> A company should have a crisis plan and policy in place that identifies key leaders who act as official spokespeople and ensures employees are directing questions to the appropriate team members in communications, PR, and legal.
>
> A big contributor to a company's reputation and ability to move past a crisis is how actively and quickly it acknowledges an issue and how it responds to it."

Transparency

Dixon suggests that:

> "Internal and external stakeholders, customers, media, and the general public expect transparency, a show of concern, and promise of action. To not be visible when a crisis is swirling—even though the company might be actively investigating and fact finding—is very detrimental and can easily be perceived as the company not caring, acting selfishly, and refusing to accept any responsibility."

Don't Wait for All the Facts

Dixon goes on:

> "One of the biggest mistakes companies make is waiting until they have all the facts before responding. Or the review and response process is so complicated that the key leaders are unable to gain consensus and respond quickly. It is fine to say, 'We are investigating and don't have all the facts yet ...'
>
> Preparing and delivering a holding statement that demonstrates awareness and concern as well as the known facts can help dispel rumors and untruths. It may also help to keep the crisis from escalating."

Saying Zip About Zillow

In a November 2021 story headlined "What Went Wrong With Zillow? A Real-Estate Algorithm Derailed Its Big Bet," the *Wall Street Journal* reported that:

> "This month, Zillow conceded failure in what amounts to one of the sharpest recent American corporate retreats. It announced that it would close Zillow's offices, which [were] responsible for the majority of the company's revenue but none of its profits; cut about 2,000 jobs, or a quarter of its staff; and write down losses of more than a half-billion dollars on the value of its remaining homes.
>
> 'This is code red,' Joshua Swift, senior vice president of Zillow Offers, said during [a] virtual meeting, according to the person who attended. Mr. Swift declined to comment through the company."

CHAPTER 72
Tractor Supply Company

Abandoning Corporate Values

A company that publicly proclaims and touts a set of principles and values but suddenly walks away from them runs the risk of creating a crisis for the organization and its brand.

Tractor Supply Company, which bills itself as the US's largest rural lifestyle retailer, is a case in point. The company's sudden reversal in 2024 of its publicized years-long commitment to diversity, equity, and inclusion (DEI) is a cautionary tale about the challenges when serving a diverse customer base in these highly politicized times.

It is also instructive on what can go wrong when making public statements about sensitive hot-button issues.

Setting and Achieving DEI Goals

In 2021, Tractor Supply strengthened and increased its goals in several DEI-related areas, *Retail Dive* reported.

In 2023, the company received national recognition for its inclusive workplace when it was featured on *Bloomberg's* Gender Equality Index for the second year in a row, and in *Newsweek's* inaugural list of America's Greatest Workplaces for Diversity.

Changing Direction

But Tractor Supply's embrace of DEI changed abruptly in June 2024 when it was the target of a social media campaign by Robby Starbuck, a conservative podcast host and unsuccessful Republican congressional candidate in Tennessee.

Starbuck wrote on X "that it was 'time to expose Tractor Supply" which he said was one of conservatives' most beloved brands but was at odds with their values. He pointed to its DEI hiring practices, in-office Pride Month decorations, climate change activism, and 'funding sex changes,' among other complaints," *NPR* reported.

Starbuck's campaign took its toll on Tractor Supply.

Three weeks later the company announced it was abandoning its embrace of DEI by eliminating its DEI goals and staff would stop providing data to the Human Rights Campaign, cancel sponsorships of Pride festivals, and no longer pursue its carbon emission goals.

What Drove Tractor Supply to Take These Steps?

"We have heard from customers that we have disappointed them. We have taken this feedback to heart," the company said.

"These changes mark a stunning shift in policy and messaging from Tractor Supply, which once touted its diversity and inclusion efforts. Just earlier this month, Tractor Supply President and CEO Hal Lawton maintained that the company remained 'very consistent' in how it approaches its own DEI and ESG—environmental, social and governance—programs for a number of years," according to the *Associated Press*.

Backlash

Tractor Supply's efforts to stem criticism about its policies—while putting out one fire—simply created a new fire of criticism when groups including the Human Rights Campaign, GLAAD, and the National Black Farmers Association denounced the company's actions.

"Embarrassing Capitulation"

"Tractor Supply's embarrassing capitulation to the petty whims of anti-LGBTQ extremists puts the company out of touch with the vast majority of Americans who support their LGBTQ friends, family, and neighbors," GLAAD president and CEO Sarah Kate Ellis told *The Advocate*. "It sends an appalling message, during Pride month, to see a rural staple go out of their way to bring harm to their LGBTQ customers and employees," *NPR* reported.

"Appalled by This Decision"

The National Black Farmers Association called on Tractor Supply president and CEO Hal Lawton to resign, following the retailer's decision to back away from its equity and climate goals.

"I am appalled by this decision, which is reflective of the ongoing racial tension and division in America," John Boyd, president of the association, said in a statement. "This affects our 130,000 members, many of whom regularly shop at Tractor Supply. Having repeatedly attempted to discuss our concerns with Mr. Hal Lawton, I am now calling for his immediate resignation."

Avoiding No-Win Situations

Tractor Supply's experience demonstrates a hard truth for companies that seek to serve diverse customers: by publicly catering to the concerns or demands of one segment of customers, you might alienate and upset *another* segment.

There is one strategy businesses could follow for those who want to do something about controversial hot-button issues and still avoid these no-win situations: don't brag about or tout their actions or the success of their efforts.

While this stealth approach would not please some public relations professionals, crisis management consultants would likely nod their heads in approval.

Having It Both Ways

Ernan Haruvy, a marketing professor at McGill University, comments:

> "We live in a cancel culture that seeks to identify and hurt companies perceived to be politically aligned ... The problem for Tractor Supply was in announcing initiatives that had the appearance of being politically aligned, and then retreating from these same initiatives, thereby upsetting absolutely everybody.

> On the one hand, it is regrettable that corporate social responsibility is now subject to political backlash. On the other hand, if cancel culture leads companies to pursue social responsibility with genuine intentions and less fanfare, this could be a net positive to society."

"A Big Mistake"

A big mistake Tractor Supply made was "assuming that the loudest people are [in the] majority," Charlotta Hellichius, a brand and business strategy expert, points out:

> "In research on public sentiment across divisive issues, this has been proven wrong. Look at gun violence, where there—similarly—a small group of vocal activists that take up the majority share of conversation but definitely don't represent the much larger silent majority that wants to have a more honest and nuanced conversation about how to solve the very real societal challenges that plague American society right now."

Reality Check

Business leaders should think strategically before issuing statements or taking public positions on hot-button issues. That means carefully considering the impact a publicized position would have on different segments of their customer base and how those customers might react.

CHAPTER 73
University of Pennsylvania

Saying the Wrong Thing at the Wrong Time

In responding to any crisis, what leaders say and do about the situation—and how they say and do it—matters.

A good example is the resignation of Liz Magill, the president of the University of Pennsylvania, who faced backlash over her testimony at a congressional hearing in 2024 concerning antisemitism. Her departure was announced by Scott Bok, chair of the university's board of trustees.

Crisis Response Lessons

Be Prepared

Jeffrey Sonnenfeld, dean for leadership studies at the Yale School of Management, said in a statement that Magill and her peers were underprepared before the House committee, according to *CNN*:

> "University leaders have an elevated duty to fortify the truth and protect their campus communities from hate, threats, and violence. Freedom of expression is NOT an absolute right anywhere in society. Hate speech is different from speech. These college leaders were over-lawyered but still underprepared and [showed] an absence of judgment."

Get It Right the First Time

When publicly addressing a crisis, business leaders need to get it right—and get it right the first time.

The day after her congressional testimony, Magill expanded on one of her responses to the committee, saying a call for the genocide of Jewish people would be considered harassment or intimidation.

"I was not focused on, but I should have been, the irrefutable fact that a call for geno-cide of Jewish people is a call for some of the most terrible violence human beings can perpetrate," Magill explained in a video statement released by the university. "It's evil, plain and simple," according to the *Associated Press*.

Timing Is Critical

Magill had an opportunity to issue a call for action or reforms when she spoke to Congress. But it was not until the next day that she "called for a review of Penn's poli-cies, which she said have long been guided by the US Constitution but need to be 'clar-ified and evaluated' as hate spreads across campus and around the world 'in a way not seen in years,'" the wire service reported.

The Importance of Sound Bites

When crafting a statement or answers to possible questions, think through what brief snippet or excerpt news organizations may use. That sound bite, which could only be a few seconds long, could be all people hear or see about what you say about a crisis.

Bok acknowledged in his statement that "Magill erred during her disastrous testimony, describing a 'dreadful 30-second sound bite' following a lengthy hearing," according to *CNN*.

Connect With Audiences

It is critical to know and keep in mind the audiences that will hear and see what you have to say—and customize your messages and comments accordingly.

David Thalberg, a media trainer and president of marketing and public relations agency Stryker-Munley Group, says:

> "You must reach your audience—show you care that you've heard their pain and will take action to fix or improve the situation ... President Magill was cold and steely. People are hurting, and she did not show any care for them when she could have easily expressed empathy."

Know When to Go

It is not unusual for one or more top executives to resign from an organization because of their handling of or response to a crisis.

"Former President Liz Magill last week made a very unfortunate misstep—consistent with that of two peer university leaders sitting alongside her—after five hours of aggressive questioning before a congressional committee," Bok said. "Following that, it became clear that her position was no longer tenable, and she and I concurrently decided that it was time for her to exit."

Magill's resignation was followed the same day by the resignation of another university official: board of trustees chair Scott Bok—the same person who had announced Magill's departure.

"While I was asked to remain in that role for the remainder of my term in order to help with the presidential transition, I concluded that, for me, now was the right time to depart," he wrote in an email to *USA Today*.

CHAPTER 74
UPS

Strikes

The good news for business leaders in 2023 was that a threatened labor strike by the Teamsters union against UPS was averted when UPS agreed to raise the pay for its employees. The strike would have been one of the largest strikes in US history. But while companies dodged that crisis bullet, the agreement was no guarantee against other potential strikes or disruptions that could create a crisis for them.

As is the case with strikes and any other type of crisis, don't wait until they happen to find out if you're prepared for them.

Company executives can take the following steps to help protect their organizations against future strikes.

Update or Prepare Plans

Review your crisis management plans to ensure they are up to date and account for the latest possible threats; if you do not have a plan in place, prepare one ASAP. The sooner the better.

Andy Barr, a crisis communication expert and CEO of the 10 Yetis digital marketing agency, says in an article for *Forbes.com*:

> "Ensure your crisis communication policies and procedures are current and include a process for reaching everyone impacted by a crisis. Anticipate and prepare for more customer service inquiries.
>
> Have your communication team prepped and ready to go. Typically, you will have a reply playbook where you can tweak pre-prepared replies to fit the question. Never do a copy-and-paste job, though."

Inventory Resources and Skills

Based on the crises you are planning for, take stock of the resources and skills you'd need to respond effectively to them. If they are not available in-house, contact the people or companies that can provide them.

Conduct Scenario Exercises

Test the effectiveness of crisis plans before they are needed by conducting a regular series of exercises to see how your company would respond to different crisis situations.

If, for example, there had been a strike against UPS, how would your organization have responded to it?

Spokesperson Training

Know in advance who will represent your company to the public when a crisis strikes and ensure they have received spokesperson training.

Learn from Others

Pay close attention to how others respond to their crisis, and what you can learn from their experiences, successes, or failures.

Supply Chain Disruptions

Valerie Blatt, Global Head, SAP Business Network Customer Success, explains in an article for *Forbes.com*:

> "Companies that have taken steps to transform supply chain operations from traditional, linear supply models to more resilient and collaborative supply chain networks have distinct advantages.

> First, they can see into their supply chains to anticipate and act on disruptions before they paralyze operations; and second, they have the agility to locate and engage with alternate suppliers–such as providers of materials and finished goods, logistics services, or even contingent labor."

Royal Mail Strike

According to Andy Barr:

"In the United Kingdom, when the Royal Mail went on strike (in 2022-2023), small and medium-sized companies were left to frantically search around for an alternative provider for delivering products to consumers.

This meant fast-tracking new operating procedures and processes and relying on new delivery companies to offer a level of service that customers expected. It resulted in increased demand and costs for customer service channels and even increased costs for consumers directly as shipping cost increases needed to be passed on because of tight product margins.

Even worse, when the strikes happened, deliveries stacked up in the depots and in the case of fresh produce, much of it ended up having to be returned. The number of lost parcels also increased, and it took months for the backlogs to be cleared, which resulted in consumers demanding refunds from the companies that they were expecting deliveries from."

CHAPTER 75
Verizon

Lawsuits

Litigation can create unwanted headline-making news and a crisis for companies. That is especially true for businesses and organizations that are on the losing end of class action lawsuits that result in multi-million-dollar settlements.

"A company's market share and corporate reputation are often implicated by a class action, and these exposures and risks put immense pressure on corporate decision-makers," according to the editors of the 2024 Duane Morris Class Action Review.

In a $100 million class action lawsuit settlement against Verizon in 2024, the plaintiffs alleged that Verizon harmed "wireless subscribers with a 'deceptive fee scheme' in which extra charges were not adequately disclosed. The communications giant denies any wrongdoing but has agreed to the nine-figure payout," *Forbes* reported.

At issue was Verizon's "administrative charge," which, according to *CNN*, "the plaintiffs said were 'misleading' because that fee wasn't disclosed in their plan's advertised monthly price and was charged in a 'deceptive and unfair manner.'"

Verizon claimed the charges were clearly identified and described the consumer administrative charge several times "during the sales transaction, as well as in its marketing, contracts, and billing," according to the news organization.

A company spokesperson explained that the fee "helps our company recover certain regulatory compliance and network-related costs," *CNN* reported.

Although 2023 was not a banner year for class action and government lawsuit settlements, it came in a close second—more than $51 billion. That is according to the 2024 Duane Morris Class Action Review which analyzed 1,300 class action decisions, up from 545 in 2022. The rulings in 23 areas of the law came from all state and federal courts, including private plaintiff class actions, collective actions, and government enforcement actions.

According to the survey, the largest settlements occurred in these five areas:

- Product liability ($25.82 billion total).
- Antitrust ($11.74 billion total).
- Securities fraud ($5.4 billion total).
- Consumer fraud ($3.29 billion total).
- Privacy ($1.32 billion total).

"As the ultimate referee of law, the US Supreme Court has continued to define and shift the playing field for class action litigation," says Gerald Maatman, Jr. who chairs the class action practice at the Duane Morris law firm and is an adjunct law professor at Northwestern University. "The Supreme Court's rulings in 2022 were no exception. Consistent with its approach over the past several years, the Supreme Court issued three key rulings that impact the plaintiffs' bar's ability to bring and maintain class actions."

Advice

Maatman claims there are several things that companies can do to protect these values against class action lawsuits.

Enforcement

"Of all defenses, a defendant's ability to enforce an arbitration agreement containing a class or collective action waiver may have had the single greatest impact in terms of shifting the pendulum of class action litigation."

Data Breaches

"Companies that fall victim to data breach attacks have to contend not only with the significant costs of responding to the data breach and potential of government fines but also the high costs of dealing with high-stakes class action lawsuits."

Compliance with Procedures

"A company's programs designed to ensure compliance with existing laws and strategies to mitigate class action litigation risks are corporate imperatives.

To help guard against expensive and time-consuming litigation, business leaders should consider implementing and monitoring early warning detection systems that enable their staff to quickly learn about and address issues and problems."

The procedures are important "so that employee and customer complaints can be investigated immediately and remediated where appropriate in order to avoid them growing into class action lawsuits."

Facing New Challenges

Business leaders "are facing challenges posed by social media and negative publicity that inevitably accompanies workplace class action litigation. In this environment, the fundamentals of legal compliance with employer workplace obligations have never been more important."

CHAPTER 76
Volkswagen, Taco Bell, and Hooters

April Fool's Jokes

Sometimes there is nothing funny about April Fool's jokes or pranks, especially those by companies and their employees that are taken seriously or create a crisis because the humor was lost on others.

Volkswagen

Volkswagen announced in 2021 that it would rebrand itself as "Voltswagen" to help call attention to its growing line of electric vehicles.

Poor Timing

"German automaker Volkswagen published on its website what was thought to be a draft press release about plans to change the name of its American division to 'Voltswagen,' the swapping out of the 'k' for a 't' as a commitment to electric vehicles," *USA Today* reported.

Volkswagen's prank a few days before April Fool's Day in 2021 was a joke that went too far, Columbia Business School professor and corporate strategy expert Rita McGrath told the news organization. "(It) was a mistake," she said.

The Taco Liberty Bell

As recounted by the *Philly Voice*, on April Fool's Day in 1996:

> "Taco Bell purchased full-page advertisements in seven major newspapers, including *The Philadelphia Inquirer*, announcing that it had purchased—and renamed—the Liberty Bell. The cracked American relic would now be called The Taco Liberty Bell.

The company said in an ad, 'The Taco Liberty Bell will still be accessible to the American public for viewing. While some may find this controversial, we hope our move will prompt other corporations to take similar action to do their part to reduce the country's debt.'

News of the alleged purchase had ears ringing across the country. Talk show hosts questioned the country's values. And the National Park Service, which houses the Liberty Bell, received hundreds of phone calls from furious Americans."

Hooters

An April Fool's prank by restaurant chain Hooters on an employee in 2001 ended up in litigation when server Jodee Berry was told that she had won a new Toyota.

Instead of a car, however, she received a Yoda doll when she went to pick up her new vehicle. She later sued the company and settled out of court. The terms of the agreement were not announced.

Advice

Unless they have reason to believe otherwise, people are usually inclined to take what they see, hear, or are told very seriously—especially if the source of a joke comes from people or organizations that they respect and trust.

A prank that violates that trust can turn into a crisis for the organizations that are behind them. And the bigger the joke, the bigger the risk that it could backfire.

Because of the proliferation of misinformation and the speed at which it can spread, an April Fool's joke can get out of control in the blink of an eye, with potential legal and reputational repercussions.

CHAPTER 77
Web Summit

Expressing Personal Opinions

Paddy Cosgrave, CEO and founder of Web Summit, one of Europe's biggest technology conferences, is an example of how executives can get in trouble for expressing their personal opinions.

Cosgrave resigned in 2023 after major sponsors and speakers dropped out of a conference amid the backlash over his public criticism of Israel's response to the Hamas attacks, *The New York Times* reported.

"Comments Drew Rebukes"

"His comments drew rebukes from prominent technology executives, particularly those from Israel. 'I'll never be part of your future initiatives, and we'll never work together again,' Adam Singolda, the Israeli-born founder of the advertising company Taboola, replied," according to the news organization.

"Unfortunately, my personal comments have become a distraction from the event, and our team, our sponsors, our start-ups and the people who attend," Cosgrave said in a statement. "I sincerely apologize again for any hurt I have caused."

Not the First

Cosgrave "isn't the first, and he certainly won't be the last corporate head to feel compelled to 'weigh in' and take political/social issue stands," according to Ryan McCormick, co-founder and media specialist at Goldman McCormick Public Relations:

> "Under no circumstances should high-level executives share or promote their political perspectives online. Doing so can risk alienating loyal customers or potential customers who share different perspectives. Our current climate is one where many individuals feel that when someone disagrees with their political points of view—they feel personally attacked."

Reality Checks

Cosgrave's experience is a timely reminder for all business leaders about two critical realities: Words matter. And those words can upset others.

That's why it is important for executives to do a reality check before taking a public stand on hot-button issues. Unless done properly and carefully, what they say and how they say it could create a crisis for them and those they work for.

Igniting Publicity Storms

"Of course, everyone has their own personal opinions about certain issues," Sam Patchett, client director at public relations firm Transmission Private, pointed out. "But when you represent an organization or lead a company, it only takes one poorly worded comment or off-the-cuff remark to ignite a publicity storm.

"The public spotlight is far more intense in the days of a [24-hour] news cycle and social media, and senior leaders are hitting the headlines with increasing regularity. Disney CEO Bob Iger's well-publicized criticism of the writer and actor strikes is [another] high-profile example of a CEO landing themselves in hot water for expressing an opinion, while Elon Musk seems to take great pride in rubbing people up the wrong way," Patchett observed.

Reversal?

Those sensitivities could be an early indication of a reversal in the attitude of some people about when, why, and how CEOs should speak out on hot-button issues.

A survey in 2022 found that most people *wanted* company executives to be visible and *expected* them to speak out on controversial issues and topics. According to the 2022 Edelman Trust Barometer:

- 81 percent believed CEOs should be personally visible when discussing public policy with external stakeholders or the work their company has done to benefit society.
- 60 percent said that when considering a job, they expect the CEO to speak out publicly about controversial social and political issues that the prospective employee cares about.

Perhaps people still want CEOs to publicly express personal opinions—but *only* if they agree with theirs.

CHAPTER 78
WeightWatchers

Competition and Trends

The sudden departure in 2024 of WeightWatchers CEO Sima Sistani, who had been in the job for less than three years, was the latest bump in the road for the weight-loss company.

New Trends and Competition

The company renamed and rebranded itself as WW in 2018 when the body-positivity movement became popular and said it would seek to transform itself from a weight-loss company into a wellness company. It also encountered stronger competition from self-care and nutrition companies, and demand for new medications like Ozempic, Wegovy, and Zepbound that help people lose weight, according to *The New York Times*.

Oprah Winfrey

In December 2023, board member and celebrity endorser Oprah Winfrey announced that she was taking an unnamed drug to help manage her weight, *The New York Times* reported. "The fact that there's a medically approved prescription for managing weight and staying healthier, in my lifetime, feels like relief, like redemption, like a gift, and not something to hide behind and once again be ridiculed for," she told *People* magazine.

In February 2024, the company's stock took a hit "after it disclosed that Winfrey would exit its board and donate her stock to the National Museum of African American History and Culture," *Reuters* reported.

Declining Market Value and Subscribers

WeightWatchers started 2024 with a market value of nearly $700 million, which had tumbled to $65 million in late September 2024, according to *Axios*.

In second-quarter results that were released on August 1, 2024, "the company reported net income down 54.2% to $23.3 million, with subscribers declining by 6.1%. The company also launched a 2024 restructuring plan to save $100 million annually through operational optimization," according to *The Business Journals*.

Sima Sistani's Resignation

Then came the sudden departure of CEO Sima Sistani. WeightWatchers explained in a press release how Sistani had:

> "... led the Company's transformation to a modern digital health organization and extended the Company's portfolio of solutions into the telehealth space with the acquisition and integration of Sequence (now WeightWatchers Clinic). This expanded the Company's offerings to include high-touch clinical weight management solutions alongside its science-backed behavioral programs."

Board member Tara Comonte was named interim CEO. She previously served as president and CFO of burger chain Shake Shack, *Axios* wrote.

WeightWatchers said Comonte would "sharpen its strategic focus and evolve its behavioral and clinical offerings to drive growth" and acknowledged that "Ms. Comonte steps into the role at a time when the Company is focused on improving its operational and financial performance while continuing to build on its product innovation and solutions for members."

Morningstar analyst Sean Dunlop told *Axios* that Sistani's departure "doesn't bode well" because weight-loss drugs are replacing WeightWatchers for many people who are looking for ways to lose weight.

How the Company Could Bounce Back

Public relations and marketing experts weighed in with their advice on how the company could rebound.

Get Back to Basics

"WeightWatchers' issues likely come from losing sight of their core customers' needs. They should refocus their messaging around the real value of their program," Josh Cremer, founder and CEO of marketing firm The Rohg Agency, comments.

Sistani's unexpected resignation could be a sign of deeper problems for the organization. Cremer goes on:

> "Flexible pricing and packaging to meet changing lifestyles may also help. But the CEO's resignation suggests bigger internal issues. WeightWatchers needs to get back to basics: know your customers, speak to them clearly, and give them a genuine experience worth coming back for. With focus on their strengths, they can overcome this. But they must act fast. The clock is ticking."

"A Robust Social Media Presence"

Courtney Haywood, the head of Haywood Agency Partners, a strategic communication firm, suggests that:

> "A robust social media presence could offer WeightWatchers a lifeline, especially if it ties its content to the broader conversation on medical weight-loss solutions. Leveraging influencers, 'realistic' success stories, and integrating digital tools would help the brand align with today's consumer expectations while maintaining its core principles. In doing so, WeightWatchers could potentially carve out a space for itself amidst the rapid shifts in the weight-loss industry and ensure its longevity."

Reconnect

To survive the sudden departure of Sistani and the company's other challenges, WeightWatchers "will have to make up with its first love, the Baby Boomer and Gen X lifetime members who preferred, enjoyed, and benefited from the social interactions of weigh-ins and meetings," Tiffany Joy Murchison, founder and CEO of TJM & Company Media Boutique, recommends. Maintaining the loyalty of key customers could also buy time for the interim CEO, or her successor:

> "Reconnecting with the in-person and lifetime member audience would not only retain their loyalty but also create a stable environment, providing the new CEO with the necessary time and resources to get the company back on track."

The crises and challenges that have faced the company—and will continue to face it in the days ahead—are enough to challenge many business leaders. In the aftermath of Sistani's unexpected departure, add to the list of challenges that was facing the company the importance of finding a new permanent CEO to lead the organization.

Public relations and marketing experts weighed in with their advice on how the company could rebound.

Pivot Quickly

Ryan Waite, vice president of public affairs at consultancy Think Big, points out how "WeightWatchers has been facing significant challenges, from shifting consumer preferences and rising competition in the weight-loss industry to a steep financial burden." A lot was riding on how fast and how well WeightWatchers would respond to a changing and challenging marketplace:

> "The company's future hinges on its ability to pivot quickly, especially with the growing popularity of prescription weight-loss drugs like Ozempic. To survive, WeightWatchers needs to redefine its role in a changing market, focusing on being more than just a weight-loss brand by expanding its health and wellness offerings while re-engaging its community through digital innovation."

CHAPTER 79
Volodymyr Zelensky

Controlling the Message

Control is an important factor in helping to ensure the effective and successful delivery of messages during a crisis.

On two different occasions, Ukraine President Volodymyr Zelensky showed the world the benefits and advantages of control—and what could happen when there are no controls or safeguards to prevent the delivery of messages from going off the rails.

His meeting in the Oval Office of the White House with President Donald Trump and Vice President JD Vance on February 28, 2025 was a worst-case communication scenario that became a nightmare reality for the Ukrainian president and his supporters.

The purpose of Zelensky's visit to Washington was to sign an agreement with Trump that would give the US rights to rare minerals in Ukraine. The day got off to an encouraging start when Trump met Zelensky as he arrived at the White House. The two leaders shook hands and posed for pictures.

But in the Oval Office meeting the conversation, which unfortunately took place in front of reporters and cameras, soon dissolved into an unexpected and headline-making confrontation.

Zelensky attempted to tell his side of the story about Russia's invasion of Ukraine but was interrupted by a combative and argumentative Trump, who repeatedly accused the Ukrainian president of "gambling with World War III."

"In one jaw-dropping meeting, the once unthinkable fear that Ukraine would be forced to engage in a long war against a stronger opponent without US support appeared to move exponentially closer to reality," according to *The New York Times*.

"All it took was 90 seconds for weeks of tortured diplomacy to unwind in spectacular fashion," the *Associated Press* reported.

> "The sudden blowup was the most heated public exchange of words between world leaders in the Oval Office in memory, as the usual staid work of diplomacy descended into finger-pointing, shouting and eye-rolling. The encounter left the

future of the US-Ukraine relationship, and Kyiv's ability to defend itself in the brutal conflict with Russia, in mortal jeopardy," according to the news organization.

The planned signing of the mineral agreement did not happen, a scheduled joint press conference with Trump and Zelensky was cancelled, and some Republicans said Zelensky should resign.

The blowup had implications for America's continued support of Ukraine and how Europe would deal with Russia.

Compared with the disastrous Oval Office meeting, Zelensky's speech to a joint session of Congress in December 2022 was a masterclass in crisis communication. His televised remarks provided several lessons business executives should remember when telling their side of the story about a business crisis.

Deliver Your Message in Person

Moshe Cohen, who teaches leadership, negotiation, organizational behavior, and mediation at Boston University's Questrom School of Business, comments:

"President Zelensky's speech to Congress reminds us foremost how important it is for business leaders to be physically present in times of crisis.

While he could have delivered the same message electronically or by video, his choice to come to Washington demonstrated commitment, created connection, and increased alignment to his cause. During a crisis, people can feel anxious or lost, and the leader's physical presence provides them with direction, stability, and hope."

Know Your Audience

Zelensky's speech "demonstrates how important it is for leaders to know their audience and speak with them rather than at them," Cohen notes:

"Just as Zelensky's references to our shared values, narratives, and history as well as his use of powerful imagery made his words resonate with us, business leaders can use their organizations' core values and mission to reassure their people and guide them through crises."

Capture Attention

A first step in persuading others to support your cause is to get their attention.

Zelensky did that by comparing the American troops who fought against Hitler on Christmas in 1944 to the Ukrainian soldiers who would fight against Putin that Christmas.

Explain What's at Stake

"This battle is not only for the territory, for this or another part of Europe," Zelensky told Congress. "The battle is not only for the life, freedom, and security of Ukrainians or any other nation which Russia attempts to conquer. This struggle will define in what world our children and grandchildren will live, and then their children and grandchildren."

Convey a Sense of Urgency

Zelensky told Congress that "Ukraine holds its lines and will never surrender. So, so, here [on] the front line, the tyranny which has no lack of cruelty against the lives of free people—and your support is crucial, not just to stand in such [a] fight but to get to the turning point to win on the battlefield."

Make Comparisons

To help establish an emotional connection with the lawmakers and the American public, Zelensky compared Russians to the Nazis at the Battle of the Bulge.

Battlefield Flag

Visuals were another effective tactic that the Ukrainian president used.

He presented a battlefield flag to House Speaker Nancy Pelosi, which helped to underscore the fact that the war was being waged against Ukraine, that Ukrainians were in the fight, and that his country was grateful to the United States for its help and support.

Military Green Activewear

Another powerful visual was the fact that Zelensky wore green military activewear instead of a suit when he delivered his speech. It sent the signal that he was in the trenches with his countrymen.

Advice

Business leaders should carefully consider the circumstances surrounding the delivery of their messages about a crisis. To help guarantee success, how, when, where, and why they tell their side of the story should ensure that there is no one who could interrupt the organization's spokesperson or take control of the situation.

Otherwise, the news coverage corporate executives receive may not be the news coverage and results they were expecting or wanted.

CHAPTER 80
Jeff Zucker

Full Disclosure

Full disclosure is an important best practice when communicating about a crisis. As Jeff Zucker's sudden resignation in 2022 as president of *CNN* showed, the failure to disclose important information can lead to a crisis.

CNN reported that:

> "*CNN* Worldwide president Jeff Zucker, the influential news executive who reshaped the iconic network, announced Wednesday morning that he has resigned from his position effective immediately.
>
> Zucker's stunning announcement came less than two months after he fired prime time anchor Chris Cuomo for improperly advising his brother, then–New York Gov. Andrew Cuomo, about how to address sexual misconduct allegations."

According to *The Washington Post*:

> "Zucker said that his relationship was probed following the network's decision to fire anchor Chris Cuomo in early December. 'As part of the investigation into Chris Cuomo's tenure at *CNN*, I was asked about a consensual relationship with my closest colleague, someone I have worked with for more than 20 years,' he said. 'I acknowledged the relationship evolved in recent years. I was required to disclose it when it began but I didn't. I was wrong. '"

CNN reported that "Zucker did not name his colleague, but the relationship is with Allison Gollust, his key lieutenant for the last two decades. Gollust is remaining at *CNN*:

> "Zucker and Gollust began working together at *NBC* in 1998. They rose through the ranks at the network together, and when Zucker joined *CNN*, Gollust was among his first hires. Just before coming to *CNN* Gollust had worked briefly as communications director for Andrew Cuomo. She is currently executive vice president and chief marketing officer at *CNN*."

"Another Striking Example"

Kia Roberts, founder and principal of Triangle Investigations, notes that:

"Zucker's resignation from *CNN* is yet another striking example of the dramatic shift in how the public perceives and feels about ethically questionable behavior from persons in powerful positions.

"What is especially fascinating about Zucker's resignation is that it seems to be triggered not because of allegations of misconduct by the person whom he was involved in an admittedly consensual relationship with, but because Zucker did not disclose the existence of the relationship to human resources within the organization."

Resignation Says Volumes

Roberts goes on:

"There isn't a lot of sizzle or fizz to the relationship between Zucker and his colleague, a high-ranking executive within the *CNN* organization. Both parties are divorced and were consenting adults when the relationship began.

That someone as powerful as Zucker would resign due to what is essentially a technicality—him not disclosing the existence of this consensual relationship—says volumes about the rigid and firm stance that employers are now taking when it comes to fraternization and dating within the workplace."

"Zucker Was Right to Resign"

Debra Caruso Marrone, president of DJC Communications, a media relations and crisis management firm, believes that:

"Zucker was absolutely right to resign. He's the top guy. If he doesn't follow the rules, he has no credibility as a leader at *CNN*, or in the greater media industry. If he wants to avoid being canceled permanently, it's his responsibility to do the right thing.

Leadership is as much about setting an example as it is about managing an organization. A good leader sets the tone and models the type of behavior employees should follow. If someone in Jeff Zucker's position does not conform to company policies, how can anyone else be expected to do so. He had no choice."

An Ethical Obligation to Disclose

Robert Foehl, professor of business ethics at the College of Business at Ohio University and a former corporate ethics practitioner, explains that:

"As the leader of one of the world's most prominent news organizations, Jeff Zucker had an ethical obligation to disclose to his superiors at WarnerMedia his romantic relationship with an employee under his direction and supervision."

Relationship a Concern

Foehl observes further:

"Mr. Zucker's romantic relationship with a subordinate is a concern given his positional power, as well as the potential impact that such a relationship could have on his ability to make unbiased decisions.

Romantic relationships in the workplace are not uncommon and most organizations of *CNN*'s size have established policies on how such relationships are to be handled. The crux of those policies is that employees must affirmatively disclose any such romantic relationships."

"A Blatant Disregard of Corporate Policy"

Foehl explains why Zucker needed to be held to high standards of conduct:

"Unfortunately, Mr. Zucker did not make any such disclosure. His relationship was discovered by happenstance during an unrelated investigation by his employer. His lack of disclosure was, at best, a blatant disregard of corporate policy. At worst, it was designed to conceal the relationship from his employer.

Given that the position of president in a company is critical in setting the ethical tone of the entire company and given that the leader of an organization should be held to higher standards of conduct, Mr. Zucker was right to tender his resignation."

CHAPTER 81
10 Rs of Crisis Management

I began my previous book about crisis management, *Crisis Ahead*, with a set of rules to help ensure you are as ready as possible for any crisis.

I think it's fitting that, based on the examples in this book, I end *The Crisis Casebook* with those same rules.

1. **Risk.** Identify the risk triggers that would cause a crisis for your organization. Some risks may be unique to your company because of the nature of your business. For example, if you're an airline, a risk trigger would be a plane crash. Other triggers could apply no matter what type of business you are in, such as embezzlement or sexual harassment.
2. **Reduce.** Take the steps that are necessary and prudent to lessen known risks. These steps can be as basic as following common-sense accounting procedures to help prevent fraud and forgery to more extensive actions such as providing appropriate training or retraining to employees.
3. **Ready.** Have a crisis plan in place and ready to implement when it is needed. Because one size will not fit all companies, the plan should be customized to meet the needs and realities of your organization and industry.
4. **Redundancies.** Have backup and contingency plans in case they are required. Since it is impossible to plan for every eventuality, a Plan B, Plan C, or Plan D may be needed, just in case.
5. **Research.** Get all the information you can about your crisis, including details about what just happened, is happening now, or what you expect to happen. Knowing the who, what, when, where, why, and how of the situation is essential in helping to respond strategically, effectively, and efficiently.
6. **Rehearse.** Practice implementing your plan on a regular basis—at least once a year. Having a plan and not practicing it is not much different than having no plan at all. The more you practice implementing the plan, the more prepared you will be if and when you need to use it.
7. **React.** Activate your plan when necessary. Know what will trigger a crisis and how you would respond to different crisis scenarios. A crisis is no time to try to learn as you go along.
8. **Reach out.** Immediately communicate with those who are affected by or concerned about the crisis. Your company or organization may have different publics and

stakeholders who would be affected by the situation and would be interested in the outcome.

9. **Recover.** Know how you would bounce back from a crisis. Planning your recovery from a disaster, scandal, or other emergency is just as important as planning your response to it. You will need to get back to normal as quickly as possible, and a recovery plan will help you do just that.

10. **Remember.** Keep in mind the experiences of those who have already gone through a crisis. What would you do to repeat their successes and avoid their mistakes? There is no need to reinvent the wheel when it comes to the best ways to respond to, manage, and recover from a crisis. There are plenty of lessons from which you can learn.

Acknowledgments

Pamela Kervin Segal played a behind-the-scenes and essential role in the publication of *The Crisis Casebook*. I owe her a big debt of gratitude for her proofreading and editing skills and spot-on suggestions as I researched and prepared the manuscript.

Thanks to my friends and colleagues who generously shared their advice and recommendations about early drafts of the cover of the book. They include David Nellis, Arnold Sanow, Ed Barks, Nancy Kervin, Stephen Tull, Bob and Karen Sachs, Marissa Eigenbrood, Erin MacDonald-Birnbaum, Rachel Fischer, Jeff Peckins, Bob James, and Ann Ramsey.

I want to express my appreciation to the team at John Murray Business for their great work in turning my manuscript into a published book. The team members include Iain Campbell, Meaghan Lim, Antonia Maxwell, Vivienne Church, Kim Birchall in the editorial department; Diana Talyanina in the production department; Matt Young and Kaitlyn Shokes in the marketing department; and Aaron Munday in the art department.

The Crisis Casebook would not have been possible without the help and cooperation of the thousands of public relations, branding, marketing, crisis management, and other experts and executives who shared their advice and insights for the hundreds of articles I've posted on *Forbes.com* on a wide variety of topics, ranging from Airbnb to Zelensky. I've included the comments of many of these individuals (or those who were quoted by other news organizations) in this book, and those who are quoted in the previous pages are also listed in the List of Sources section.

Charlie, my longtime faithful canine companion, was always nearby when I wrote several of my earlier books. This time around, Tootsie Roll and Buddy Holly helped ensure that I took breaks during the course of the researching, writing, and editing of the manuscript for *The Crisis Casebook*. And, of course, there is Rocky the cat, who sat on Pamela's lap as she edited and proofread my manuscript.

List of Sources

Adrienne Uthe, founder and strategic advisor at Kronus Communications

Alice M. Walton, president of Walton Strategies

Amanda Orr, public relations expert at Orr Strategy Group

Amani Wells-Onyioh, Democratic political strategist and partner and operations director at Sole Strategies

Amy Clark, chief human resources officer of the Better Business Bureau National Programs and founder of the Growth Minded Leadership group

Amy Levy, president of Amy Levy Public Relations

Andrea B. Clement, media relations and communication expert and founder of Clem.co

Andy Barr, CEO and founder of the 10 Yetis digital marketing agency

Andy Whitehouse, assistant professor at Columbia University

Ann Skeet, senior director of leadership ethics at Santa Clara University's Markkula Center for Applied Ethics

Art Ocain, vice president of service delivery at Airiam

Ben Michael, attorney with Michael & Associates

Brian Alster, CEO of Altrata, global wealth intelligence company, and former general manager at Dun & Bradstreet's North American finance and risk business

Bridget Arik, chief operating officer at Redmill Solutions

Bruce Dahlgren, CEO of MetricStream

Bryan Hornung, founder of Xact IT Solutions, and a co-author of books about cyber-security, including *Adapt and Overcome* and *Under Attack*

Cameron Gawley, co-founder and chief growth officer at Arrival, a social commerce app

Captain (Retd) Barbara Bell, adjunct professor of leadership and ethics at the United States Naval Academy, and author of *Flight Lessons: Navigating Through Life's Turbulence and Learning to Fly High*

Carla Bevins, associate teaching professor of business management communication at Carnegie Mellon University's Tepper School of Business

Caroline Sapriel, founder and managing partner at CS&A International

Casey Jones, founder and head of marketing at CJ&CO

Cassandra Burke Robertson, law professor and director of the Center for Professional Ethics at Case Western Reserve University's School of Law

Catherine Rymsha, visiting lecturer in management at the University of Massachusetts Lowell

Charity Lacey, principal at you+me marketing

Charlie O'Toole, senior account manager at SourceCode Communications

Charlotta Hellichius, brand and business strategy expert

Cheryl Fenelle Dixon, marketing and communication executive and adjunct professor in the M.S. strategic communications program at Columbia University

Christina Eyuboglu, public relations and crisis communications consultant

Christine Haas, CEO and founder of Christine Haas Media

Christy Reiss, crisis communication professional

Clifford Oliver, former senior executive at FEMA and now principal at Nanticoke Global Strategies

Colin Ram, civil litigation attorney with Colin Ram Law

Collen Clark, attorney with law firm Schmidt and Clark

Courtney Haywood, head of Haywood Agency Partners

Curt Aubley, managing director at Deloitte Risk & Financial Advisory

Danielle Grossman, senior media consultant at Sevans PR

Darcy Eikenberg, leadership and executive coach

David Braun, founder and CEO of Capstone Strategic

David Greiner, corporate law and governance attorney

David Moody, senior associate at Schellman

David Thalberg, media trainer and president of marketing and public relations agency Stryker-Munley Group

David Thomson, president of Thomson Communications

Dawn Cone, management consultant and executive coach at DSC Consulting Solutions

Deanne Criswell, former FEMA administrator

Debra Caruso Marrone, president of DJC Communications

Denise Graziano, strategic advisor and expert in organizational transformation and growth, and CEO of Graziano Associates

Dr. Allen Sills, NFL's chief medical officer

Dustin Siggins, business writer and founder of Proven Media Solutions

Emily Walton, certified executive coach and founder of Alo Coaching

Emily Williams, content strategist and CEO of Web Copy Collective

Ephraim Schachter, leadership strategist and C-suite coach

Ernan Haruvy, marketing professor at McGill University

Gerald Maatman, Jr., chair of class action practice at the Duane Morris law firm and adjunct law professor at Northwestern University

Gigi Marino, communications consultant

Greta Maiocchi, head of marketing and recruitment at the Open Institute of Technology

Haiko de Poel, branding expert

Heather Stratford, founder of Drip7

Irina Tsukerman, president of Scarab Rising

Jack Spaulding, executive director of strategy at Planit

Jake Holyoak, digital public relations expert

Jeff Pedowitz, business consultant

Jeffrey Sonnenfeld, dean for leadership studies at the Yale School of Management

Jennifer Donahoe, group account director for public relations and social media at Planit

Jo Caruana, founder and CEO of Finesse group

John Goodman, CEO of John Goodman PR

John Yarbrough, senior vice president of corporate marketing at Alert Media

Jonathan Hemus, managing director and crisis management consultant at Insignia

Josh Cremer, founder and CEO of marketing firm The Rohg Agency

Josh Yavor, chief information security officer at Tasian

Julianna Sheridan, vice president of precision and crisis communications at Matter Communications

Justin Goldsberry, CEO and founder of Goldsberry Management Group

Katie Waldron, public relations consultant

Kevin Breen, director of cyber threat research at Immersive Labs

Kia Roberts, founder and principal of Triangle Investigations

Kirk Hazlett, adjunct professor of communication at the University of Tampa

Kojenwa Moitt, CEO of Zebra Public Relations

Kraig Kleeman, founder and CEO of CEO Branding Worldwide

Kristen Gall, president of Rakuten Rewards

Lakesha Cole, founder and principal publicist at she PR

Lance Kinney, associate professor of advertising and public relations at the University of Alabama's College of Communication and Information Sciences

Laura Guitar, leader at rbb Communications' Reputation & Risk Advisors

Laura Meyers, director of corporate communications for The Bonadio Group

Laurie R. Barkman, CEO of Business Transition Sherpa

Lesli Franco, vice president of O'Connell & Goldberg

Lindsey Chastain, founder and CEO of The Writing Detective

Lindsey Walker, owner of the Walker+Associates Media Group

Luc Wathieu, professor of marketing at Georgetown University's McDonough School of Business

Lucas Botzen, CEO and HR expert at Rivermate

Luke Blaney, CEO of Chief Negotiation

Lynn Neils, former in-house lawyer at Johnson & Johnson

Malika Begin, business consultant and an adjunct professor at Pepperdine University

Marc Lewis, attorney specializing in sexual abuse cases

Maria Correa, career expert at Resume Help

Martha Holler, founder of Shine PR

Melissa A. Poole, vice president of investor relations for The Hershey Company

Michael Grimm, vice president of Reputation Partners

Michael Toebe, trust and reputation risk management and executive communications specialist at Reputation Intelligence-Reputation Quality

Mike Campbell, CEO of Fusion Risk Management

Mitchell A. Thornton, professor and director of the Cyber Security Institute at Southern Methodist University

Mitchell S. Muncy, executive vice president, Ethics and Public Policy Center, Prospera

Moshe Cohen, founder of The Negotiating Table and a senior lecturer at Boston University's Questrom School of Business

Nesochi Okeke-Igbokwe, health expert and CEO of the Dr. Nesochi LLC internal medicine practice

Nicholas Creel, an associate professor of business law at Georgia College and State University

Nick Kalm, founder and CEO of Reputation Partners

Nikki Jain, CEO and founder of The Sprout PR

Nikkia Adolphe, founding partner and head of media strategy at Tenet Consultancy

Niles Koenigsberg, digital marketing specialist at Real Fig Advertising + Marketing

Paddy Cosgrave, CEO and founder of Web Summit

Patricia Harned, CEO of Ethics & Compliance Initiative

Paul Wertheimer, nationally recognized crowd safety expert and founder of Crowd Management Strategies

Peter Loge, director and associate professor in the School of Media and Public Affairs at George Washington University

Peter Schwartz, international business consultant

Rabbi Yonason Goldson, author of *Grappling With Gray: An Ethical Handbook for Personal Success and Business Prosperity*

Ray Hennessey, executive partner and CEO of Vocatus

Rhea Freeman, public relations, marketing, and social media consultant

Rob Britton, principal of RealWorld Leadership and an adjunct professor at Georgetown University

Robert C. Bird, professor of business law and Eversource Energy Chair in Business Ethics at the University of Connecticut

Robert Foehl, professor of business ethics at the College of Business at Ohio University and former corporate ethics practitioner

Ryan McCormick, co-founder and media specialist at Goldman McCormick Public Relations

Ryan Waite, vice president of public affairs at Think Big

Sarah Mitchell, marketing director for Relyir

Scott Sobel, crisis, media, and litigation communications counsellor

Shane Allen, public relations consultant

Shannon Peel, branding expert

Smita Das Jain, personal empowerment life coach and executive coach from India

Stacy Elmore, co-founder of The Luxury Pergola

Stacy Rosenberg, associate teaching professor at Carnegie Mellon University's Heinz College of Information Systems and Public Policy

Steve Taplin, CEO of Sonatafy Technology

Tara Furiani, CEO of Not the HR Lady

Tenyse Williams, adjunct digital marketing instructor at Columbia University, George Washington University, and University of Central Florida

Terry M. Isner, owner and CEO of Jaffe PR

Tiffany Joy Murchison, founder and CEO of TJM & Company Media Boutique

Tracy Pearson, J.D., Ed.D., investigation and implicit bias expert

Valerie Blatt, Global Head, SAP Business Network Customer Success

Victoria Clark, licensed mental health counselor and executive coach

Wendy L. Patrick, lecturer at San Diego State University's Fowler College of Business

Zach Friend, national public policy, political campaign, and communications expert

Bibliography

Introduction

Segal, Edward. *As Ukraine Resists Russian Invasion, Zelensky Demonstrates These Leadership Lessons.* March 3, 2022. Forbes.com. https://www.forbes.com/sites/edwardsegal/2022/03/01/as-ukraine-resists-russian-invasion-zelenskyy-demonstrates-these-leadership-lessons/

Segal, Edward. *Zelensky's Most Effective Crisis Communication Strategies, Tactics And Techniques.* May 7, 2022. Forbes.com. https://www.forbes.com/sites/edwardsegal/2022/03/05/zelenskys-most-effective--crisis-communication-strategies-tactics-and-techniques/

Segal, Edward. *FEMA Launches National Risk Index Update That Businesses Can Use To Prepare For Nature-Related Crises.* August 18, 2021. Forbes.com. https://www.forbes.com/sites/edwardsegal/2021/08/17/fema-launches-national-risk-index-update/

Segal, Edward. *How Dashboards Are Helping To Monitor, Manage And Prevent Crisis Situations.* November 9, 2021. Forbes.com. https://www.forbes.com/sites/edwardsegal/2021/11/05/how-dashboards-are-helping-to-monitor-manage-and-prevent-crisis-situations/

Segal, Edward. *The Important Roles War Rooms Play Before And During A Business Crisis.* November 18, 2022. Forbes.com. https://www.forbes.com/sites/edwardsegal/2022/11/18/the-important-roles-war-rooms-play-before-and-during-a-business-crisis/

Segal, Edward. *How FEMA's New University Can Help Companies Prepare For Disaster.* August 29, 2024. Forbes.com. https://www.forbes.com/sites/edwardsegal/2024/08/29/how-femas-new-university-can-help-companies-prepare-for-disasters/

Chapter 1

Segal, Edward. *Chris Rock's Joke About Actress Jada Pinkett Smith Creates Crisis For Academy Awards.* March 30, 2022. Forbes.com. https://www.forbes.com/sites/edwardsegal/2022/03/28/chris-rocks-joke-about-actress-jada-pinkett-creates-crisis-for-academy-awards/

Segal, Edward. *What Business Leaders Can Learn From Will Smith's Apology For Slapping Chris Rock.* March 28, 2022. Forbes.com. https://www.forbes.com/sites/edwardsegal/2022/03/28/what-business-leaders-can-learn-from-will-smiths-apology-for-slapping-chris-rock/

Segal, Edward. *The Messages Will Smith's Resignation From The Academy Are Sending To Business Leaders.* April 1, 2022. Forbes.com. https://www.forbes.com/sites/edwardsegal/2022/04/01/the-message-will-smiths-resignation-from-the-academy-sends-to-business-leaders/

Segal, Edward. *As Punishment For Slapping Incident, Will Smith Is Barred From Attending Oscar Ceremonies For 10 Years.* April 11, 2022. Forbes.com. https://www.forbes.com/sites/edwardsegal/2022/04/08/as-punishment-for-slapping-incident-will-smith-is-barred-from-attending-oscar-ceremonies-for-10-years/

Segal, Edward. *How Will Smith's New Movie Could Repair Image After Slapping Incident.* June 10, 2024. Forbes.com. https://www.forbes.com/sites/edwardsegal/2024/06/10/how-will-smiths-new-movie-could-repair-image-after-slapping-incident/

Chapter 2

Segal, Edward. *Adidas Responds To Its Kanye West Crisis.* October 25, 2022. Forbes.com. https://www.forbes.com/sites/edwardsegal/2022/10/25/how-brands-are-responding-to-their-celebrity-related-crises/

Chapter 3

Segal, Edward. *How Airbnb Is Responding To A Mass Shooting At Pittsburgh Rental Property.* April 18, *2022.* Forbes.com. https://www.forbes.com/sites/edwardsegal/2022/04/17/how-airbnb-is-responding-to-mass-shooting-at-pittsburgh-rental-property/

Chapter 4

Segal, Edward. *Grounding Of Boeing 737 MAX 9 Planes Is A Key Crisis Management Lesson.* January 7, 2024. Forbes.com. https://www.forbes.com/sites/edwardsegal/2024/01/06/grounding-of-boeing-737-max-9-planes-is-a-key-crisis-management-lesson/

Chapter 5

Segal, Edward. *Amazon Responds To Release Of Leaked Documents Showing 150% Annual Employee Turnover.* October 24, 2022. Forbes.com. https://www.forbes.com/sites/edwardsegal/2022/10/24/amazon-responds-to-release-of-leaked-documents-showing-150-annual-employee-turnover/

Chapter 6

Segal, Edward. *How And Why Businesses Are Vulnerable To Email-Based Cyberattacks: New Study.* November 10, 2022. Forbes.com. https://www.forbes.com/sites/edwardsegal/2022/11/10/how-and-why-businesses-are-vulnerable-to-email-based-cyberattacks-new-study/

Chapter 7

Segal, Edward. *How And Why The Ads Of 4 Companies Created Controversies.* October 26, 2024. Forbes.com. https://www.forbes.com/sites/edwardsegal/2024/10/26/how-and-why-the-ads-of-4-companies-created-controversies/

Chapter 8

Segal, Edward. *8 Early Crisis Management Lessons From The Travis Scott Concert Tragedy.* December 27, 2021. Forbes.com. https://www.forbes.com/sites/edwardsegal/2021/11/09/early-crisis-management-lessons-from-the-travis-scott-concert-tragedy/

Chapter 9

Segal, Edward. *Audi Comes To The Rescue Of "Wheel Of Fortune" And Their Self-Inflicted Crisis.* February 2, 2022. Forbes.com. https://www.forbes.com/sites/edwardsegal/2021/12/25/audi-comes-to-the-rescue-of-wheel-of-fortune-in-their-crisis-situation/

Chapter 10

Segal, Edward. *These 6 Best Practices Could Help Jeep And Other Brands Avoid A Crisis.* March 1, 2021. Forbes.com. https://www.forbes.com/sites/edwardsegal/2021/03/01/these-6-best-practices-could-help-jeep-and-other-brands-avoid-a-crisis/

Segal, Edward. *What Companies Can Do When They Wind Up On The Wrong Side Of Issues.* April 6, 2022. Forbes.com. https://www.forbes.com/sites/edwardsegal/2021/04/06/what-companies-can-do-when-they-wind-up-on-the-wrong-side-of-issues/

Chapter 11

Segal, Edward. *What Leaders Can Learn From Defense Secretary Austin's Apology.* February 2, 2024. Forbes.com. https://www.forbes.com/sites/edwardsegal/2024/02/01/what-leaders-can-learn-from-defense-secretary-austins-apology/

Chapter 12

Segal, Edward. *Death Of Bed Bath & Beyond CFO Creates New Crisis For Company.* September 6, 2022. Forbes.com. https://www.forbes.com/sites/edwardsegal/2022/09/04/death-of-bed-bath-beyond-cfo-creates-new-crisis-for-company/

Segal, Edward. *By Naming Interim CFO, Bed Bath & Beyond Underscores Need To Respond Quickly To A Crisis.* September 7, 2022. Forbes.com. https://www.forbes.com/sites/edwardsegal/2022/09/06/by-naming-interim-cfo-bed-bath--beyond-underscores-need-to-respond-quickly-to-a-crisis/

Chapter 13

Segal, Edward. *What The Activism Of Ben & Jerry's Can Teach Business Leaders.* March 24, 2024. Forbes.com. https://www.forbes.com/sites/edwardsegal/2024/03/24/what-ben--jerrys-activism-can-teach-business-leaders/

Chapter 14

Segal, Edward. *Biden's Decision To 'Step Aside' Has Parallels In The Corporate World.* July 21, 2024. Forbes.com. https://www.forbes.com/sites/edwardsegal/2024/07/20/bidens-refusal-to-step-aside-has-parallels-in-the-corporate-world/

Segal, Edward. *The Unusual Aspects Of Harvard President Claudine Gay's Resignation.* January 3, 2024. Forbes.com. https://www.forbes.com/sites/edwardsegal/2024/01/02/the-unusual-aspects-of-harvard-president-claudine-gays-resignation/

Segal, Edward. *8 Best Practices For Responding To Criticism Of How A Crisis Was Managed.* June 10, 2024. Forbes.com. https://www.forbes.com/sites/edwardsegal/2024/01/02/the-unusual-aspects-of-harvard-president-claudine-gays-resignation/

Chapter 15

Segal, Edward. *Pharma Shows Business Leaders How To Recover From A Crisis.* May 23, 2021. Forbes.com. https://www.forbes.com/sites/edwardsegal/2021/03/23/pharma-shows-business-leaders-how-to-recover-from-a-crisis/

Chapter 16

Segal, Edward. *Meghan, Harry And Buckingham Palace Are Providing Key Crisis Communication Lessons.* March 8, 2021. Forbes.com. https://www.forbes.com/sites/edwardsegal/2021/03/07/meghan-harry-and-buckingham-palace-are-providing-key-crisis-communication-lessons/

Segal, Edward. *How And When Queen Should Have Responded To Harry And Meghan's Interview With Oprah Winfrey.* March 11, 2021. Forbes.com. https://www.forbes.com/sites/edwardsegal/2021/03/09/how-what-and-when-queen-should-respond-to-harry-and-megans-interview-with-oprah-winfrey/

Segal, Edward, *Fallout And Lessons Continue From Meghan And Harry's Interview With Oprah Winfrey.* March 15, 2021. Forbes.com. https://www.forbes.com/sites/edwardsegal/2021/03/13/fallout-and-lessons-continue-from-meghan-and-harrys-interview-with-oprah-winfrey/

Segal, Edward. *Royal Family's Crisis Has Lessons For All Family Businesses.* March 16, 2021. Forbes.com. https://www.forbes.com/sites/edwardsegal/2021/03/14/royal-familys-crisis-has-lessons-for-all-family-businesses/

Chapter 17

Segal, Edward. *What To Do When Your Company Gets Unwanted Publicity.* August 2, 2021. Forbes.com.https://www.forbes.com/sites/edwardsegal/2021/08/02/what-to-do-when-your-company-gets-unwanted-publicity/

Chapter 18

Segal, Edward. *How California Pizza Kitchen Made The Best Of A Bad Situation. October 27, 2024.* Forbes.com. https://www.forbes.com/sites/edwardsegal/2024/10/27/how-california-pizza-kitchen-made-the-best-of-a-bad-situation/

Chapter 19

Segal, Edward. *How Firing People On Zoom Can Create Another Crisis.* May 15, 2022. Forbes.com. https://www.forbes.com/sites/edwardsegal/2022/05/12/how-firing-employees-via-zoom-can-create-crisis-situations-for-companies/

Wayland, Michael, and Wapner, Scott. *Carvana Lays Off 1,500 Employees Following Stock Free Fall.* November 18, 2022. *CNBC.* https://www.cnbc.com/2022/11/18/carvana-to-lay-off-1500-employees-amid-economic-uncertainty-.html

Chapter 20

Segal, Edward. *Kate Middleton's Two Doctored Photos Are A Cautionary Tale For Executives.* May 19, 2024. Forbes.com. https://www.forbes.com/sites/edwardsegal/2024/03/11/kate-middletons-doctored-photo-is-cautionary-tale-for-executives/

Chapter 21

Segal, Edward. *Crisis Management Lessons From The Planned Shake-Up Of The CDC.* August 18, 2022. Forbes.com. https://www.forbes.com/sites/edwardsegal/2022/08/18/crisis-management-lessons-from-the-planned-shake-up-of-the-cdc/

Chapter 22

Segal, Edward. *9 Crisis Lessons From General Mills' Response To Allegation Of Shrimp Tails In Cereal Box.* March 27, 2021. Forbes.com. https://www.forbes.com/sites/edwardsegal/2021/03/25/9-crisis-lessons-from-general-mills-response-to-allegation-of-shrimp-tails-in-cereal-bo

Chapter 23

Segal, Edward. *Licht's Rocky Tenure As CNN's CEO Provides Crisis And Leadership Lessons.* June 7, 2023. Forbes.com. https://www.forbes.com/sites/edwardsegal/2023/06/07/lichts-brief-tenure-as-cnns-ceo-provides-crisis-and-leadership-lessons/

Chapter 24

Segal, Edward. *7 Crisis Management Lessons From Colonial Pipeline's Response To Cyber Attack.* May 8, 2021. Forbes.com. https://www.forbes.com/sites/edwardsegal/2021/05/08/colonial-pipeline-cyber-attack-is-providing-crisis-management-lessons-in-real-time/

Segal, Edward. *SolarWinds And Colonial Pipeline Crises Showed 7 Ways To Respond To Cyberattacks.* May 31, 2021. Forbes.com. https://www.forbes.com/sites/edwardsegal/2021/05/31/solarwinds-and-colonial-pipeline-crises-showed-8-ways-to-respond-to-cyberattacks/

Segal, Edward. *1 Year Later: Actions Taken, Lessons Learned Since The Colonial Pipeline Cyberattack.* May 9, 2022. Forbes.com. https://www.forbes.com/sites/edwardsegal/2022/05/07/1-year-later-actions-taken-lessons-learned-since-the-colonial-pipeline-cyberattack/

IBM. *IBM Report: Half Of Breached Organizations Unwilling To Increase Security Spend Despite Soaring Breach Costs.* July 24, 2023. IBM. https://newsroom.ibm.com/2023-07-24-IBM-Report-Half-of-Breached-Organizations-Unwilling-to-Increase-Security-Spend-Despite-Soaring-Breach-Costs

Chapter 25

Segal, Edward. *6 Crisis Lessons From How Universities Responded To The Student Protests.* May 25, 2024. Forbes.com. https://www.forbes.com/sites/edwardsegal/2024/05/25/6-lessons-from-how-universities-responded-to-the-student-protests/

Chapter 26

Segal, Edward. *The Global IT Outage Provides Several Crisis Management Lessons.* July 19, 2024. Forbes.com. https://www.forbes.com/sites/edwardsegal/2024/07/19/global-it-outage-provides-several-crisis-management-lessons/

Chapter 27

Segal, Edward. *What The Pentagon Can Teach Business Leaders About Crisis Communication.* February 21, 2022. Forbes.com. https://www.forbes.com/sites/edwardsegal/2021/10/18/what-the-pentagon-can-teach-business-leaders-about-crisis-communication/

Chapter 28

Segal, Edward. *How Homeland Security Responded To Its Own Disinformation Crisis.* May 19, 2022. Forbes.com. https://www.forbes.com/sites/edwardsegal/2022/05/18/how-dhs-is-responding-to-their-own-disinformation-crisis/

Chapter 29

Segal, Edward. *China's Didi And UK's Metro Bank Show How And Why To Respond Quickly To Rumors.* July 8, 2021. Forbes.com. https://www.forbes.com/sites/edwardsegal/2021/07/08/chinas-didi-and-uks-metro-bank-show-how-and-why-to-respond-quickly-to-rumors/

Chapter 30

Segal, Edward. *ExxonMobil, Fauci Set Record Straight After Comments By Trump And Campaign Ad.* October 27, 2020. Forbes.com. https://www.forbes.com/sites/edwardsegal/2020/10/26/set-the-record-straight-asap-to-protect-your-companys-image-and-reputation/

Chapter 31

Segal, Edward. *Facebook Name Change Is Example Of Marketing Tactic Used By Companies Under Fire.* October 29, 2021. Forbes.com. https://www.forbes.com/sites/edwardsegal/2021/10/28/facebook-name-change-is-example-of-marketing-tactic-used-by-companies-under-fire/

Segal, Edward. *How Facebook's Response To Whistleblower Could Make Their Crisis Worse.* December 10, 2021. Forbes.com. https://www.forbes.com/sites/edwardsegal/2021/10/06/how-facebooks-response-to-whistleblower-could-make-their-crisis-worse

Chapter 32

Segal, Edward. *8 Best Practices For Responding To Criticism Of How A Crisis Was Managed.* June 8, 2024. Forbes.com. https://www.forbes.com/sites/edwardsegal/2024/06/09/8-best-practices-for-responding-to-criticism-of-how-a-crisis-was-managed/

Chapter 33

Segal, Edward. *What Corporate Executives Can Learn From How FE MA Prepares For Disasters.* May 24, 2021. Forbes.com. https://www.forbes.com/sites/edwardsegal/2021/05/24/what-corporate-executives-can-learn-from-how-fema-prepares-for-disasters/

Segal, Edward. *6 Lessons From FEMA's Response To Thousands Of Crisis Situation.* April 13, 2024. Forbes.com. https://www.forbes.com/sites/edwardsegal/2024/04/13/6-lessons-from-femas-response-to-thousands-of-crisis-situations/

Chapter 34

Segal, Edward. *New Reports About SVB's Collapse Underscore Question Of Who Should Investigate A Crisis.* April 30, 2023. Forbes.com. https://www.forbes.com/sites/edwardsegal/2023/04/29/new-reports-about-svbs-collapse-underscore-question-of-who-should-investigate-a-crisis/

Chapter 35

Segal, Edward. *How Companies Are Trying To Discourage And Detect Misconduct By Executives.* February 10, 2021. Forbes.com. https://www.forbes.com/sites/edwardsegal/2021/02/09/how-companies-are-trying-to-discourage-and-detect-misconduct-by-executives/

Fernholz, Tim. *Firefly Aerospace Investigates CEO's Alleged Inappropriate Relationship.* July 15, 2024. Payload.com. https://payloadspace.com/firefly-aerospace-investigates-ceos-alleged-inappropriate-relationship/

Jones, Andrew. *Firefly Aerospace CEO Leaves Company Amid Misconduct Investigation.* July 19, 2024. Space.com. https://www.space.com/firefly-aerospace-ceo-misconduct-investigation

Chapter 36

Segal, Edward. *The 6 Crisis Management Lessons From Peloton's Delayed Recall Of Treadmills.* May 5, 2021. Forbes.com. https://www.forbes.com/sites/edwardsegal/2021/05/05/the-6-crisis-management-lessons-from-pelotons-delayed-recall-of-treadmills/

Segal, Edward. *Fisher-Price Recall Shows Again Why Company Actions And Values Should Be In Sync.* June 11, 2021. Forbes.com. https://www.forbes.com/sites/edwardsegal/2021/06/11/fisher-price-recall-shows-again-why-company-actions-and-values-should-be-in-sync/

Chapter 37

Segal, Edward. *How Goldman Sachs Responded When Publicly Criticized By A Departing Employee.* April 21, 2021. Forbes.com. https://www.forbes.com/sites/edwardsegal/2021/04/20/goldman-sachs-lessons-for-responding-when-departing-workers-criticize-their-companies/

Chapter 38

Segal, Edward. *How Companies Can Avoid Political Arguments From Becoming A Crisis.* April 29, 2024. Forbes.com. https://www.forbes.com/sites/edwardsegal/2024/04/27/how-companies-can-avoid-political-arguments-from-becoming-a-crisis/

Chapter 39

Segal, Edward. *Factors Executives Could Consider When Choosing A Second In Command.* August 6, 2024. Forbes.com. https://www.forbes.com/sites/edwardsegal/2024/08/06/factors-executives-could-consider-when-choosing-a-second-in-command/

Chapter 40

Segal, Edward. *A Sweet Lesson From Hershey: How, When—Or If—To Advertise During A Crisis.* November 1, 2021. Forbes.com. https://www.forbes.com/sites/edwardsegal/2021/11/01/a-sweet-lesson-from-hershey-how-when---or-if---to-advertise-during-a-crisis/

Chapter 41

Segal, Edward. *How And Why Jeep Responded To The News Of Springsteen's Arrest On DUI Charges.* February 15, 2021. Forbes.com. https://www.forbes.com/sites/edwardsegal/2021/02/15/how-and-why-jeep-responded-to-springsteens-arrest-on-dui-charges/

Chapter 42

Segal, Edward. *Backlash Over "Jeopardy!" Guest Host Dr. Oz Provides Lessons For Protecting Brands.* March 26, 2021. Forbes.com. https://www.forbes.com/sites/edwardsegal/2021/03/26/blowback-over-jeopardy-guest-host-oz-provides-insights-for-protecting-brands/

Segal, Edward. *Sudden Departure Of New "Jeopardy!" Host Creates Another Crisis For Popular Game Show.* August 22, 2021. Forbes.com. https://www.forbes.com/sites/edwardsegal/2021/08/20/sudden-departure-of-new-jeoprady-host-creates-another-crisis-for-popular-game-show/

Segal, Edward. *Naming Of Bialik And Jennings To "Jeopardy!" Hosting Duties Does Not End Game Show's Crisis.* September 16, 2021. Forbes.com. https://www.forbes.com/sites/edward-segal/2021/09/16/naming-of-bialik-and-jennings-to-split-jeopardy-hosting-duties-does-not-end-shows-crisis/

Segal, Edward. *Naming Jennings New Sole Host Could End "Jeopardy!"'s Recent Rocky Ride.* December 26, 2023. Forbes.com. https://www.forbes.com/sites/edwardsegal/2023/12/18/naming-jennings-new-sole-host-could-end-jeopardys-recent-rocky-ride/

Chapter 43

Segal, Edward. *Kellogg Shows The Importance Of Considering The Impact Of Words.* February 29, 2024. Forbes.com. https://www.forbes.com/sites/edwardsegal/2024/02/28/kellogg-shows-the-importance-of-considering-the-impact-of-words/

Chapter 44

Segal, Edward. *KFC's Apology For Sending Promotional Message To Germans Provides 7 Crisis Management Lessons.* November 13, 2022. Forbes.com. https://www.forbes.com/sites/edwardsegal/2022/11/13/kfcs-apology-for-sending-promotional-message-to-germans-provides-7-crisis-management-lessons/

Chapter 45

Segal, Edward. *King Charles III's First Public Speech Sets Tone And Direction For Monarchy.* September 13, 2022. Forbes.com. https://www.forbes.com/sites/edwardsegal/2022/09/10/king-charles-iiis-first-public-speech-sets-tone-and-direction-for-monarchy/

Chapter 46

Segal, Edward. *How And Why Competing Companies Work Together To Tackle A Crisis.* November 23, 2022. Forbes.com. https://www.forbes.com/sites/edwardsegal/2023/11/22/how-and-why-competing-companies-work-together-to-tackle-a-crisis/

Chapter 47

Segal, Edward. *Impact Of Suez Canal Crisis On Companies Around The World Could Last Weeks.* March 21, 2021. Forbes.com. https://www.forbes.com/sites/edwardsegal/2021/03/31/impact-of-suez-canal-crisis-on-companies-around-the-world-could-last-weeks/

Segal, Edward. *How Businesses Can Protect Their Supply Chains After Bridge Collapse.* March 29, 2024. Forbes.com. https://www.forbes.com/sites/edwardsegal/2024/03/27/how-businesses-can-protect-their-supply-chains-after-bridge-collapse/

Peek Behind The Scenes At How Target's Prepping Our Supply Chain To Deliver Holiday Joy All Season Long. September 1, 2021. https://corporate.target.com/news-features/article/2021/09/supply-chain-prep

Chapter 48

Segal, Edward. *Maui Shows What Can Happen When Crisis Safeguards Fail Or Are Ignored.* August 16, 2022. Forbes.com. https://www.forbes.com/sites/edwardsegal/2023/08/16/what-can-happen-when-protections-against-a-crisis-fail-or-are-ignored/

Chapter 49

Segal, Edward. *Executives Can Learn From Ouster Of House Speaker Kevin McCarthy.* October 21, 2023. Forbes.com. https://www.forbes.com/sites/edwardsegal/2023/10/04/executives-can-learn-from-ouster-of-house-speaker-kevin-mccarthy/

Chapter 50

Segal, Edward. *McDonald's Shows Why Perspective Is Important Before Responding To A Crisis.* September 6, 2021. Forbes.com. https://www.forbes.com/sites/edwardsegal/2021/09/06/mcdonalds-shows-why-perspective-is-important-before-responding-to-a-crisis/

Chapter 51

Segal, Edward. *What Executives Can Learn From Eric Adams' Bribery-Related Indictment.* September 26, 2024. Forbes.com. https://www.forbes.com/sites/edwardsegal/2024/09/26/what-executives-can-learn-from-eric-adams-bribery-related-indictment/

Chapter 52

Segal, Edward. *In Face Of Blowback, NBC Reverses Decision To Hire Ronna McDaniel.* March 27, 2024. Forbes.com. https://www.forbes.com/sites/edwardsegal/2024/03/25/blowback-to-nbcs-hiring-of-former-rnc-chair-underscores-hr-priorities/

Chapter 53

Segal, Edward. *Elon Musk Shows How A Business Leader's Ego Can Create A Crisis.* November 22, 2022.Forbes.com.https://www.forbes.com/sites/edwardsegal/2022/11/19/elon-musk-shows-how-a-business-leaders-ego-can-create-a-crisis/

Chapter 54

Segal, Edward. *What Company Executives Can Learn From NFL's Latest Response To Concussion Crisis.* October 9, 2022. Forbes.com. https://www.forbes.com/sites/edwardsegal/2022/10/09/what-company-executives-can-learn-from-nfls-latest-response-to-concussion-crisis/

Chapter 55

Segal, Edward. *Lessons From The National Women's Soccer League Crisis.* October 4, 2022. Forbes.com. https://www.forbes.com/sites/edwardsegal/2022/10/04/lessons-from-the-national-womens-soccer-league-crisis/

Chapter 56

Segal, Edward. *Dolly Parton As Crisis Manager And Communicator.* January 19, 2021. Forbes.com. https://www.forbes.com/sites/edwardsegal/2021/01/19/dolly-parton-as-crisis-manager-and-communicator/

Chapter 57

Segal, Edward. *Merger With LIV Golf Threatens PGA Tour's Image And Reputation.* June 18, 2023. Forbes.com. https://www.forbes.com/sites/edwardsegal/2023/06/09/merger-with-lvi-golf-threatens-pga-tours-image-and-reputation/

Chapter 58

Segal, Edward. *What Presidential Candidates Can Teach Business Leaders About Branding.* October 8, 2024. Forbes.com. https://www.forbes.com/sites/edwardsegal/2024/10/06/what-presidential-candidates-can-teach-business-leaders-about-branding/

Chapter 59

Segal, Edward. *Crisis Communication Lessons From Jen Psaki's Successful Tenure As White House Press Secretary.* May 6, 2022. Forbes.com. https://www.forbes.com/sites/edwardsegal/2022/05/05/crisis-communication-lessons-from-jen-psakis-successful-tenure-as-white-house-press-secretary/

Chapter 60

Segal, Edward. *Here's What Executives Need To Know Before Responding To Consumer Protests.* February 22, 2021. Forbes.com. https://www.forbes.com/sites/edwardsegal/2021/02/22/heres-what-executives-need-to-know-before-responding-to-consumer-protests/

Chapter 61

Segal, Edward. *Corporate Succession Lessons From The Death Of Queen Elizabeth II.* September 9, 2022. Forbes.com. https://www.forbes.com/sites/edwardsegal/2022/09/08/corporate-succession-lessons-from-the-death-of-queen-elizabeth-ii/

Chapter 62

Segal, Edward. *How To Respond To Multiple Crisis Situations Created By The Coronavirus And Other Emergencies.* January 4, 2021. Forbes.com. https://www.forbes.com/sites/edwardsegal/2021/01/04/how-to-respond-to-and-recover-from-back-to-back-crisis-situations/

Chapter 63

Segal, Edward. *The Secret Service Faces Another Unfolding Crisis Situation; 4 Agents Are Suspended.* April 9, 2022. Forbes.com. https://www.forbes.com/sites/edwardsegal/2022/04/07/the-secret-service-faces-another-unfolding-crisis-situation-4-agents-are-placed-on-leave/

Segal, Edward. *Fake Federal Agents "Created A Potential National Security Risk," According To U.S. Government.* April 14, 2022. Forbes.com. https://www.forbes.com/sites/edward-segal/2022/04/09/fake-federal-agents-created-a-potential-national-security-risk-according-to-us-government/

Tucker, Eric; Amri, Farnoush; Santana, Rebecca; and Lauerlitics Claudia. *Acting Secret Service Director Says He's 'Ashamed' After The Trump Assassination Attempt.* July 30, 2024. AssociatedPress.https://apnews.com/article/trump-assassination-attempt-fbi-secret-service-a382e3ec081dd13e85eaa9e726cca02c

Chapter 64

Segal, Edward. *Communications Lessons From Silicon Valley Bank's Crisis.* March 14, 2024. Forbes.com. https://www.forbes.com/sites/edwardsegal/2023/03/14/communications-lessons-from-silicon-valley-banks-crisis/

Chapter 65

Segal, Edward. *What Business Leaders Can Learn From Will Smith's Apology For Slapping Chris Rock.* March 28, 2022. Forbes.com. https://www.forbes.com/sites/edwardsegal/2022/03/28/what-business-leaders-can-learn-from-will-smiths-apology-for-slapping-chris-rock/

Chapter 66

Segal, Edward. *Crisis Management Lessons From Southwest Airlines' Meltdown.* December 29, 2022. Forbes.com. https://www.forbes.com/sites/edwardsegal/2022/12/29/crisis-management-lessons-from-southwest-airlines-meltdown/

Chapter 67

Segal, Edward. *What Boards May Look For When Hiring CEOs To Turn Around Companies.* September 4, 2024. Forbes.com. https://www.forbes.com/sites/edwardsegal/2024/09/01/what-boards-may-look-for-when-hiring-ceos-to-turn-around-companies/

Chapter 68

Segal, Edward. *What Companies Can Learn From The Supreme Court's First Code Of Ethics.* December 31, 2023. Forbes.com. https://www.forbes.com/sites/edwardsegal/2023/11/25/what-companies-can-learn-from-the-supreme-courts-first-code-of-ethics/

Chapter 69

Segal, Edward. *T-Mobile Data Breach Underscores Importance Of Crisis Management Best Practices.* August 20, 2021. Forbes.com. https://www.forbes.com/sites/edwardsegal/2021/08/18/t-mobile-data-breach-underscores-importance-of-key-crisis-management-best-practices/

Chapter 70

Segal, Edward. *Taylor Swift And Ticketmaster Are Providing Crisis Response Lessons For Business Leaders.* November 21, 2022. Forbes.com. https://www.forbes.com/sites/edwardsegal/2022/11/21/taylor-swift-and-ticketmaster-are-providing-crisis-response-lessons-for-business-leaders/

Segal, Edward. *Taylor Swift's Crisis Management Lessons For Business Leaders.* July 16, 2024. Forbes.com. https://www.forbes.com/sites/edwardsegal/2024/07/16/taylor-swifts-crisis-management-lesson-for-business-leaders/

Chapter 71

Segal, Edward. *Tesla's Silence About Sexual Harassment Lawsuit Underscores Importance Of Crisis Communication.* November 22, 2021. Forbes.com. https://www.forbes.com/sites/edwardsegal/2021/11/19/teslas-silence-about-sexual-harassment-lawsuit-underscores-importance-of-crisis-communication/

Chapter 72

Segal, Edward. *Lessons From Tractor Supply's Sudden Reversal On Its Commitment To DEI.* July 24, 2024. Forbes.com. https://www.forbes.com/sites/edwardsegal/2024/07/13/lessons-from-tractor-supplys-sudden-reversal-on-its-commitment-to-dei/

Chapter 73

Segal, Edward. *The Unusual Aspects Of Harvard President Claudine Gay's Resignation.* January 3, 2024. Forbes.com. https://www.forbes.com/sites/edwardsegal/2024/01/02/the-unusual-aspects-of-harvard-president-claudine-gays-resignation/

Segal, Edward. *Resignation Of Penn's President Provides Crisis Response Lessons.* December 11, 2023. Forbes.com. https://www.forbes.com/sites/edwardsegal/2023/12/09/resignation-of-penns-president-provides-crisis-response-lessons/

Segal, Edward. *How Executives Could Respond To Calls That They Resign After A Crisis.* December 11, 2023. Forbes.com. https://www.forbes.com/sites/edwardsegal/2023/12/11/how-executives-could-respond-to-calls-that-they-resign-after-a-crisis/

Chapter 74

Segal, Edward. *How Companies Can Prepare For The Next Potential Strike.* July 25, 2023. Forbes.com. https://www.forbes.com/sites/edwardsegal/2023/07/25/how-to-prepare-for-the-next-strike/

Chapter 75

Segal, Edward. *Class Action And Government Lawsuit Settlements Topped $51 Billion In 2023.* January 9, 2024. Forbes.com. https://www.forbes.com/sites/edwardsegal/2024/01/09/class-action-and-government-lawsuit-settlements-topped-51-billion-in-2023/

Segal, Edward. *Class Action Lawsuits Set New Billion Dollar Settlement Records In 2022: Report.* January 4, 2023. Forbes.com. https://www.forbes.com/sites/edwardsegal/2023/01/04/class-action-lawsuits-set-new-billion-dollar-settlement-records-in-2022-report/

Valinsky, Jordan. *Today Is The Final Day To Claim Your Slice Of A $100 Million Verizon Settlement.* April 15, 2024. *CNN.* https://www.cnn.com/2024/04/15/tech/verizon-class-action-settlement-deadline/index.html

Chapter 76

Segal, Edward. *Why April Fool's Jokes Can Be No Laughing Matter For Companies And Organizations.* April 4, 2022. Forbes.com. https://www.forbes.com/sites/edwardsegal/2022/04/01/why-april-fools-jokes-can-be-no-laughing-matter-for-companies-and-organizations/

Chapter 77

Segal, Edward. *How CEOs Could Damage Careers And Companies By What They Say.* October 24, 2023. Forbes.com. https://www.forbes.com/sites/edwardsegal/2023/10/24/how-ceos-could-damage-careers-and-companies-by-what-they-say/

Chapter 78

Segal, Edward. *The Sudden Departure Of WeightWatchers' CEO Is Latest Jolt For Company.* October 24, 2024. Forbes.com. https://www.forbes.com/sites/edwardsegal/2024/09/29/the-sudden-departure-of-weightwatchers-ceo-is-latest-jolt-for-company/

Chapter 79

Segal, Edward. *Why Zelensky's Speech To Congress Was A Masterclass In Crisis Communication.* December 22, 2022. Forbes.com. https://www.forbes.com/sites/edwardsegal/2022/12/22/10-crisis-communication-strategies-and-tactics-zelensky-used-in-speech-to-congress/

Segal, Edward. *Ukrainian President Volodymyr Zelensky Underscores Need For More Military Aid In Speech To Joint Session Of Congress.* March 18, 2022. Forbes.com. https://www.forbes.com/sites/edwardsegal/2022/03/16/zelensky-underscores-need-for-more-military-aid-in-speech-to-joint-session-of-congress/

Santora, Marc, and Kramer, Andrew E. *Shocked By Trump, Zelensky And Ukraine Try To Forge A Path Forward.* March 2, 2025. *The New York Times.* https://www.nytimes.com/2025/03/01/world/europe/trump-zelensky-us-ukraine-russia-meeting.html?smid=nytcore-ios-share&referringSource=articleShare

Miller, Zeke. *Trump's Oval Office Thrashing Of Zelenskyy Shows Limits Of Western Allies' Ability To Sway US Leader.* March 1, 2025. Associated Press. https://apnews.com/article/trump-zelen-skyy-oval-office-ukraine-russia-blowup-8aa63e55c859e8fea963911478c376ee#

Chapter 80

Segal, Edward. *Jeff Zucker's Resignation Underscores Importance Of Full Disclosure To Help Avoid A Crisis.* February 9, 2022. Forbes.com. https://www.forbes.com/sites/edwardsegal/2022/02/02/zuckers-resignation-underscores-importance-of-full-disclosure-to-help-avoid-a-crisis/

Index

About the Author

Edward Segal serves as a Leadership Strategies Senior Contributor for *Forbes.com*, where he covers crisis-related news, topics, and issues.

He is the author of the award-winning and bestselling book, *Crisis Ahead: 101 Ways to Prepare for and Bounce Back from Disasters, Scandals, and Other Emergencies* (Nicholas Brealey, 2020), which was also published in a Chinese-language edition.

Segal hosts the *Crisis Ahead* and *Crisis Management Minute* podcasts on Apple Podcasts, Federal News Network, and wherever else podcasts are found. He has more than 30 years' experience as a crisis management consultant, commentator, and trainer.

© Benedict Bacon

Segal managed crisis situations as the CEO of two trade associations; advised and helped organizations survive disasters, scandals, and emergencies, including the arrest and firing of corporate officers, hate crimes, and sexual harassment; and conducted crisis management and communication training for hundreds of executives and their staffs.

He is the former marketing strategies columnist for the *Wall Street Journal*'s StartUpJournal.com and a senior media relations consultant for Ogilvy Public Relations.

Segal has provided crisis management and public relations advice, counsel, and services to Fortune 500 corporations and organizations, including Marriott, Ford, Humana, Airbus, the National Association of REALTORS®, and the American Academy of Physical Medicine and Rehabilitation.

Contact Segal at crisiscasebook@gmail.com or visit his websites at CrisisCasebook.com, PublicRelations.com, and EdwardSegal.com.

Crisis Ahead: 101 Ways to Prepare for and Bounce Back From Disasters, Scandals, and Other Emergencies

By Edward Segal

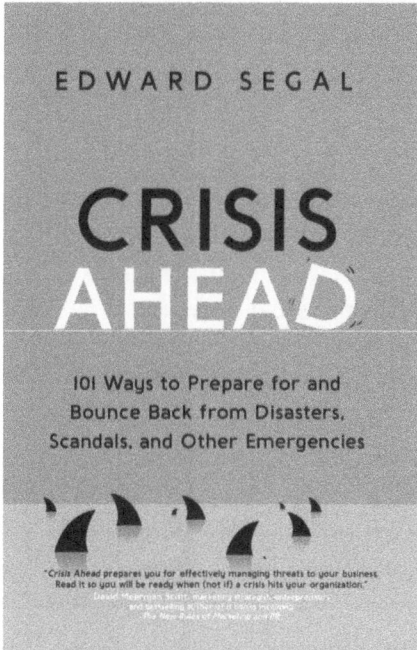

EDWARD SEGAL

CRISIS
AHEAD

101 Ways to Prepare for and
Bounce Back from Disasters,
Scandals, and Other Emergencies

"Crisis Ahead prepares you for effectively managing threats to your business.
Read it so you will be ready when (not if) a crisis hits your organization."

It's not a matter of IF a scandal or crisis will hit, it's WHEN.

How a company deals with a crisis will have lasting impact on their reputation, profits, and more. But for most organizations, when a crisis hits, they're caught off guard and ill-prepared.

Crisis Ahead shows what levers to pull and what moves to make in real time when faced with a crisis, scandal, or disaster. It includes dozens of anecdotes, stories, and lessons about how companies, organizations, and individuals have prepared for, created, and managed crisis situations.

'*Crisis Ahead* is the ultimate and invaluable survival guide for business executives who are knee-deep in a crisis and a handy reference book for company officials who want to prepare for the inevitable.

Edward Segal helps you assess your readiness to handle a crisis and provides a practical handbook—packed with exciting real-world examples that required real-world solutions—for crisis communication planning everyone can benefit from. Edward's conversational writing style makes *Crisis Ahead* a quick and easy read and its innovative design ensures you can immediately find the advice and information you need before, during, or after a crisis.'

Mitchell Marovitz, director and professor, Communications, Journalism, and Speech Program at the University of Maryland Global Campus

9781529361421 Crisis Ahead, 224pp, 6×9 inches